The Performing Art of Therapy

The Performing Art of Therapy explores the myriad ways in which acting techniques can enhance the craft of psychotherapy. The book shows how, by understanding therapy as a performing art, clinicians can supplement their theoretical approach with techniques that fine-tune the ways their bodies, voices, and imaginations engage with and influence their clients. Broken up into accessible chapters focused on specific attributes of performance, and including an appendix of step-by-step exercises for practitioners, this is an essential guidebook for therapists looking to integrate their theoretical training into who they are as individuals, find joy in their work, expand their empathy, increase self-care, and inspire clients to perform their own lives.

Mark O'Connell, LCSW-R, MFA, is a New York City-based psychotherapist in private practice, an author, and an actor. For more information, see www.markoconnelltherapist.com.

"*The Performing Art of Therapy* is a significant contribution to the field of counseling and psychotherapy. Mark O'Connell has given us a smart, practical, and deeply personal book that will be useful to therapists of all orientations. So much of psychotherapy is taught by text, in a removed, scientific, objective style. O'Connell presents therapy as a creative art, emphasizing performance and the experiential dimension of the encounter. This is not a list of techniques but rather a journey into the use of oneself as the essential instrument of therapeutic engagement."

—**Lewis Aron, PhD**, director of the New York University postdoctoral program in psychotherapy and psychoanalysis and author of *Dramatic Dialogues: Contemporary Clinical Practice*

"Mark O'Connell writes to enliven therapists' use of their selves as creative artists. He situates himself at the intersection of acting and psychotherapy, from which he offers practical exercises that focus on mind, body, emotion and breath; he does so not in the manner of a how-to guide, but in keeping with a therapist's reach for the freedom of potential and the luxury of being. Sweetening the read, O'Connell serves up wonderful anecdotes from well-known actors who help bring to life his valuable psychotherapeutic suggestions."

—**Ken Corbett, PhD**, assistant professor in the New York University postdoctoral program in psychotherapy and psychoanalysis

"*The Performing Art of Therapy* brilliantly explores the nuances of therapist and patient on the therapeutic stage. O'Connell's creative, useful, and inspiring work offers us new ways of thinking about our clients as well as our own aliveness, engagement, and self-care."

—**Galit Atlas, PhD**, author of *The Enigma of Desire: Sex, Longing, and Belonging in Psychoanalysis* and *Dramatic Dialogues: Contemporary Clinical Practice*

"This revelatory book proposes that the elements of observation, empathy, and truthful self-examination so essential to the art of acting are also fundamental to the practice of therapy. In clear, readable, almost conversational prose that is remarkably free of scientific jargon, Mark O'Connell shares insights learned through years of training and practice that are equally applicable to artists and mental health professionals. Any student actor could open a page of this delightful, thought-provoking book and find a nugget of wisdom or practical advice, and any seasoned professional could find, analyzed with simple clarity, the lessons of a lifetime of experience and training. This book, written in a voice that is at once wise and wise-cracking, serious and ironically self-effacing, is a great gift to the field of therapy."

—**Brian McEleney, MFA**, director of the Brown University/ Trinity Rep MFA program in acting

The Performing Art of Therapy

Acting Insights and Techniques for Clinicians

Mark O'Connell
Drawings by Erin Lombardi

 Routledge
Taylor & Francis Group

NEW YORK AND LONDON

First published 2019
by Routledge
52 Vanderbilt Avenue, New York, NY 10017

and by Routledge
2 Park Square, Milton Park, Abingdon, Oxon, OX14 4RN

Routledge is an imprint of the Taylor & Francis Group, an informa business

© 2019 Mark O'Connell

Library of Congress Cataloging-in-Publication Data
Names: O'Connell, Mark (Psychologist)
Title: The performing art of therapy : acting insights and techniques for clinicians / Mark O'Connell ; drawings by Erin Lombardi.
Description: New York, NY : Routledge, 2019. |
Includes bibliographical references and index.
Identifiers: LCCN 2018045907 (print) | LCCN 2018046619 (ebook) |
ISBN 9781138737624 (hbk) | ISBN 9781138737631 (pbk) |
ISBN 9781315175683 (ebk)
Subjects: LCSH: Psychotherapy. | Client-centered psychotherapy. |
Psychotherapist and patient.
Classification: LCC RC489.A7 (ebook) |
LCC RC481 .O26 2019 (print) | DDC 616.89/1656–dc23
LC record available at https://lccn.loc.gov/2018045907

ISBN: 978-1-138-73762-4 (hbk)
ISBN: 978-1-138-73763-1 (pbk)
ISBN: 978-1-315-17568-3 (ebk)

Typeset in Bembo
by Newgen Publishing UK

The actor is an instant analyst.

(Peter Brook, Theater Director, 1994)

Psychotherapy is, like other therapies, a creative art…

(Edith Weigert, Psychoanalyst, 1964)

I became an artist—and thank God I did—because we are the only profession that celebrates what it means to live a life.

(Viola Davis, Actress, 2017)

This book is dedicated to all of my clients, past and present. Thank you for daring to explore your *selves* through our "scene work," and for inspiring me to do the same.

Contents

Acknowledgments

It takes an ensemble to write a book. Many thanks to:

Alice Speilburg: you are more than an agent; you're a creative partner. Anna Moore, Jamie Magyar, and the Routledge team: you have set a wonderful stage for these musings.

Robin Weigert!: our dialogues. Erin Lombardi!: your artwork. Ida Rothschild!: your editing. All three of you opened up the possibilities of this project with your deep listening, imaginative suggestions, and careful attention. <3

My acting mentors: Brian McEleney, Carol Gill Malik, and Mark Alan Gordon (all of whom contributed to this text), as well as Stephen Berenson, Anne Scurria, and Julia Carey: You all saw my potential before I did; I use what you taught me every day. My therapy mentors: Ken Corbett, you emboldened me to trust my creative instincts, and you continue to influence me with yours; Lewis Aron, you constantly challenge me to embody different points of view; Al Sbordone, you empowered me to personalize my clinical work; Virginia Goldner, Fiona True, and Charles Silverstein, I not only learn from what you do but more significantly from how you do it.

Lew Aron's Thursday group, whose dynamic conversations influence my thinking and my work: Catherine Basile, Grant Brenner, Susannah Falk Shopsin, Susan Gill, Jerry Katz, Madeline Rhum, Claire Steinberger, Liat Tsuman, Avital Woods, and Merav Ben-Horin. The performers who shared your personal insights, methods and approaches with me: Lian-Marie Holmes, Allison Langerack, Susan Ferrara, Krystel Lucas, Arbender Robinson, Paul Ricciardi, and the incomparable Olympia Dukakis. My yoga teacher, Nancy Elkes: your guidance keeps me in mental, physical, and emotional shape. Each of my clients, to whom this book is dedicated: we are in this together.

The variously trained clinicians who reviewed these pages gave me generous feedback, and helped to sharpen my intentions: Jamie Weiner, Jessica Moskowitz, Scott Kramer, Philip Ringstrom, James Pollock, and Benet Hennessey.

My father, the late Stephen P. O'Connell: I still feel seen and held by you. My mother, Mary O'Connell: I continue to follow my dreams, like you always encouraged me to do. My mother-in-law, the late Sandy Deabler: Your belief in me endures. My aunt Connie Lopez, the actor/psychiatric nurse: You inspire me to navigate the unknown. All the members of my chosen family: I am not me without you.

My husband, Justin Deabler: You listened this book into existence, just as you give meaning to everything significant in my life. And our incredible son, Robin Baxter: You endlessly expand my capacity to love.

Prologue

Where does the actor acquire the understanding that for the doctor takes years of study?

(Peter Brook, Theater Director, 1994)

Therapist, you are a performing artist, whether you realize it or not.

The moment a client enters your office, you are on stage, face-to-face with an audience, a scene partner, and a variety of characters that you do not yet know how to play (after all, our clients both become *and* cast us in all of these roles faster than we can say, "How can I help you?"). And every move you make—or don't make—influences the treatment, the play, and the story you tell together.

Like actors, as therapists, our appearance, aura, voice, and relational responsiveness often leave stronger impressions on clients than the words we say or the techniques we use. This is not to say that our clinical training is of no use; of course it is. But effective technique is less about *what* we do—less about reading a script by rote—and more about *how* we do it, how we use ourselves, how we perform our interventions.

When you watch actors performing in movies or plays, do you think about their techniques?—whether they used Strasberg, Adler, or Meisner? Probably not. You are more likely moved by the performers themselves—their ineffable presence, their use of self. Likewise, our clients are more affected by *us* than by our schools of thought—whether we studied psychoanalysis, CBT, or family systems.

No matter what kind of therapist you are, if you approach your work like a performing artist, I promise you will become more awake, alive, and engaged with your clients, while also having a greater capacity to care for yourself. I offer this promise as a psychotherapist who has used my experience as a trained, professional actor every day.

This book is for therapists of all types who are ready to face what you actually bring to the consulting room; what you actually have to work with as a clinician in the way of mind, body, and voice; and what you actually do with yourself in a session, moment to moment—as opposed to what you think you do, in theory.

Granted, I'm sure you already use yourself effectively in your work. What I offer you in the pages ahead are some specific ways in which the art of acting can help you use your instrument as a therapist. This approach has enhanced my capacity to be curious, empathic, imaginative, creative, energetic, spiritual, humble, reflective, generous, self-caring, and joyful in my practice. I hope this book helps you to do the same.

For many of us, the thought of looking at ourselves closely in the mirror is dreadful. We became therapists so we could shirk the spotlight and give it to our clients instead. But just as the actor who disappears into her roles inevitably awakens to an audience looking at her—not just at her character, but at *her*—we too must face the raw fact that our clients look at *us*, beneath our methods and degrees. Thinking like an actor helps to navigate the discomfort of this vulnerability. Just as an actor learns to face her fear of being glimpsed behind the curtain, even eventually learning to harness and make creative use of it on stage, so therapists can learn to utilize a similar self-awareness in session.

Let's talk about fear. Since psychotherapy requires our clients to trust us with their private thoughts and emotions, we are easily governed by our fear of harming them; the Hippocratic oath, "First do no harm," rings like a warning bell in our ears. This fear, I believe, is why we cling so tightly to our credentials and by-the-book interventions, which we wear like life-jackets—the way actors hide behind their scripts—as each new client sweeps us into a wild sea of uncertainty. We look away from the mirror and disavow what we are beneath the professional polish: idiosyncratic bodies, minds, and personalities that influence the therapeutic journey—just as actors can't help but color their performances with who they are in real life. We armor ourselves with the promise that we know what we're doing. And, not unlike the professional actor who shields her stage fright by memorizing her lines, we often do. But likewise, similar to the artistic actor who allows her fear, curiosity, and natural instincts to lead her to the character beyond the text on the page, we sometimes do not. At least, not at first.

Each client is so unique that we must give them time and space to find their own sense of self—or what psychologist Christopher Bollas calls, "idiom."[1] We must allow their life experience to find its way into our office (the rehearsal room) before we can even begin to help create meaning out of it. This zen-like process of doing by not doing may seem lazy or unprofessional to some, but it is hardly without discipline. This artistic practice is perhaps more used by actors than by therapists, but it is one from which therapists can greatly benefit.

(Again, you don't go to the movies to watch actors "Act," but to experience a story and have a good time. Likewise, you don't visit a therapist to watch her "do therapy." As psychoanalyst Adam Phillips says, "I do very little psychoanalysis when I'm doing psychoanalysis."[2])

My experience as an actor has taught me to actively engage the unknown, to follow my curiosity, and to have faith that by deferring hasty answers

I can provide my clients with the necessary space to arrive on their own terms—the way actors take time to discover their characters. (A recent study determined that actors possess an aptitude called "foresight," which is "the talent to envision many possible outcomes,"[3] various line readings, possible backstories, and different interpretations of characters and scenes).

When I practice my clinical work like an artist, I am less likely to panic in moments of uncertainty—out of feelings of failure or inadequacy. Therefore, I am also less likely to hide behind knee-jerk interventions based merely on assumptions, projections, and diagnostic manuals before the client has even had the chance to explore the range of her own voice.

As an actor, I have learned to be aware of myself and to use myself in the present moment—reflectively, adaptively, and creatively. This approach empowers me to stay attuned to my clients as we discover the unknown together, without getting shut down by fear. I can assist, if not model a way for, them to be their fullest, freest selves, and to develop their own capacity to relate, reflect, adapt, and make meaning of their lives. I think most of us consider these to be among our primary clinical goals, regardless of our theoretical orientations.

When we follow theories and techniques by the book (or memorize our lines), we may disguise our fear of not having answers with the mask of professionalism. But to play the part of *therapist* authentically and effectively, we must be able to use our unmasked selves—as artists—in the moment. In the words of seminal psychoanalyst/psychiatrist Dr. Edith Weigert, the therapist "is an artist who may learn something new every day…"[4]

Consider the jazz musician who looks away from his sheet music and freestyles without losing the thread of the piece, and in this process actually discovers deeper, richer meanings in the experience. Likewise, imagine the actor who improvises off-script and finds vital aspects of both her character and her scene partner that initially escaped her. Similarly, as therapists, we can engage in what psychoanalyst Ken Corbett calls "a mode of not knowing." We can be led by nothing more than our client, our self, and our creative curiosity for periods of time, not only without doing harm, but even as a means to discover various versions of ourselves and them. This is what I call *the performing art of therapy*.

But before we continue, let's check in. Red flags may have gone up for those of you hearing me suggest that you throw your psychotherapy training to the wind. I'm not. Nor am I offering this book as a replacement for texts about clinical theory or technique. I presume you already have enough training, education, and supervision to practice therapy ethically, responsibly, and with a relatively clear sense of purpose. What I propose here is that approaching therapy as a performing art can help us to balance our theoretical frameworks with the unpredictable realities of our job—and, more significantly, to transcend the preconceived limitations we impose on our work, our clients, and ourselves.

Theories and techniques are useful and even necessary—especially when we are completely at a loss. But as you know, we are in the business of human minds, emotions, and relationships, none of which can be reduced to paint-by-number instruction manuals. As with any art form, we need a way to think about what we do that allows erratic flickers of life to interfere with our intended (and often abstract) goals—an approach that helps us balance the need to be both expert practitioners and naive caregivers for each unique individual who seeks our help.

So, to be clear, this book is meant as a companion to whatever training, philosophies, or techniques help you to organize what you already do as a therapist. Theories and methods help us to carve out the canals of our clinical treatments, but the art of using our idiosyncratic selves lets the water flow through.

Just as actors balance the technical demands of their jobs with their unique instruments, therapists are also required to be in *two places at once*. We must hold the parameters of a clinical frame alongside the chaos of life, knowing alongside not knowing, not doing alongside doing, the temperature in the room alongside the temperature we aim to achieve.

This concept of holding two opposing ideas at the same time has been a vital part of psychotherapy discourse, especially since psychoanalyst Jessica Benjamin introduced the terms *complementarity* (a black-and-white conflict in which each opposing side stubbornly insists they are right) and *mutual recognition* (in which two different realities can coexist).[5] Benjamin wrote that in both therapy and life we are constantly thrust into complementary collisions—e.g., chaos vs. control, hope vs. dread, certainty vs. doubt—and that the only way out of these dilemmas is to maintain two opposing perspectives equally at once. This is a challenging and often confounding prospect that we must face as therapists, and it requires us to find a place in our minds from which we can observe multiple possibilities—much like the actor's sense of *foresight*. Psychotherapists often refer to this sort of mental observation deck as *the third*,[6] and we can all learn a great deal from actors who necessarily and openly approach their paradoxical work from a *third* position.

Every aspect of the actor's craft requires her to hold clashing concepts at once, beginning with the very premise of her job: to find truth in a given (often fictional) set of circumstances. She must reveal herself openly and vulnerably, but through the safety of a proscenium frame. She shows us like no one else can how to be both professional and personal, without letting one extinguish the other. From the actor we learn to be stabilized and guided by theories (our scripts) while also surfing on the instability of each new session (on stage) in the spotlight, where we encounter a bit of spontaneous life that has not yet been written.

Here again, "not knowing" becomes crucial to both therapy and acting. Like actors, we work with a scene partner who shows up (to the office/ the set/the rehearsal room) with her own ideas, her own perspective, her own subjectivity. Together, through a process of creative collaboration—of listening with curiosity and humility, of pushing and pulling, of giving and receiving—we discover a life (a "character," if you will) and make meaning out of it. This co-created, relational, intersubjective process is very similar to Jessica Benjamin's groundbreaking take on *the third*, which, in her view, is beyond the vantage point of observation.[7] Rather than simply holding a static *third* position as therapists, Benjamin proposes we *surrender* to it in each new session as we do in a partnered dance.[8] This surrender allows us to discover new dynamic and creative possibilities for both our clients and ourselves.

According to actress Robin Weigert—who played Nicole Kidman's therapist in the award-winning series *Big Little Lies*, and is also the grand-daughter of Dr. Edith Weigert, quoted above—the idea of a *third* space of surrender and collaboration between people applies to both acting and therapy. She says:

> Three is a very important number when talking about a relationship between two people. The ego fights to keep a relationship of two a relationship of two. Only when invited does a **third** element join the conversation and change both the speaker and the listener. Both are transformed into beings less driven by intentionality (to produce that which "I alone" would manufacture) than by receptivity (to respond to that which is).

Weigert further believes that by thinking of therapy as a performing art, clinicians can invite ourselves and our clients to participate in its mysterious, transformational power. She says:

> My experience both as an actor and as an 'analysand' [as well as an actor who has effectively played a therapist] is that when we listen with creative intent we **invite participation**. What it is exactly that comes in to the theater (set), or comes in to the therapist's office, and participates in the scene, in the session, is hard to define. Even after so many years acting, I can still only describe the experience as one of being joined. By what, exactly, I cannot say. What I can say is that creativity for me is just this, nothing more—ask, ask this way and ask that way, ask again, wait… receive."[9]

Psychoanalyst Steven Mitchell has described the creative collaboration of therapy similarly, invoking literary critic Frank Kermode who said the therapist "might be more usefully thought of as a kind of poet rather than as a kind of archaeologist."[10] Rather than the traditionally expected scenario of "expert doctor" excavating and unearthing the "submissive patient's" true self, Mitchell offered that therapist and client could each open themselves up to the mysterious *third* (or potential space,[11] as Winnicott put it) between them, and work together (as scene partners, if you will) to construct "truths in the service of self-coherence."[12] He wrote that the client's "dynamics and life history do not have an independent reality that can be uncovered or grasped from the outside—they exist in a state of complex potentiality and are actually co-created by the observer's participation."[13]

In order to invite or receive this invitation for creative participation that both Weigert and Mitchell describe, we must possess great curiosity, reflectiveness, and humility. We must have the capacity to use our self genuinely and in a variety of ways as we navigate the unknown with our scene partner. And though therapists say "use yourself" all the time, the phrase means different things to different people at different times. So, let's put those words into context.

The book *Use of Self in Therapy*, for instance, argues that, regardless of our therapeutic orientations, knowing who we are psychologically—e.g., our emotional needs and what makes us tick—is our most valuable tool. Psychoanalytic theorists—especially those of the relational, intersubjective, interpersonal, and self-psychology varieties—refer to "use of self" as they continue to theorize about the clinical benefits of the therapist's countertransference.[14] Couples, family, and group therapists use themselves as mediators, referees, and empathic listeners, depending on what is called for. Those who practice CBT and DBT say that a coachy use of self establishes greater trust with clients than does traditional psychoanalysis, which tends to cast the therapist in the role of silent follower more than interactive guide. All of these uses of self assist therapy treatments at different times and in different ways.

I propose that approaching our work like actors—or better yet, like performing artists in our own right—can help us to use ourselves in *all* these ways and more.

In my work as a therapist, the craft of acting provides tangible approaches to explore and play my unique instrument—the combination of my mind, face, body, emotions, voice, personality, energy, history, and imagination. But perhaps more importantly, it prepares me to get lost with my clients, to expand my sense of myself and them as we progress, and to return to a centered version of myself when the curtain drops and it's time to go home.

I am not necessarily advising you to deploy literal dramatic exercises during your sessions. Since I have graduate degrees in both acting and social work, people often ask me why I don't specialize in *psychodrama*, Gestalt, or some other modality in which therapists deploy theatrical interventions—sometimes to great effect. But I feel psychotherapy is a performing art in and of itself. We engage in what psychoanalysts Lewis Aron and Galit Atlas call *dramatic dialogues*,[15] whether we listen quietly to just one client in a psychodynamic situation or facilitate a behavioral-focused group of many. Everything I learned in drama school enhances the work I do as a therapist in every situation: when I dive into the deep end of each individual person's story; coach couples and families through relationship conflicts; manage and promote my business; or teach and talk about my work with peers, students, and/or the public.

The main function of therapy is actually no different than that of acting: to discover truth in a given set of circumstances.

> As psychoanalyst Kindler has suggested when comparing the two art forms, "[b]oth are endeavors involving the imaginative collaboration of the two participants."[16]

Again, I know you already have your own way of collaborating with your clients, which is why you're a therapist. I suggest here that owning ourselves as performing artists can help us to confidently reach beyond the surface of each "script" we are given without unnecessary hang-ups about which "technique" is best. Perhaps one-day conservatory acting training will even be offered as an essential part of psychotherapy, social work, and psychology curriculums. But in the meantime, you can refer to this book.

Structure of the Book

Act I: Prepare

Therapists and actors are both on the receiving end of the frequent misperception that our jobs are easy (e.g., "All you do is sit there?" "You just show up and say your lines? Must be nice."). To be sure, we're most effective with our clients—scene partners or audiences—when we seem to be doing nothing at all. But such clarity, ease, and openness to possibility are ironically achieved by a great deal of preparation. And as with any performing art, much of our work takes place offstage/outside the office.

In this section I share how I prepare for my "scenes" with clients—the live moments of exchange when I am in the hot seat with them. Granted, one never knows what will happen from one scene to the next, so this prep is not intended to control exactly what will take place. Instead, it helps me to enter that mysterious, unknown, third/potential/rehearsal space, armed and ready to maximize the creative possibilities of our time together.

The tools in this section give me a framework to fall back on when the client and I are both completely at a loss. When we need something technical to refocus us and "get on with the show." Just "showing up" and "being yourself" can certainly work as an actor or therapist, but only until it doesn't. As my graduate acting teacher, Brian McEleney, used to say, "[d]on't wait for the acting gods to strike, they may never arrive." The ideas, suggestions, and exercises in this section have prepared me to embrace even the moments when the "therapy gods" do not happen to strike.

In these chapters, I discuss the art of listening: our main action as therapists. I show how to get a sense of what you look and sound like, and how that awareness can be used in clinical work. I offer practical strategies for being present and using breath—in order to stay centered and attuned to our scene partners, but also to shift focus, raise stakes, hold intense feelings of aggression, despair, or trauma, and assume greater authority in the room when necessary. We will talk about energy and how we can use our bodies and voices to foster greater empathy for clients while maintaining a strong sense of self. And throughout, I will remind you that it doesn't matter what you do, exactly, as long as it works.

Act II: Rehearse

This section focuses on what we actually do with each client—most of the time. This is the process of getting to know them and helping them get to know themselves better. I refer to this main body of our work as "rehearsal" because it parallels that particular aspect of the actor's process.

Rehearsal is the period during which each performer tries her wings, takes risks, fails, succeeds, explores, makes discoveries, adapts, and collaborates. All of the artists in the rehearsal studio inevitably influence each other's sense of the characters they play and the stories they co-create. These are stories they can revise again and again, much like a therapy treatment.

I must take a moment to clarify what I mean by "rehearse" and "perform," because these words can be interchanged or contrasted, depending on the context in which they are used (e.g., We could say the opening of a Broadway play marks the end of the "rehearsal" and the beginning of the "performance." But the actors in the play may actually feel, to the contrary, that their rehearsal period has only begun. After all, they may have over a year of eight shows a week ahead of them, and only three weeks of rehearsal behind them, leaving them with a great deal of room to take risks and fail and discover their characters more truthfully and deeply—as Dame Judi Dench says, "[w]hen you're in theater, you get out there the next night and do it better."[17] Likewise, a film actor may perform at 100% at every stop—whether she's doing a read through, rehearsing, or shooting a scene—because for her, to practice her craft means to seek truth with full commitment, every step of the way). For the purpose of organizing this book, I am using "rehearse" to mean the primary thrust of our clinical work, in which we invite ourselves and our clients to participate in possibility; to enter that third/potential/transitional space together. Rehearsal is the time we give ourselves to throw paint at a blank canvas, and while each participant expects the resulting image to appear one way, both discover what is actually there and continue to paint together. As Robin Weigert describes, in both the processes of acting and of therapy, "Both [scene partners] are transformed into beings less driven by intentionality (to produce that which I would manufacture) than by receptivity (to respond to that which is)."[18] I often say that no matter what happens between therapist and client during a psychotherapy treatment, it is always a dress rehearsal for life.

The chapters in this section explore the various ways I have learned to use active listening in session—as well as my body and voice—to frame the treatment and establish trust before we dive into the deep end together. We will discuss the value of curiosity, having intentions, trying, failing, failing again, failing better, adapting, and reflecting as the process evolves. I share how improvisation and the concept of play enhance my work. I share creative ways to use transference and countertransference, the way an actor might: e.g., to discover who the client is trying to be, who they want to be, who they are afraid to be, the roles in which they actively cast you, the characters they passively wish you to embody, and the characters you decide to embody for them as an intentional intervention. We will also delve into the potentially controversial topics of love and erotic feelings, which are often challenging for therapists to integrate into our professional lives—but, conversely, tend to be very business-as-usual for actors. Along these lines, we will cover the art of being vulnerable yet safe, intimate yet maintaining boundaries, paradoxes that actors navigate regularly, consciously, and openly, as part of their craft. I believe that we therapists can similarly learn to bring our emotional vulnerability, sexuality, and/or feelings of love into our work consciously, confidently, and playfully, but also with safety, purpose, and self-care.

Act III: Perform

As we have established, all performances are rehearsals, and all rehearsals are performances. But here I use "perform" to mean the technical moves we deploy to enhance the effectiveness of our contact with scene partners and audiences, with the expectation that things will go (almost) exactly as planned.

For actors, these are the moments they need to sing, dance, do stage combat, speak with an accent, or move with a specific physicality. But on a more basic level, it could simply mean the technical timing of their dialogue or the particular places on stage they need to move, stand, or sit (known as blocking).

For therapists, I think of *performance* as the moments we contract for the technical terms of each treatment; or set clear guidelines for a client who is in danger, or who is a danger to her or himself or to someone else; or intervene in any sort of crisis; or do couples, family, or group therapy, all of which require a more technical and extroverted use of self than individual treatment. But more simply and ubiquitously, we also *perform* our considered interpretations, reflections, narratives, and directions that we choose to share with clients.

There are also the non-clinical performances of publicity and self-promotion, which have always been part of the actor's job, but are increasingly necessary for therapists as well—especially as the internet becomes the primary medium through which people learn about our work. And of course the task of presenting our work—in classrooms, at conferences, on panels, or in the media—is a performance in itself.

In the final chapter, we discuss the performance of auditioning. I leave this topic for last, just as conservatory acting programs do, because as crucial as audition skills are to land a job (or book a second meeting with a client), the technical marks we prepare to hit at an audition—e.g., to make a good first impression, convey confidence and competence, convince the casting director or client that we are the best possible person for the job—do not necessarily help us with the creative voyage we will embark on once we book the role. Nonetheless, audition tools are necessary for all performing artists, and I will give you several to add to your professional arsenal.

Once again, before we begin, please keep in mind that you already know how to perform therapy in your own way.

Like actors, therapists tend to go blank when offered advice about our craft. We can suddenly forget the wealth of natural resources we bring to the job that are 100% our own. When you receive tips as a performing artist, always consider if and how they fit with what you already do intuitively. And if they do not, please don't chop off your toes to squeeze into the glass slipper (as my yoga teacher, Nancy Elkes, says, "[t]ry the pose but don't change for me, don't change for anyone"). If the following suggestions help you to help your clients, then great; and if not, that's fine too. At the very least, they may help you to think more consciously about what you already do as a therapist.

My main intention here is to identify dynamics that are always—and have always been—in the clinical setting, whether we acknowledge them or not. I find that looking at those dynamics through a performing arts lens helps to clarify them, put them into explicit language, and to navigate them.

More than anything, I hope this book helps you to practice therapy with more access to *you*. I hope it helps you to harness all the great qualities you bring to your work intuitively, so that you can use yourself with intention—and perhaps even expand your *self* in the process. I hope it empowers you to practice your craft with less fear and more freedom and fun, less burnout and more creative energy, more willingness to join your clients emotionally while remaining securely grounded in yourself. And of course I hope this book helps you to inspire your clients to do the same for themselves.

You do not end where psychotherapy begins. Both you and your clinical work expand, creatively and continuously, when you own yourself as a performing artist.

Act I

Prepare

[L]et our unconscious, intuitive creativeness be set into motion by the help of conscious, preparatory work.

(Constantin Stanislavski, *Creating a Role*, 1946b, p. 8)

1   Listen

The first thing we do as therapists is listen. And we never stop.

We listen before we know what's happening. We listen to what clients say, and more closely to what they don't say. We listen when everything else we try fails. And we listen to our own reactions, feelings, and thoughts, during and well beyond each session.

No matter how prepared or unprepared we are to engage with a client, our main action is always to listen—in a way that invites participation. As a result, any preparation we do for our clinical work will be most useful if it makes us better listeners.

I bet your ability to listen carefully is what first made you think, "Hey, I should be a therapist." The realization of your propensity to listen was probably not unlike that moment the actor gets "bitten by the bug"—when she first captivates a crowd, gets laughs, conjures tears, and receives applause.

As therapists, we learn that listening is our way in. We feel needed, validated, and connected to other people when we care for them by genuinely listening to them. We feel rewarded when we embolden other people by demonstrating our interest in them, their story, and the particular ways they need to tell their tales.

And while the actor's way of approaching people may seem to be the opposite of ours—by entering the spotlight rather than retreating into the dark—I believe that therapists and actors represent two sides of the same listening coin.

Both art forms depend on the occurrence of what I call a **relational event**. A *relational event* is an exchange of attention, mind, emotion, energy, and imagination between at least two people: e.g., actor and audience, actor and scene partner, client and therapist. The fire of a *relational* event is sparked into flaming life through the catalytic act of listening.

And though the actor easily forgets her job requires listening (and not just showing off), and the therapist forgets listening is an action (beyond just sitting back), both artisans must listen in order for their work to breathe, fly, and have meaning. "Acting is just listening,"[1] says consummate actress, Meryl Streep, while Freud wrote that the therapist "should simply listen."[2]

Listening makes the magic happen; it is the portal through which shared experience is possible.

There is no live theater, no *relational event*, if the actors on stage don't listen to one another, the audience doesn't listen to the actors, or the actors don't listen to how the audience receives them. The texture of the actor's *next* move is determined by how her *last* move was listened to by her audience—and how she listened back. It is in this delicate dance, this subtle exchange of subjective attention, that *relational events* occur. One participant expresses herself with a sound or gesture, and through the act of another participant listening, that gesture is transformed into something new, shared, and meaningful.

Unlike their theatrical peers, screen actors do not play to their audiences directly, but their performances still depend on the presence of others. Close ups, for instance, are always more captivating and transporting to watch if the actor has someone to play to off camera instead of having to do the extraneous work of imagining a listener. Even scenes that feature only a single actor have a live "audience" on set in the form of a director—if not an entire crew—who brighten the actor's performance through the electricity of live listening.

Everything true about listening during acting is also true during therapy. Clients who complain, "If you're not going to say anything, I might as well talk to a wall" are missing the point. We rely on attuned listening to realize we exist. Not only does the light of someone else's attention make us feel recognized, but it also invites us to expand our versions of ourselves—our multiplicity—as we play various roles in our lives.

Therapists of various schools have theorized for decades that our experience of self actually depends on our relationships with other people; filmmakers have been intuiting this same truth since the dawn of cinema. Consider the infinite number of films in which we get to know a male protagonist through the lens of a woman who listens. *King Kong*, to cite an iconic example, presents a monstrous ape who we only come to know as a sensitive creature by way of an empathic, blonde beauty sitting in his palm. Michael Keaton's Bruce Wayne in Tim Burton's 1989 *Batman* also comes to mind, where we see Kim Basinger's photojournalist/love interest literally follow the mysterious protagonist throughout the film, gradually creating a picture of his true self through the lens of her camera—coupled with her unwavering curiosity and attentive heart. And of course the highly effective and deliberate conceit of the hit show *The Sopranos* is entirely predicated on an anti-hero being listened to, carefully and empathically, by a woman—his therapist, no less. By contrast, protagonists who don't have a woman to listen to them in this way—e.g., Robert DeNiro in *Taxi Driver*, or the titular Dane in Shakespeare's *Hamlet*—tend to come across as solitary, dark, and disturbed, since we have no relational access to them. Finally, and fortunately, filmmakers and television producers are beginning to take some responsibility for their influence on contemporary culture, and are casting—shocking and novel as it may seem—*Women!* as complex protagonists who are listened to, warmly and respectfully, by both men and other women. We are also starting (ever so slightly) to see more men and women of color as subjects who are listened to and respected in mainstream entertainment, as well as LGB and T people and those whose bodies or gender expressions do not conform to the norm[3]—although we clearly still have a long way to go on this front. This progress suggests that as a culture we are gradually learning how necessary it is to be the subject of someone else's active listening in order to feel alive, to feel understood, and to find the confidence to share more of our true selves. And while we wait for Hollywood to accurately represent more of us as interesting, relatable subjects on screen, we all have the opportunity to *be* on the therapy couch. There, each of us can experience an authentic sense of self, while growing through the fertile opportunity created by another person really listening to us.

The act of listening during therapy involves far more than quiet staring. Active listening is an engagement of minds, emotions, and imaginations, and it invites the person on whom we focus our attention to discover more surprising, rich, and wonderful aspects of herself than she ever would encounter by talking to a wall. Fantastic worlds of possibility open up in therapy, even in sessions in which the therapist says nothing, as long as s/he truly listens.

This realization begs an essential question: how does one truly listen?

As journalist Celeste Headlee observes, "There is no reason to learn how to show you're paying attention if you are in fact paying attention."[4] While I agree with her that, in theory, the act of listening is very simple— as is breathing, singing, and standing up straight—in reality, we make it complicated. And this digital age of screens and devices in which we live, where distraction prevails as the norm, does not help. It therefore seems worth sharing in the chapters ahead how I have used my acting training to help find the natural flow of my listening.

"How do I listen as a unique, idiosyncratic, individual?" is perhaps the most crucial question I ask myself in all of my prep work as a clinical performing artist. And when I enter the rehearsal studio/therapy office, I ask myself the equally important question of how *my* listening affects each client. This dynamic above all informs how I make adjustments during the course of a session, depending on what my scene partner seems to need. Again, most of the key *relational events* during the course of any treatment happen when we have said nothing at all; but that silence hardly means we're doing nothing.

Listening is an action, the main action that we rely on in absolutely everything we do as therapists and performers. It is the egg that keeps the dough together. Every part of this book will refer back to the essential skill of listening. As with any artistic process, in therapy we must envision goals and attempt to create structure while also accepting that every move we make is fluid and bleeds into the overall mission in no definitive order. But the one constant, from the start, is that we are always listening.

2 Know What You Look Like (And Use Your Subtext)

Subtext

"Why are you making that face?" is a question that's been posed by several of my clients—abruptly, mid-session—throughout my career.

When I was greener, I would rely on the classic "blank screen" excuse (*I'm not making a face!*, I'd think. *This has nothing to do with me! This must be his projection!*). My eyebrows would raise up inquisitively, and I'd fire back something like, "Hmm, I wonder what's happening with *you* right now…"

The event in the room probably *was* more about them than my face. But the way I listened made it about me and my lack of experience in using myself as a therapy scene partner. By default, I sent unhelpful, implicit, messages to the client like:

1) *You are breaking "the rules" by asking about me,* 2) *I am above being fully present with you because I am the "doctor" and you are the "patient,"* 3) *I am insecure about my facial expressions and therefore you should not talk about them* and 4) *I expect you to give an emotionally naked performance, alone in the spotlight, while I watch, fully clothed in the dark.*

Those who dared to question my facial expressions were met with all of that, instantly, through a mere flicker of my eyes.

That flicker is what screen actors call *subtext*, and the art of employing subtext is one of their most necessary skills. Actors who play for the camera must be aware of how their idiomatic reactions, feelings, and thoughts register, even subtly, on their faces. In the actors' medium, much of the story is told through subtext. While their mouths utter a few dry lines, their eyes express something far more evocative, perhaps even the complete opposite of the words they speak (e.g., When I say, "Tell me about your question?" with my mouth, and *how DARE you ask what I'm thinking?!* with my eyes). As a therapist, I benefit from thinking like a screen actor. Especially when I want to respond to questions of the, "What's up with your face?" variety with ease and presence of mind.

Know Your Face

What do your clients actually see as you listen? I sometimes find it helpful to see myself on video to get a sense of my natural facial responses as I listen or speak to people (Not unlike film actors checking out *dailies*—the raw footage that was shot on a particular day—to get a sense of how their work comes across). Try recording yourself doing a mock session.

As you watch your face on screen, what do you observe? Are your eyebrows tense and inquisitive? Does your jaw tighten? Do your eyes appear cold and distant? Or do you look like a warm, curious scene partner? Would you like to talk to that therapist? It's not the answers to these questions that matter as much as the questions themselves. The awareness of how I use my face when I'm "in a scene" helps me to be present in my own skin, even when I'm just listening. With such awareness, I'm not blindsided when clients react to me in various, even unexpected ways.

Make Use of Video Sessions

Observing myself during video sessions allows me to see how my face engages my clients in real time. I can watch and listen to my scene partner closely with one eye, and occasionally notice what my face looks like with the other. In my experience, holding both images in sight and mind does not distract me from the client because I can hear and see them the entire time. This technical tool has helped me to be in *two places at once*—to observe both my internal and external senses of self. Psychologist Sheldon Bach might describe this practice as oscillating back and forth between states of *subjective awareness* and *objective self reflection*.[1] You might think of it as two different movie camera angles working in tandem: One from your inner, first-person point of view, and the other looking back at you from the outside, a third-person perspective. In this sense, the computer screen serves as a mediating *third* space between your two perspectives as a clinical performer—subjective and objective.

It's easy to get lost in our analytical minds, without even realizing it, while clients are talking. As a result, we sometimes leave them alone with the empty shell of our body and face staring at them (Creepy, right? Would you bare your soul to that?). On the flip side, it can be equally off-putting when we allow too much of ourselves to intrude into their space, to be too "on," too up in their business, even just by the way we choose to listen. Having a sense of what my passive, listening face looks like when either of these things happens gives me the choice to make adjustments or not, depending on the situation. This can be done even when I'm working "live" in the office, without the aid of the screen.

After years of practicing therapy, I don't feel the need to look at myself as much as I used to. The cultivated awareness of how my thoughts and reactions register in my face helps me take responsibility for my presence in each scene, even when I think I'm doing nothing at all. At the very least, this prepares me to be less defensive and more reflective when clients accuse me of "making a face." Maybe they are indeed bothered by the way I blinked my eyes, or maybe they just find it difficult to tolerate silence. I can better determine what is happening when I have a strong visual sense of my face and how it responds.

Know Your Subtext

Our genuine feelings and thoughts are just as present in each scene as our words. For instance, I have learned that my *subtext* alone can help me to establish a safe environment for clients. I can invite them to speak and encourage them with my curiosity without having to say a word. What's more, my clients typically do not ask what I'm thinking as much when I'm present with my thoughts and aware of how I'm listening (If only I could send this bit of wisdom back in time to my less secure therapist self… Although, fumbling and reflecting on our fumbles is how our work develops).

At the same time, it's important to note that we never have complete mastery over our subtext.

More often than not, we transmit reflexive reactions, judgments, and enigmatic messages[2] to clients more quickly than our conscious minds can grasp. And regardless of how clear we believe our subtext to be, our scene partner's projections will always be a significant part of our work. So, no matter what we say or don't say, what matters most is the moment we revisit our dramatic exchanges and find out what our scene partner actually took away from the experience.

Consider the following vivid example of an audience projecting onto an actor's subtext. In 1990, director Andre Gregory saw Julianne Moore in a play and recalled, "There was one moment in her performance that was absolutely staggering. She was sitting on the floor reading a newspaper and doing absolutely nothing, saying nothing. But whatever she had going on inside was terrifying."[3] After the show, he asked Moore what she was doing during the scene, and she said she was simply counting to 60. This, Gregory said, showed "a very clever actress who understood what she didn't need to do to get the appropriate response."[4]

Obviously I'm not encouraging you to count to 60 as your client talks. But this anecdote shows how little one has to do to encourage and even stimulate the thought process of their audience or scene partner.

Whether I'm intending to convey clear and genuine emotional support for a client processing a recent loss, or I'm using my empathic curiosity to follow a client's experience of living as a minority in America, or I'm simply paying attention to whatever happens with a client in the moment, I can be sure that my subtext is being transmitted to them in some way. Even when I do nothing at all.

And when they project onto my eyes (like Andre Gregory did onto Julianne Moore) and assume my subtext is "*try harder*" when I'm really thinking "*wow, you work so hard*," I can better appreciate both of our contributions to the exchange by knowing what was actually on my mind, and what they may have seen on my face.

What is it Like to See Yourself?

Seeing our own reflection affects each of us differently. Some of us readily receive what we see and are empowered to use it creatively as we relate to the world. Others are triggered by physical attributes we'd rather disavow. Still others might find this entire activity boring. I, for one, find it helps me foster dynamic *relational events* with other people. Seeing my face and body in action forces me to confront how I feel about taking up physical space, and to articulate that experience for myself.

I have spent years of self reflection—on my own and with the help of therapists, acting teachers, and friends—to better understand my relationship to my physical self. In my case, growing up as a gender nonconforming boy in a family and town teeming with bullies contributed to my attempts to be invisible as a means of survival. And on a deeper level, my relationship with my mother also contributed to my habits of self-negation. While being extremely loving and nurturing in the broad strokes of her parenting (gifts from both of my parents included the Miss Piggy, Princess Leia, and unicorn dolls I requested—and that was back in the 1980s when gender nonconforming children were not yet discussed in the mainstream), my mother often struggled to be attuned to my granular self experience, moment-to-moment. Like many who become therapists, I often found that my mother's emotions eclipsed my own, contributing to the feeling that I was divorced from myself,[5] and specifically from my body.

These idiosyncratic bits of history inform even the most microscopic ways I inhabit and use my face and body in life, in art, and in therapy. My practice of deep self reflection—including checking in with my appearance from time to time—helps me to connect to the body and self I had disavowed as a child and adolescent. By acknowledging, naming, and appreciating the history of living in my specific body—in the specific family and social contexts in which I grew up—I can better recognize my tendencies both as a therapist and as a performing artist in general (My compulsions to over accommodate clients when they are emotionally vulnerable, for example, or my worries about not doing enough for them, or looking like I don't care enough). Self reflection—externally and internally—helps me to observe, understand, and move through my doubts about being "too" silent in session, and my fear and guilt that I will come across as cold, sadistic, or too self-involved if I "leave them alone" to process their feelings (Those are of course the ways I learned to feel as a child if I did not subsume myself entirely into my mother's emotions, or if I "invaded" her self with too much of my own. And again, my sense that too much of *me* was harmful to others was exacerbated by a town full of people who reacted negatively to my gender nonconformity).

For me, checking in with my face from time to time during video sessions reminds me that I am ***there*** with the client—visible, grounded, alive, supportive, and certainly not harmful—even when I don't speak. This approach reminds me that as long as I am tuned in—both to them and to myself—I can trust my face to be present, empathic, and curious. It shows me how effective it often is when I simply follow a client's narrative, and how much better it is to let them work through their thoughts than it would be to disrupt their flow with validating words, noises, gestures, or facial expressions. Some therapists might say this intervention gives me a boost of mirroring to affirm my own narcissistic needs, which stem from my deficit of effective mirroring as a child. But for me, checking in with my own face from time to time as I work gives me confidence to be silent in session, and to allow the client to establish their own transferential process without my neurosis getting in their way.

In looking at yourself and considering your own histories of self and body, you may discover your tendencies to take up more space or less space than necessary. Or, like me, you might be surprised to learn that you are palpably confident, warm, and present with your clients even when you think you are not. "You are enough," as my grad school acting teachers used to say.

Stay in the Shallow End of Narcissus' Pool

Be careful, because looking at yourself is a tricky business. Having a peek in Narcissus' pool can lure you into vacuous self obsession. And getting sucked into yourself is, of course, the opposite of the intended goal—which is to ***listen*** to the client with a free and open mind.

I have written elsewhere about the potential pitfalls of seeing yourself on screen, an experience that may spur you to over-identify with the image you see and attempt to replicate or control it in some way—a dilemma I call, "Oops, I'm a Celebrity" (OIAC).[6] OIAC happens to many fleeting reality-TV stars (amateur performers) who become frozen in a framed idea of self based on reductive screen clips that have been edited together to create a persona or "character." When this reductive image is internalized, the result sends one down a slippery slope of obsessive self-consciousness, and may lead to a significant break from other people, or even from reality. When I ask you to look at your face during therapy, I am not at all advising you to get lost in such a hall of mirrors. On the contrary, I want you to look at your listening face the way a true performing artist does, not an amateur "celebrity." Use what you see in the mirror to help you discover the possibilities of who you can be, as opposed to the limitations of who you think you are.

In order to stay focused on your intention, think of the lyrics of Charles Wright's song "Express Yourself." Wright's lyrics essentially say something like: *It doesn't matter what you look like. It's what you think, feel, and do to make you look that way that matters.*

Try to maintain a sense of what's happening inside you when you're working with clients, as well as what you look like when you're immersed in this process, not the other way around.

Naturally, many of you will be uncomfortable looking at yourselves, either on your own time or especially during video sessions. My proposal here may feel off-putting or misguided because to look at yourself might seem to steal focus that belongs on the client. Again, I am in no way suggesting that we fixate on our own appearance. Instead, I'm suggesting that knowing what our physical presence looks like during sessions can be a valuable tool. I'm suggesting that you develop self-awareness as opposed to self consciousness. And frankly, a complete lack of self-awareness can be dishonest. Such a state disregards the specific impact we have on our scene partner as we sit opposite them in our specific body with our specific thoughts and feelings. As Sheldon Bach observes, to negate our own sense of self and to submit entirely to being "someone else's object" is simply the other side of the narcissism coin.[7]

Observe Other Listeners

I find inspiration in what other people look like when they listen—e.g., in social and professional exchanges, during television interviews, and between actors, especially when one of them is playing a therapist. There are so many bad representations of therapy on screen, but there are also a few extra-ordinary ones—Robin Weigert on *Big Little Lies*, Gabriel Byrne, Dianne Wiest, and Amy Ryan on *In Treatment*, Lorraine Bracco in *The Sopranos*, and Viola Davis in the movie *Trust*, to name a few. No matter what lines they speak—if they speak any at all—these actors convey care, curiosity, and concern through their eyes, in addition to a strong intuitive sense of what their "client" is not saying in words, but may be thinking and feeling on some level. Great actors respond to their scene partners intuitively, with rich layers of subtext that invite them to participate and expand their sense of self. There is much we can learn by watching these artists and by allowing that inspiration to expand the ways we use our own subtext in session.

It is crucial to have our *own* sense of how we look, and rely on our own judgment of how to use it rather than to exclusively depend on feedback from clients, teachers, directors, or audiences. Throughout our careers as clinical performers, we need to find a way to oscillate between taking in feedback humbly, and maintaining our own sense of self, both from the inside out and the outside in—to be in *two places at once.*

3 Know What You Sound Like (And Face Your Inner Critic)

I bet you don't love to hear recordings of your voice; you're not alone. Instead, most therapists prefer to listen to our clients and to analyze them from a safe, clinical distance. To listen to ourselves is to open a Pandora's box of complex, deeply-rooted, experiences within our bodies—what psychoanalyst Adrienne Harris describes as, "unconscious material suspended just out of awareness."[1] "[Y]our voice is linked to the whole of your body, emotional life and psyche,"[2] says revered vocal coach/theatre director, Patsy Rodenburg, while psychoanalyst Christopher Bollas similarly observes that "[t]here are many subtle ways to express affect, but none more than 'in' and 'through' the voice."[3] We spend lifetimes finding clever ways to push this material out of mind in order to protect ourselves from…ourselves—from our internalized self-judgment, if not self-hatred.

And yet, we ask our clients to face this very fear each time they enter our office and take center couch. As celebrated drag queen and television host, RuPaul might say, "If you can't listen to yourself, how in the *hey-ell* you gonna listen to somebody else?!"[4]

Let's think about this dilemma in theater terms. Much like in therapy, at the beginning of a play, a performer needs to **frame** the event/create an environment/set the scene. This framing welcomes and orients the audience (and/or scene partner) to the world in which they will exist for the foreseeable future, a world they must trust enough to transcend their everyday selves and explore a range of experiences. It is up to the performers to establish this trust. No matter what the actors say or do, if they do not seem to trust themselves—if they are palpably disconnected from their minds, bodies, and voices—their audience will not trust them, and will therefore refrain from suspending disbelief and joining them on any potential adventures.

There are innumerable ways we can establish this trust, but as both an actor and a therapist, my primary practice is always to find connection between my mind and body in the moment. And the *clearest* indication of that connection (or lack thereof) is evident in my voice.

As Adrienne Harris puts it, we must "have access to and be comfortable with [our] subjective affect states and bodily reactivity if [we] are to experience and metabolize patients' communications."[5] In other words, we must know how our own instruments (our minds, bodies, emotions, and voices) work if we are to help clients understand and make use of their own.

Subtext manifests through our voices as palpably as it does through our eyes. Like the actor, our voices transmit volumes of information, whether we realize it or not—so we might as well realize it. Achieving that realization means taking time to locate where we live in our minds and bodies in each moment, and how that manifests through the sounds we produce.

We need not be derailed by: 1) The client who laughs at our shaky, sheepish, voice when we are CLEARLY uncomfortable about a kinky sexual experience they just described, or 2) the client who gets abruptly defensive because our unwittingly flat tone at the end of a long day suggests that she is not entertaining, or 3) the client who notices we are off our game because, as it turns out, we got into a high-stakes, political Facebook argument with a family member that morning and REALLY don't want the client to notice, but our attempt to mask those turbulent feelings manifests in a shrill, dismissive sound which inhibits him from talking freely.

In my experience, awareness of my voice helps me recover from such moments of distraction, miscommunication, and empathic failure without being defensive. If I recognize and perhaps even acknowledge how I sound—as opposed to ignoring it—I can reestablish trust, ease, and congruence within myself, and therefore with my scene partner. At the same time, I model self-awareness for my client without the need to be defensive, and from there the two of us have a safe opening to sort out any misconnection that may have taken place.

So again, the primary goal of getting to know our instrument is not necessarily to change it or cover up its flaws, but to increase our awareness of it. When in doubt, a practice of self-awareness is enough. Such an acknowledgment signals to your scene partner that you trust yourself and that they can trust you as well. Building self-awareness shows them that: 1) You are willing to look at yourself as you are, 2) you are willing to face and to own your idiosyncrasies, 3) you are willing to acknowledge and accept the presence of various emotional, physical, and mental content within you, and how that manifests in the sounds you make, and most of all, 4) it invites and encourages them to be aware of themselves.

Face Your Fear

As Patsy Rodenberg writes:

> [W]e all harbour a fundamental fear about our voices, we are all racked with severe self judgements. That fear is bound up in the way we think we sound to others. This self judgement can and does prevent us from communicating fully to the world.[6]

I agree. We fear hearing our own voices because they rarely sound the way we wish—the version of us that we imagine to be appealing. Hearing our voice forces us to consider how others actually hear us, and this spurs our *inner critics* to deride us for sounding weak, sensitive, dull, daft, earnest, dramatic, needy, crazy, or too much/not enough. And then we freeze, terrified of further judgment, whether or not anyone has actually been critical of our aural presentation. We try to push all the mortifying things our voices imply about us out of our minds, and along with that often goes our self-awareness—and with that, our accessibility to others.

But the more I understand this fear, the more I am able to get out of my own way and accept and make use of the instrument I have to work with rather than to disavow it. **In fact, one of the biggest jobs of both therapists and actors is to simply get over the fear of ourselves.** This evolution is a process most people would rather not attempt. But our continuous practice of facing our fear of *self* is a distinguishing feature of a performing artist. This process helps us to be open and available to scene partners when we're in the hot seat, and to inspire them to do the same.

Disarm Your Inner Critic

The best way to manage our fear of self is to disarm our inner critics, which is easier said than done.

First, we have to accept that the critic is here to stay. Like a nagging roommate, our inner critic will get along better with us if we find a way to coexist with it rather than try to ignore it or kick it out. I make a daily practice of getting along with my inner critic, and with all the parts of myself I don't like; consequently, this effort improves my relationships with other people.

Next, we can transform our criticisms, deprecations, and judgments, into *curiosity*. When I lead with *curiosity* as opposed to *criticism,* I can thaw my frozen, solipsistic state of fear, and move into a mode of discovery that is fluid, dynamic, and intersubjective—allowing several points of view to exist at once. Constant curiosity helps me to get out of my own way, to be aware of myself and the people around me, and to coexist with an open mind. Try asking yourself, "What do I want to express?" and "How am I being received?" at the very same time without letting one question completely dominate the other. Let these questions take priority over any judgments you have about your voice.

Sound Check

Once in a while, I like to do a self sound check by saying a few words out loud. I then reflect on the sound I produce, imagine another person listening to me, and ask myself how my voice might affect them: e.g., Would it invite them into my space, or push them away? I wonder what subtextual messages my voice might suggest: e.g., That I am ambivalent about talking to that person, that I'm nervous, or that I'm filled with unadulterated joy. I also notice how I sound and how I am received when I exchange a few words with people around me. My main objective in all this is to practice mindful reflection on where I am in *that moment*, and how my experience manifests in my voice. Try doing some sound checks of your own before you start your day. What does your voice tell you about where you are mentally, physically, and emotionally?

As you vocalize, allow your mind to roam and connect your sounds to the various thoughts, feelings, and impulses that come to you in the moment, whether or not they make sense (You can even do this as you fix your breakfast, feed your pets, or take out the trash as part of your morning routine). Be sure to express your natural thoughts and feelings with intent. Notice if you're just blurting out vague sounds in order to obey my orders like a "good" student, or if you're truly expressing what you want based on whatever flows naturally through your mind. The distinction here is key, and applies to *everything* we do as therapists and as performers in general. **Every move and sound we make—whether in preparation or performance—will *always* be most useful and effective if we execute it with personal and specific intent. This will help us to be authentic, alive, and clear in the ways we present ourselves to scene partners** (The word *intent* of course implies that we are concerned both with what we have to say and with how we are heard at the very same time). Needless to say, on the flip side, every move and sound we make without personal intent, in a mindless effort to follow "rules," will *always* be less interesting, less useful, and less effective for everyone involved.

As you do your daily sound check, remember the following: **It is the practice of mindfulness—of mind-body-voice connectedness—that matters most, not the result. The *observation* of your voice and its *intent* is much more important than the quality of the sound itself.**

Take it from consummate actress Glenn Close, who said of her preparation for the iconic role of Norma Desmond in the Broadway musical of *Sunset Boulevard* that:

> The only way I could kind of psychologically attack the big songs were thinking of them as monologues…**if I could put the thought over**, maybe people…if I didn't hit a note perfectly, maybe they wouldn't…it wouldn't be so obvious.[7]

In other words, if Close could practice making her *thoughts* and *intentions* clear to her audience, they could find a connection with her even if her singing was not conventionally beautiful (Not unlike vocal coach Patsy Rodenburg's reminder that "God doesn't mind a bum note!,"[8] or the advice from the founder of modern acting, Constantin Stanislavksy, to "[p]lay well, or play badly, but play truly,"[9] or the belief of psychologist Carl Rogers that the most important element of therapy is not for the therapist to be perfect, but to be *congruent*[10]—to be aware of and willing to represent the feelings you have in the here and now). Similarly, **our own self-awareness and specificity of thought and intention will invite clients to connect with us more than anything else we do, no matter how we sound or look.** So I am not necessarily suggesting that you change anything about your voice right now; instead, just *observe* what it tells you about your body and mind in the moment, and practice linking mind with body, voice with emotion, and voice with thought. The idea is to locate your *self* in this moment. If that is not happening for you, try it again with an even more specific and personal intention. Keep it interesting for yourself.

And as with the last chapter, think of Charles Wright's song "Express Yourself," only this time in terms of sound: e.g., *It doesn't matter what you sound like. It's what you think, feel, and do to make you sound that way that matters.*

Everyday Self and Total Self

"Our everyday self is a narrow construct… Our total self is far broader…and ultimately infinite,"[11] says master acting teacher, Richard Hornby. I take him to mean that our *total self* is like a piano, and our *everyday self* is simply the few keys we've learned to play really well—so far. So as you do your daily sound check, expect to play only the keys with which you are most familiar, and at the same time know that you have a whole instrument full of potential music you have not yet learned to produce.

The chapters ahead in this section—on breathing, expanding our capacity to physicalize, vocalize, and speak—will all suggest ways to play our untapped keys. But first, I find it useful to hear how my instrument sounds. This experience gives me a sense of how my voice works—what parts I use, and what parts I avoid, try to hide, or have never even tried to play. I then notice where in my body I tend to push sound out, and ask myself why that is.

Practice observing your *everyday self*, and at the same time, increase your curiosity about your *total self*—the potential *you*, which is far greater than you can know at any given moment. This mental exercise in self-awareness accomplishes two crucial things for you as a performer:

1) It sends a significant, implicit message to your clients, something like, "I'm human like you. I've got some things figured out about myself, and many more things that I don't. I expect the same is true for you, and I'd like to help you explore that for yourself." 2) It also informs you what specific technical tools might help you to engage yourself more fully as a clinical performer, whether you hope to find more poise in your everyday version of self, or to explore untapped versions of your vulnerability, assertiveness, or playfulness, well beyond your familiar range.

Record Your Voice

Try recording yourself speaking as if to a client, a partner, a friend, a parent, or even a customer service rep. As you listen to the recording, notice the sounds and how different they are when directed at different people. Where in your body does sound seem to be coming from? What muscles are you using to produce sound? Why do you suppose that is?

For example, I tend to clench and push sound out from my throat, especially when I'm nervous or intimidated, which I believe is a knee-jerk attempt to control how I'm received—a neurotic habit derived from a fear of being misunderstood, based largely on a childhood of having my own self-narrative taken away from me. I am reminded of this habit when I hear recordings of my voice ("Ugh," I say to myself, "Why am I so clenched, so forced, so nasal?") This tells me that I may need to do some deep breathing that day (see Chapter 5: Breathe), and perhaps practice making sounds lower in my body (see Chapter 7: Speak) as I reflect on my unique fear of freely expressing emotion. At the same time, the practice of listening to my voice simply reminds me how I operate, and I try to be *curious* about that rather than *critical*. I can make adjustments to my instrument if I wish, but most importantly I'm aware of how my instrument works.

You might notice your tendencies to overcompensate with your voice for things you fear you lack—such as masculinity, femininity, authority, charm, humor, or gravitas. You might notice your tendency to be rushed or slow in your speech patterns, and have an idea of why you behave in that manner. You may catch your repetitive cadences or tendencies to drop the end of your thoughts, or give all of your thoughts the same tonal weight. You'll notice your use of pitch, or lack thereof. Do you emphasize important words when you speak?—or do you tend to mute yourself or mumble because you don't want to seem like you're "trying too hard?" Where do these habits come from? What does your voice reveal about you, and what does it conceal? Be *curious* instead of *critical*.

4   Be Present

The scene work of therapy requires us to **be present** because we never know what will happen each day, in each session, with each client.

But what do you *do* to **be present**?—straighten your back, widen your eyes, and cock your head forward, as if to be present is to be hypervigilant? Talk loudly, smile big, and make jokes—as if to be present is to be extroverted? Or do you just sit back and wait—as if to be present is to do nothing at all? How do you know if your efforts to *be present* are just right? What does it mean to *be present*?

I suggest that the present is not a static state into which we can force ourselves. **To *be present* is to vacillate continuously back and forth between our internal and external senses of *self* within the here and now.**

Achieving this state means that however I show up for work—whatever meditations or exercises I did or did not do, whatever exchanges I had with my husband and neighbors, and whatever transportation made my commute smooth or rough—**I can always practice being present, as long as I have the capacity to *observe* and *experience* where I am, both internally and externally, at any given moment.**

Where Are You?

I'm sure you've had the dream in which you're about to take an exam for which you haven't studied, or deliver a speech without any clothes—in the theater we refer to this as *the actor's nightmare*.[1] Being unprepared under pressure can be terrifying and immobilizing. But in psychotherapy, there is no script or answer key we can memorize to prepare for each session.

What we can practice is our own authentic use of self, moment-to-moment, which also happens to be our greatest resource. As award-winning actress Mary Louise Parker has said, "I don't think you can know someone else if you don't know yourself."[2] So the more we mine our *selves*, and locate where we are at any given time, the more prepared we are to face the unknown with our clients and help them to be present with themselves.

Consider the following actor's nightmare come to life: A friend of mine once escorted a legendary entertainer to the stage for a concert at Sotheby's in New York City. As with any extraordinary life in show business, this one came at great personal cost. My friend witnessed some of that cost firsthand when he arrived at our diva's dressing room to find her slumped face down on a table—conscious, but disoriented. She grabbed my friend's arm, and frantically cried, "Where am I?…". After he reminded her reassuringly, he beheld a magical metamorphosis: Our diva's face lit up, her heels rooted into the floor, and her entire frame became rapturously poised as she waved a jazz-hand from left to right and called out "Sotheby's" with Fosse-style staginess. She then sashayed confidently into the spotlight and delivered a flawless, larger-than-life performance, as if she knew not only *exactly* where she was, but also that she *owned* the place.

This superstar had the capacity to exist fully within the present, when the present was comprised of an audience, stage lights, and a flashy venue. But she lost track of herself offstage, when circumstances were more pedestrian. This is a dilemma many performers face: How do you transition from manic showbiz life to depressive real life? And many clinicians—especially those who specialize in trauma, severe mental illness, or personality disorders— face a similar dilemma of needing to be ON at work, only to be depleted and adrift when we return home.

As a therapist, a regular practice of asking, "where am I?"—internally and externally, offstage and on, moment-to-moment—helps me to: 1) Transition between On and Off with self-awareness, congruence, and self-care, 2) Join my clients wherever they are in the here and now, and help them locate themselves, 3) Recognize how different their experience of self is from mine, and, 4) Identify moments when clients are unable to be in the present due to trauma, cognitive or emotional challenges, or some other reason we need to explore further.

Mind/Body Practices

If you don't exercise, then…exercise. At the very least, a cardio or strength building workout—such as running, cycling, yoga, or pilates—keeps us holistically healthy and provides the physical, mental, and emotional stamina to endure and excel at our work. Beyond that, exercise provides tangible opportunities to practice *being present*.

When we commit to a physical activity, we automatically straddle *two ideas at once*—our expectations and our often vastly varying experiences, a finish line and different ways to reach that goal. This vacillation mimics the dichotomy we face with each therapy session. Just as an actor balances the **super objective**—the ultimate story they aim to tell—along with a series of **objectives** they play moment-to-moment in order to tell that story,[3] therapists too must balance the structure of a session along with infinite possibilities within that frame. Physical exercise presents an opportunity to practice straddling between structure and possibility while engaging mind and body.

The highly specific goal of running, for example, allows indeterminate means (objectives) to get to the finish line (the super objective). As I traverse the expanse between point A and point B, for instance, I am free to observe my body, breath, mind, emotions, and surroundings, and expand the quality of my journey as I go. The trick with running—or any meditative exercise—is not to simply "play the end of the scene," as my actor friend Susan says, but to *commit* to each step of the way. This commitment prepares us to find each present moment with each scene partner. As my acting teacher, Anne Scurria used to say, "Let what's for later be for later." Approaching running with this concept in mind helps me to not only increase patience, tolerance, and endurance, but with each inhale of fresh air, with each observation of passing trees, squirrels, dog-walkers, and laughing children, and with each movement I make, I create infinite space in my mind to reflect, ponder, expand, and most importantly, *experience* my life in real time. Paradoxically, this process of being present, of staying mindful in the moment, occurs even as I ultimately aim toward a predetermined, finite goal or destination.

The Best Day of Your Life

A yoga teacher who once substituted for my regular instructor Nancy (by default heightening my awareness) once said, "You could practice today like you do every day, but you could also practice like it's the best day of your life."

We get so caught up in "getting things done" that we forget to maximize the potential of *how* we do things in the here and now. So ask yourself what happens when you decide to engage in *this* yoga practice, *this* run, *this* scene, as if *today* is the best day of your life.

What's it like on your best day?—fun? Empowering? Challenging? Do you just want the activity to be over; too much to do with too little time? What if you permit yourself to release those worries? Tell yourself, *this* is your moment to live. If you feel less than optimal, move *as if* you're in top form, *as if* you are the strongest, calmest-under-pressure, most open, inspired, generous version of *you*. Fake it before you make it.

What happens to your body and mind when you move with confidence? What is your posture like? How does the energy flow through you? Where is your focus? What is it like to fully inhabit *this* body and *this* mind, with all of its specific advantages and limitations, including the tight shoulders, the shortness of breath, the obsessive thinking, or the headache you may have right here and now?

Stay in There

When I say to approach an exercise like it's "the best day of your life," I do not mean you should ignore its challenges. But as the activity becomes strenuous—as you encounter fatigue, boredom, and impatience—rather than quitting or tuning-out until it's over, you can choose to believe you are resilient enough to meet any obstacles you may encounter. Be open to whatever sensations come over you, and be willing to stay with them, second by second, unless of course you are in severe physical pain related to an injury or potential injury, in which case you should unequivocally stop the exercise. But if the pain you feel is related to healthy muscle soreness, complex emotions, or mental static, try to stay with it. You might even practice a mantra along the lines of, "[h]ere and now, what do I see? What do I hear? What do I feel?…"[4] to guide and enhance your experience.

During strenuous activities, I also find it helpful to think of the supportive voices of my friends, family, and mentors. "Each of us is a company of many,"[5] said psychoanalyst Joan Riviere, and we need to remind ourselves of this essential wisdom when we're under pressure, especially when we're alone. What we call a self is made of myriad relationships, which help us find our individual footing. So even when we fly solo—as we run, cycle, write case notes, devise treatment plans, or study lines—we often rely on the relational support of those significant people whose motivating voices have permanent residence in our minds. For me, this includes my grad school acting teacher, Brian McEleney, who would say, "stay in there," in a tone that conveyed tough love, whenever I'd try to wriggle out of vulnerable emotions while performing a scene. Brian's combination of authority, warmth, no-nonsense, and faith, helped me to stay "dropped in" during difficult emotional scenes. His voice continues to play in my mind when I get fussy during a run, when I rush a yoga practice, or when I catch myself daydreaming to avoid heavy, complex material that a client has brought into session.

Of course the most surefire way to *stay in there* is to risk making eye contact with a real live person. Many times we would simply rather not face such a confrontation—literally. Other people can throw us off our intended course. But at the same time, eye contact is an instant portal to the present. Actors find this concept to be a revelation, again and again, no matter how experienced we are. The monologue we labor on for weeks, alone in our bedroom, comes to life when we look a real person in the eyes and simply say the words *to them*. No amount of rehearsing alone can get us to that place—or keep us there. Rehearsal grounds us in the monologue or scene, but sharing it with another person gives us wings. The world opens up when you look away from the script and into the eyes of another person. You might find the same to be true when you look up and smile at a friendly dog walker in the park when you run, or exchange laughter with your yoga teacher when she adjusts your body, or make genuine eye contact with your client during a session.

The trick of course is to not submit entirely to the other person's experience to the exclusion of your own, but to use the opportunity of this engagement to be connected to them and to yourself—to be in two places at once. The eye contact may inform you that you need to take a private moment to orient yourself before opening up with confidence, and that too is part of being present.

Loss and Vulnerability

We associate exercise with gain more than loss (unless we're talking weight), but we do in fact lose something whenever we commit to a workout. We gain health and strength, but we lose opportunities to pay bills, pick up prescriptions, buy groceries, call friends, and write books! If we must let "what's for later be for later" in order to be present—and we must—then we must also face corresponding feelings of *loss*. Exercise routines are great opportunities to practice experiencing feelings of loss, and to move through them mindfully at the same time. Such mindfulness is not unlike the practice we ask our clients to engage in each week.

My previous suggestion to approach every exercise like it's the best day of your life does not prevent you from experiencing feeling loss. In fact, on our best days, we can experience loss more consciously, deeply, and thoroughly than usual. And the truth is that loss is with us whether we acknowledge it or not. As Adam Phillips writes, "[o]ur lives are defined by loss…loss of what might have been…of things never experienced."[6]

How can we encourage our clients to experience and survive feelings of loss, vulnerability, and suffering—as we all do as therapists—if we don't practice what we preach? My clients definitely sense both when I am connected to my emotional vulnerability, and when I try to avoid those feelings and hide behind the mask of professionalism or expertise. If I want them to both trust me and themselves, I have to show them—not just tell them—that I too am vulnerable.

Similarly, as audiences, we trust actors who connect personally with their character's vulnerability, and do not trust, and are even repelled by, actors who attempt to rise above the character's emotions (as I had inadvertently tried to do in Brian McEleney's class). As I've already suggested, actors and therapists have to face our fears of self and go to emotional places that most people would simply rather not experience. But we can go there if we trust that our vulnerability will ultimately produce strength—as Freud observed.

As you exercise, notice the tension in your jaw, neck, and shoulders. Try to let that tension go, and permit yourself to feel all the sensations from which it was protecting you—especially worries about all the things you're not doing. Allow the feelings of loss to flood your body. Feel the chill of weakness, the punch of inadequacy, or the sting of failure, wherever it hits you.

Now here's the trick: At the very same time, keep your mind awake (as unpleasant as that may be), continue the exercise (*stay in there*), and allow yourself to *think* as the sensations come over you. **The capacity to think creatively and judiciously as we experience a spectrum of emotions—including loss—is a crucial internal resource for performing artists.** Through this practice, we remind ourselves—and our clients, scene partners, and audiences—that it's ok to feel, AND to think, AND to move, AND to live, all at once.

I find it especially effective to practice thinking through feelings of loss while in plank pose. It's hard to be still for an extended period, especially in a push-up position. But, as my yoga teacher Nancy says, "rivers flow within mountains." As I hold myself steady in plank, allowing my core to do most of the work, I let all of the physical and emotional sensations flow freely through the stillness of my body. At the same time, I keep my mind awake. I try to continue this mindful practice while doing pushups. I feel the tension in my muscles, and rather than rush through to the end of the "scene," I *stay in there*, and think as I move through the discomfort of each push (I think of this as a tangible way to practice what founding psycho-analyst Melanie Klein called *the depressive position*,[7] as I literally feel myself pushing through a position that feels depressing. This physical struggle costs me energetically, muscularly, and emotionally, but, at the same time, grounds me in the reality of the present moment).

The practice of thinking through loss not only increases my capacity to locate and take ownership of my genuine emotions, but also helps me to empathize with clients, and to establish trust with them. When I am connected to both my vulnerability and my presence of mind, my scene partners can feel invited to engage bravely in the plank poses and push-ups of their own lives.

Furthermore, the greater my capacity to identify with each client's vulnerability, the more I can determine, in each moment, how to best help them be present with themselves—if not also with me. I may choose to get ahead of them, follow behind them, or attempt to join them exactly where they are, depending on what they seem to need.

Harry

Harry is a highly motivated professional who typically enters my office like he's in a race against time. He never takes downtime, unless he gets sick, and he has described his experience of stillness as being "trapped in a basement without stairs." This alarming sensation floods him whenever he takes a break. A "relaxing bath" is stressful, a nap means losing income, and exercise means failing to be productive. And yet, he began therapy hoping to find "balance."

I often get pulled along by Harry's energetic narratives and concerns, and find myself offering futile, life-coachy advice to keep him feeling "productive" (e.g., "Me: Have you tried yoga?… Him: Yep, that makes me *more* anxious…"). Each time this dynamic occurs, I feel the **loss** of being left behind as he races ahead.

But, with the help of my regular mind/body practices, I have learned to drop into my own fears of stillness at these times. This connection allows me to not just empathize, but to identify with Harry's underlying vulnerability— which is obscured by his confident exterior. From there, I might choose to **get ahead** of him, take a breath, slow down the pace of the session, and say something like, "I feel like I can't catch up to you, like I constantly let you down. I wonder if that's how you often feel." I might then once again suggest he try a practice like yoga, but this time, I'll let him know I understand how hard it is for him to take time for himself, and recognize what such choices cost him emotionally. As with most things we say in therapy, it's not necessarily the content of the lines that matter most, but the underlying intention. In this case, I intend to normalize Harry's fears of stillness and assure him that I share some of those fears by naming and describing them in detail. Sometimes, this exercise invites him to identify, experience, and express his feelings of loss in real time, and to move through them rather than away from them, knowing that I too experience the cost of being present.

Wade

Wade called me to set up couples therapy, but his husband was ambivalent, so he decided to start sessions alone until his husband was willing to join. I suggested we frame our work as Wade's individual therapy, and that I would recommend a couples therapist when his husband was ready. This understanding allowed us to start where Wade was. But before I knew it, I was coaching him to play the end of a scene *I* had written for *him*.

My intentions were good: I wanted Wade to express his feelings independently of his husband. But this goal was far ahead of where he was at the time. Notably, Wade is from an extremely emotionally enmeshed family, which makes him particularly anxious about issues of separation and individuation. Each week in session, he would report on his husband's mood swings, impulsive behaviors, rude comments, and lack of affection. But when I tried to locate how that made Wade feel, he'd go blank, get irritated, and say, "I don't know, I'm just worried about him." I would then (unintuitively) push further, and try to narrate *my* sense of where he was, or rather where *I* thought he *should* be, saying things like, "You do so much for your husband, but get so little in return. Can you set boundaries? Let him know how you feel?" I realize now that my clunky interventions were a reaction to how hard it was for me to tolerate Wade's fear of losing his husband. I would rush to the finish line as if trying to get a painful workout over with. But in so doing, I failed to connect with his vulnerability in the present. And though he was too accommodating to tell me in words, his face, voice, and body said, "Wait. I'm not there yet."

It wasn't until I played back our scenes in my mind—often during a run—that I truly received those messages. *Why does he flinch when I talk?*, I pondered, *Why do my insights and suggestions bother him?*

I finally realized I was moving too fast for Wade. With this realization in mind, I slowed myself down—as I do when I find myself rushing a yoga practice—and tried to **follow behind** him. I stayed mentally attuned to him, moment to moment, as he took the lead, however slowly. I practiced thinking through my frustration and impatience, as I do when I mindfully practice push-ups or run uphill. And all the while, I remained poised, waiting for a moment of connection.

After a few months, Wade reported that he had acted out of character the night before, and threw a book at a wall in response to something offensive his husband had said. "I have a long fuse," he said, "but when it blows it blows." His family was often in conflict when he was a kid, and he learned to disavow his feelings in order to maintain stability. "I need to get better at recognizing my anger in the moment. This has come up with my mother a lot," he acknowledged, admitting, "She tells me how I'm feeling, and I don't tell her that she's wrong, even when she is. I hate that."

I observed that Wade often seemed irritated with me when I tried to reflect back his feelings, and I wondered if I reminded him of his mother at those times. He seemed relieved that I brought this tension up. He then took the lead, and shared how he often struggles to assert his feelings for fear of conflict, guilt, and the risk of separation from his attachments. We both agreed we would look out for moments in session when this situation arose.

I continue to *stay in there* with Wade, and though we both acknowledge—often playfully—that I'll never be perfect at this, I'm much better at it now. I *follow* his complex journey through painful emotions, step by step, even when it's like watching grass grow. And I try to acknowledge each nuanced, micro-progression in which he allows himself to *experience*, *observe* and *express* his own feelings of anger, fear, and loss, in the present.

Tim

Tim, a gay man in his forties, survived severe abuse as a child. He would often dream of being rescued by a man with whom he'd fall "madly in love." But that never happened. The boyfriends throughout his life were either abusive or neglectful—with the exception of his current partner, who is stable and kind, but not particularly affectionate or emotionally available. For our first two years working together, we mostly focused on the traumas of Tim's past, and the fantasy of his desired future. His dreams had motivated him to create a life for himself—his family of origin did not give him emotional or financial support, and he relied completely on himself to get through school. He is now a successful artist and healer. But the cost of getting there makes it hard for him to celebrate his accomplishments.

One day, Tim entered our session unusually depressed. He had come from a rally attended by throngs of young gay men. "I wanted to hit them," he said, explaining, "They have the opportunity to fall in love; to do whatever they want. They don't know anything about the eighties. The years we fought for visibility. For HIV treatments and equal rights." To Tim, these men were all living his childhood dream. They had the opportunity to be themselves openly, and to fall "madly in love." "I'm too old to enjoy the changes we fought for," he lamented, confessing, "Sometimes I think I'll never be happy. I didn't even want to come to therapy today. What's the point?"

I was tempted to get ahead of him and make him feel better, but I resisted; he didn't need more false promises. I was then tempted to follow behind him and "wonder" what he was feeling, but I resisted that too; he definitely didn't need the insult of clinical distance in this state of raw despair.

So I looked into his eyes, and **join**ed his feelings of disappointment, regret, and loss. My own eyes teared up as I *stayed in there*—with myself and with him. He went on: "You know that movie *The Hours*? The scene where Meryl Streep tells her daughter about a time in her past when she was happy? And she thought there would be 'more' of that throughout her life? But she realizes that moment *was* happiness… I feel that way. Like I missed my chance at happiness."

I happen to love *The Hours,* and that scene in particular. So to be truly in the present with Tim meant to not only share his feelings of loss and despair, but also our mutual enthusiasm for movies, great acting, and Meryl Streep. "I do remember that scene," I responded, adding, "I love the way she touches her daughter's face, gently, as she tells the story." I mimed the gesture, as if to recall the scene, but also (probably) to convey my wish to comfort him the same way. "As she explains to her daughter that happiness is behind her, she seems to realize, in real time, that hope is right in front of her. She discovers that life is not the fantasy she once craved, but her losses can be heard and recognized by people who care about her." He smiled through his tears, and said, "I think I'll watch that movie again."

The next week Tim, shared C. P. Cavafy's poem *Ithaca* with me, a work about the motivation of our dreams and the journey that happens instead.

The Present Includes the Past and the Future

Here's a practical tool that can help you find the present even if your mind is diverted. If you haven't seen the film *Arrival*, you should (because it's good, but also) because it plays with time in a way that all therapists and actors do, whether we know it or not. The main character, played by Amy Adams, is preoccupied with the past and the future, but learns that rather than being distracting, these thoughts actually help her to live more fully and purpose-fully in the present.

As therapists, we use our minds in this way all the time. We consider the client's history and desired treatment goals while simultaneously assessing their present concerns. Meanwhile, our own histories unwittingly show up, as do our desired treatment outcomes, as we engage our clients in the present. Actors similarly juggle in their minds the lines and blocking they've rehearsed in the past with their performance goals for the future, along with the events that actually unfurl live on stage. Like actors—and Amy Adams in *Arrival*—we therapists can use our tendency to daydream of the past and the future to maximize the potential of every moment in the present.

You can practice using your mind this way during workouts, or even as you perform mundane activities—such as walking between meetings, or doing the dishes. Notice where your mind naturally drifts to the future (e.g., all the bills you need to pay; client calls you need to return; or perhaps jumping ahead many years from now, to a holiday with your future grandchildren) or to the past (e.g., the unresolved conflicts with your family; nourishing memories of receiving high praise; holiday meals with people you have loved and lost). Rather than resist these thoughts (which will only make you more distracted), go ahead and give in to them. Think of your future self—either later today, a year from now, or many years from now—and imagine thinking back on *this very moment* from that point in time. From that perspective, how would you like to have used this moment?—worrying, distractedly, about what you might not get done?—or truly living in the full potential of your mind and body? Likewise, imagine your younger self thinking forward to this moment. Recognize all the things you didn't have back then, and all the things you do have now—both the internal and external resources you currently possess as an adult. How would your younger self like you to use this moment? Worrying about what you don't have?—or making full use of what you do have?

Miles

Like me, Miles was a gay man in a long-term relationship who had experienced great loss—his mother died due to illness around the same time my father had passed away. He contacted me shortly after my book about modern weddings had been released, a text in which I openly discussed my own marital process. As Miles was struggling with normative expectations about what was next in his life with regard to marriage, family, and career, he wanted a therapist who not only seemed like him, but who also seemed to be "on track"—as if Erik Erikson had devised a timeline of maturational stages[8] for queer people like us, and I was advancing on it like a "normal" gay man.

What Miles didn't know is that, much like him, I too struggled with the concepts of time and milestones. I was in love and married, so naturally the next step would be to raise a baby. But as much as I wanted to start a family, and as much as that step toward the future made linear sense, I was a bit disoriented and melancholic. I missed my father. I also missed my mother who had just moved to a senior facility halfway across the country (Erikson didn't warn me about any of that). And while I was passionate about raising a child, gone were the illusions of moving through time as a normal-looking family with a normal set of parents (now grandparents) sagely guiding my husband and me to the next milestone. In fact, my parenting fantasies went well beyond taking home a baby. My mind flashed forward eighteen years to having a happy healthy young adult with whom we could share a meal and sit on the couch and hear stories. What I wouldn't give to have such a moment with my dad today! Like Miles, I longed for the past and for the future.

Then Miles got married. The wedding was gorgeous and meaningful. I know because he showed me pictures, kneeling next to my chair and swiping his phone with a child's glee. I absorbed each image like a proud parent. In that moment, we were two peers, two married gay men in our thirties, and at the same time we were father (or mother) and son. But the dark came after the dawn, and as the weeks went by, Miles dropped into a depression, wondering, "Then comes…what?" He literally asked me this on occasion, and to his surprise, I never had a good answer.

One day Miles was especially forlorn. His father had just visited and spent the entire time belittling him for all the things he had not yet accomplished. I felt awful for him, but as with previous sessions in which he looked to me for "sage wisdom," I didn't know what to say. I felt I had let him down (*What kind of queer marriage expert are you?*, I imagined him thinking). It was like running uphill, out of breath, losing the will to continue. To escape the pain, I let my mind wander. I thought of the next ream of adoption papers my husband and I had to fill out —ugh—and then, I drifted to something more fun: My dream of the future, the simple weekend visit with my grownup kid, and how nice that would be.

"What are you thinking about?" Miles asked. Oops. He caught me. I felt a rush of embarrassment. But rather than disavow this feeling of guilt and inadequacy, I gave in to it, and allowed it to pull me into the here and now. As I inhaled (deeply and pensively), I looked into Miles' eyes, and began to realize how relevant my daydream actually was to the present. I suddenly remembered how lovely it was to sit and look at wedding pictures with him—not unlike my fantasy of visiting with my future child. And I thought how sad it was that his father overlooked that opportunity during his visit.

"I was thinking that your father could have told you how lucky he is to be alive and to have you," I finally responded, continuing, "how happy he is that you've made an interesting and loving life for yourself, and how rewarding it is just to sit and visit with you now."

"Wow," Miles said, tearing up. "Yes. He could have said that." We shared a smile and sat together silently. The past and the future, the lost and the longed for, were all commingling, awake and alive in the present.[9]

Limitations are Liberating

My acting teacher Annie used to say that life's limitations—such as scheduling conflicts and illnesses—can be great opportunities for actors because "they force you to be where you are." Sickness, for example, restricts our body and voice, but it also keeps us focused without getting too lofty or abstract in our creative efforts, since there's only so much we can actually do. Similarly, as clinicians, strict parameters can help us focus on our main task, which is simply to recognize our client's story and help them tell it their own way.

Case in point: my work with a married couple who sought my counsel to help their son reduce anxiety. The difficulty was that their son refused to meet with me. So our scenes proved to be a bit like the play *Who's Afraid of Virginia Woolf?*, in which a married couple pretends to have a child that doesn't exist. I tried to be a good therapist and provide the practical advice they wanted, but I ended up feeling bad instead. When I asked any questions about them, they would blow me off, acting as if my questions were silly and off topic.

Finally, rather than cover up my own anxiety about not being good enough, I decided to let them know how they made me feel, and to address the elephant in the room—which was that there were obvious limits to what I could do without meeting their son. I asked if perhaps they felt as limited in their ability to help him as I did in being able to help them. And through this intervention—which was borne in the present and not by attempting to "play the end of the scene" or impersonate some sort of adolescent expert/miracle worker—I could begin to help them open up about themselves and process their anxieties. This challenge turned out to be their primary issue after all.

Here, I'm reminded of another great quote from my acting teacher, Annie: "Just because you start a scene badly doesn't mean it has to end badly." Being present is not about getting something right the first time. It's about being aware of what happens—the combination of things that we intend and expect, as well as everything else that happens that may be beyond our control—and making sure we have space in our mind to reflect on all of it as we take each step, from the beginning of the scene to the end.

This observation brings me to my main criticism of the mental health industry's tendency to prioritize diagnosis and treatment plans over process. Like a play or movie script, these things can provide an organizing frame, but as life happens—in session, or rehearsal, as it were—we must be prepared to adapt our preconceived ideas of how the story is told.

For example, when I got to play Hamlet in college, rather than impersonate Laurence Olivier or Mel Gibson, I wanted to be creative with that opportunity of a lifetime—to do it *my* way, and to play it like it was *the best day of my life*. But creative play was not what the studious actor playing Polonius had in mind. On the contrary, he showed up each day with a "treatment plan" for each scene. I'll never forget rehearsing the scene in which Polonius sees Hamlet acting strangely, and fires questions at him. Hamlet chooses to answer Polonius teasingly, playfully. The script simply indicates that Hamlet is reading, but there are no other stage directions. So when I responded to Polonius, sometimes I would keep walking without acknowledging him, sometimes I'd turn around and chase him, and other times I would walk in circles around him. This was not the treatment plan Polonius had devised when he read his script. He explained, "Polonius is a follower. He needs to follow Hamlet." "Ok…" I replied. "So, follow me…" But he was unwilling (unable?) to adapt his vision. In the end, it was I who had to accept the limitations, and adapt my idea of how to play the scene in order to ensure we were both present together.

As clinicians, we can learn from performing artists who show up for work prepared to adapt depending on what actually happens on set. We can develop a practice observing both where we are and where we are headed, what we expect to happen, and what happens instead. And we can commit to being in a state of constant inquiry and reflection about how the process unfolds. We can ask how the limitations of our present circumstances might actually be liberating opportunities, and find the rivers flowing within the mountains.

5 Breathe

"Breathing is hard," my conservatory singing coach replied when my classmates and I had asked her why our teachers always barked, "Breathe!" at us, whether we were acting, singing, or gossiping in the hall. No matter what, we always failed to breathe properly. How could something so basic be so complicated? But it is.

"The True Self comes from the aliveness of the body…including the heart's action and **breath**ing,"[1] wrote Winnicott (think of happy babies taking full-bodied breaths as they crawl). As babies, we breathe freely and unselfconsciously, if we are lucky enough to be raised in a safe and loving home. But as time passes, we subconsciously contort our breath to protect ourselves from self-consciousness, shame, criticism, rejection, and emotional (if not bodily) harm. We allow ourselves just enough air to *survive*, but not enough to *live*—to express ourselves freely, expansively, and enthusiastically. It's as if by denying ourselves breath we won't feel, and if we can't feel, we can't be harmed—or at least we won't be aware of the harm; out of breath, out of mind.

As adults we must re-learn to breathe (like babies) in order not just to *survive*, but to *live*—fully, freely, and enthusiastically—especially if we want to perform as actors, singers, dancers, athletes, educators, leaders, or therapists. And we often don't even realize we need to relearn these basics until we do, until we hear, "Breathe!"

Fortunately, I learned breathing techniques in drama school that help me achieve two primary goals as a performer:

1) To find my **natural breathing rhythm**, which allows me to pursue the following goals: a) access my natural instincts, b) *be present* with other people without shutting down, c) tolerate emotions and stay mentally alert at the same time, and d) express myself authentically with a clear and accessible sound (In other words, *to survive*, to be secure in my own skin, and to maximize my use of *everyday self*).
2) To expand my **breath capacity and control**, which allows me to develop my abilities in the following areas: a) increase and decrease my vocal volume at will, b) create an *event* with my voice and body that commands

attention without sacrificing truth, clarity, or accessibility, and c) increase my *versatility*—i.e., the varieties of emotional, mental, and physical life I can tolerate, experience, and express (In other words, to *live*, to *do*, and to explore my *total self*).

Breathing techniques would also be useful in psychotherapy training programs for many of the same reasons. The ability to access our **natural breathing rhythm** can help us to **survive** and to **be** in the room with our clients: to be aware of what we look and sound like, and how that appearance may affect them; to be aware of our own thoughts, feelings, and reactions in the moment; and of course, to truly listen—all the strategies we've discussed so far.

But expanding our **breath capacity and control** can also help us to **live** in the room with our clients—to **do**: to control our volume depending on what the moment calls for—e.g., to produce a strong, authoritative voice, or one that is nurturing, a voice that joins the client's joy, or one that makes room for their despair; to create an *event*—e.g., such as heightening a client's level of concern when that awareness is necessary in a way that is commanding but also loving; to increase our versatility so that we have the capacity to receive, tolerate, and express a range of emotions; and as with all the work we do on ourselves, our breathing can also implicitly inspire our clients to adopt self-nurturing and self-expansive practices of their own.

But again, breathing is hard. Here are a few straightforward approaches that help me access and use this elusive element called breath.[2]

Don't Breathe: Do By Not Doing

The first step towards breathing naturally is not to breathe. As I've already observed, when we are directed to BREATHE! by teachers, guidebooks, or even ourselves, we tend to create unnecessary effort. So, don't breathe. Instead, *allow* your body to receive the oxygen it needs to do what it wants (just as babies allow their body to find the air they need to crawl across the floor). This way, before you DO anything to improve your breathing technique, you will have an intuitive sense of why you're breathing in the first place.

Remember, our goal is to use breath in order to live as freely and fully as possible, not to be ★expert breathers.★ We breathe to live, we don't live to breathe.

In this vein, one of my mentors, Carol Gill Malik, uses the mantra, "Do by not doing," when teaching actors to breathe. Carol teaches the Alexander Technique, which helps actors "find the true coordination of breathing, in an indirect way,"[3] in order to speak and move with ease. Many teachers push students to improve their breathing mechanics too forcefully and abruptly— to play "the end of the scene," if you will. And, according to Carol, this type of instruction is partly responsible for the "unwanted effort, and eventual strain" we put on our bodies when we practice breathing.

Before any other performance prep, I practice finding my *natural breathing rhythm* with an exercise I call "Book Rest" (**Exercise I; Drawing 1**), based on the Alexander Technique. I lay on my back with my head supported by a book, knees bent, and my feet flat on the floor. Gravity helps my back lengthen and widen, while my neck releases. This helps me find my impulse to breathe with minimal effort.

I also like to do a warm up I learned from my acting teacher Brian McEleney, which is to literally pant like a baby (**Exercise II**). This and several other exercises (**Exercise III and IV**) help me find my body's primal motivation to breathe—or, as my conservatory voice teacher Julia Carey would say, to "let the body breathe you."

When I breathe naturally, I can foster a clinical environment of relaxation, curiosity, and levity. I signal to my scene partner(s) implicitly that I feel safe within myself, which invites them to feel safe with me. This way we can both breathe, exist, and think in each other's presence.

Intentional Images

I always try to have an intention to breathe—what Carol Gill calls a *flicker*. This flicker wakes our human instrument to life. "In fact," Carol says, "one's capacity for expression may well be determined by whether the flicker will originate in the first place."[4] In other words, the authentic use of our instrument depends on a natural breath, and a natural breath manifests from a *flicker* of inspiration. And the more personal and specific the flicker, the better. Recall the image of our happy baby crawling toward something—e.g., a cooing adult, a fluffy cat, another happy baby.

As part of my everyday practice as a performing artist, I try to connect to a flicker of intent for every exercise I do in private, and every performance I offer in the spotlight. This goal is not one that I will ever master. But the very practice of specifying my intention establishes a connection between my mind and body, and allows me to breathe, listen, and express myself without extraneous effort.

My flicker doesn't have to be literal or even make sense. For example, the logical instruction, "Breathe!" certainly has intent, but lacks inspiration. It will lead me to an overdetermined brow and tense throat. But if I imagine a visceral image, my body will be inspired to receive breath involuntarily.

Some of my intentional images include the following imaginative scenarios: Ocean water flowing in and out of my lungs; happy butterflies awakening my chest as breath rushes in, and dispersing tension as breath flutters out; the smiling face of someone I love.

Images like these help me to *be* in my body as I breathe, rather than to remain outside of it, thrashing about, trying to make it *do* what I want. They also inspire me to *be present* with my clients wherever they are in their process, rather than trying to force them to "play the end of the scene."

Breathe, Breathe Again, Breathe Better

I find Samuel Beckett's words, "Try again, Fail again, Fail better,"[5] to be a great mantra for acting, therapy, and breathing. When I accept that I'll never breathe perfectly, and that perfection is not the point, I free myself to breathe and live as naturally as I can.

Even now, after years of practice, I struggle to breathe without effort. My first instinct is to tense my throat and shoulders and squeeze air in and out, actions which are obviously counterproductive. But my awareness of this persistent need to control the uncontrollable is what matters most. Starting from this awareness, I can work with the unique instrument that I have, and maximize its potential. **Our self-awareness and willingness to address our obstacles awaken us as performing artists—much more than our technical proficiency.** Our personal limitations and capacity to work within them keep us in the present (see Chapter 4) and connected to ourselves and to our scene partners (Consider, for example, singers who produce lovely sounds, but who struggle to be fully present with their audience—who do not have a specific and personal need to share a story when they sing, or who lack an intentional flicker. Sometimes we prefer to watch a self possessed actor sing truthfully, albeit imperfectly—like Glenn Close in *Sunset Boulevard*, as we discussed in Chapter 3—to a technically perfect singer who can belt out clear sounds perfectly on key, but who lacks any specific, personal connection to the song).

So, as often as possible, and especially when I'm preparing for a high stakes performance, I do my best to breathe naturally, using the aforementioned exercises. And when I notice that I'm still pushing (which is most of the time), I breathe again. And when that next breath is too strained, I let the next one soothe me. And when that next breath is too lazy and unfocused, I let the next one engage my mind and body with a specific motivation. And when that next one seems too indulgent, I then imagine looking into the eyes of another person as I continue breathing. This meditative practice in itself is great preparation for our clinical work in which we often begin with a specific intention, often miss the mark somehow, and then must reflect on what happened as we proceed with a new intention (as Judi Dench says of live performance, we can always "get out there the next night and do it better"[6]).

The *Doing* of Breathing

Breathing is the single most important technical tool we have as performers. We can always rely on a natural inhale to move us closer to the present, and to give us the strength to listen.

When we're caught in the hot seat with a scene partner, the act of breathing (along with listening) is always the best next move we can make. When we inhale, we take in the client's hurt, ambivalence, worry, joy, excitement, and aggression; but we also take in nourishing air, which provides us the motivation, energy, and will to be awake and alert as we parse through the incoming, jumbled information and stimuli and consider how it affects us mentally, emotionally, and physically. Our inhale provides mental space to think, feel, and reflect, in a state of *thirdness*, that is both shared with and separate from the client[7]—space that allows us to process how he/she affects us, even as we are entangled in an emotional dance together. Breathing empowers us to experience the client's unique perspective deeply, but without drowning in it—to be in *two places at once*, with him/her, and with ourselves.

My yoga practice is particularly helpful in showing me how to take nourishing breaths on cue, deeply and effectively, without extraneous effort. For example, Ujjayi Pranayama [ooh-JAH-yee prah-nah-YAH-mah] (which means "victorious" in Sanskrit), not only helps me breathe deeply, but it also calms my mind and warms my body. This move begins by breathing through the nostrils, but taking the breath as if the air were entering through the back of the throat (Yogi Nancy refers to this as "Darth Vader Breathing," because it creates a Vader-like noise). After letting the air fill my chest and diaphragm, I then let it out the same way it entered. I repeat this cycle until a natural rhythm takes over. This exercise is very straightforward; I even teach it to my clients when they need some help to stabilize, regulate, and/or orient themselves.

Breathe Your Feelings

"It feels depressing sometimes to breathe. But at the same time, breathing reminds me that I'm not dead yet," one of my clients observed during a recent session.

Deep breathing connects us to a wide range of primal emotions, including those associated with the trauma of birth.[8] One of the subconscious reasons we may breathe shallowly as we grow is to distract ourselves from the primal fear, pain, and chaos of that first, mother-of-all-separations. The emotional memory lives in our bodies, often dormant, but easily awakened by a deep breath (sometimes all it takes for any of us to instantly tear-up is to breathe). Good parenting, secure attachments, and validating recognition help us to live in our bodies with confidence, exuberance, and happiness, to greater and lesser degrees, without getting swallowed by an internal emotional abyss. But even the most sturdy among us have physio-emotional memories of our birth—and of all the consecutive relational ruptures that trigger it—stored in our bodies. And our breath gives us direct access to those feelings.

Although breath momentarily destabilizes us emotionally, it also creates a flow within the system of our instrument which allows us to move through life awake, alive, and connected to one another (This is how babies raised in safe and loving homes find the will to take full, enthusiastic breaths as they move across the floor). Breath throws us off balance from time to time, but as my yogi Nancy says, "The only people who have absolutely perfect balance are dead."

Reflecting back on the previous chapter about the cost of being present and the vulnerability and loss that can overwhelm us, we can think of breath as the tool we can use to *stay in there*. Breathing is the key to living in our body with its gamut of feelings, but without being debilitated by them. Our mindful practice of breathing keeps us fully engaged in strenuous exercises—like running and push-ups—and helps us to not just *survive* emotional disturbances, but to *live* through them as well, connected to ourselves and to our scene partners.

An actor client of mine who performs in a Broadway musical once offered me an evocative example of this dynamic. He was about to perform a big, sparkly number when he learned that his aunt, with whom he was very close, had to enter hospice. As he tap danced into the lights, smiling at the audience with enthusiasm, he expected to dissociate from the news. But with each breath, each move, and each flicker of inspiration as he engaged the smiling children in the audience, he "found life." As he breathed and danced, he reflected on his ailing aunt. He thought deeply and empathically about *her* point of view at that moment. Tears dripped down his genuinely smiling face. His breath connected him to dreadful pain and hopeful joy in the very same moment. Most rewarding of all, he felt more connected to the crowd than ever before—which, as he put it, is "the gift of acting."

Peter

"I'm holding my breath and I don't know why," my client Peter confessed. After a decade of working together, this issue had never come up. Or had it?

I suggested the obvious: his wife of fifty years had passed away only months prior, and perhaps breathing deeply would flood him with grief, regret, and confusion (Peter came out as gay, to his wife and to the world, very late in life). I also recommended he check in with his medical doctor, just in case. I then searched through my digital notes on Peter for the word "breath" to see if he had ever reported anything similar. The following passage came up from our first year of work:

> Peter says he is aware he projects his desire for a loving, sexual relationship onto others, and that he is at war with himself. He both wants his romantic fantasies to be true, but also wants to **stop** himself from feeling them. He describes a cyclical pattern of projecting desires onto an "object" who is "out of reach," which leads him to feel rejection, anger, withdrawal, and loneliness, at which point the cycle of projection starts over. We explored the origins of this cycle in his adolescence. I validated his need to **hide** his desires at that time, which was an effort to **survive** (Homosexuality was not deleted from the DSM until 1973, when Peter was twenty seven). I helped him to reframe his romantic

fantasies, which he could now talk about openly. Rather than "problematic projections" we could think of them as generative. An indication that he is beginning to feel entitled to his desires; to take up space; to **live** and **breathe.**

I had chosen the word "breathe" to symbolize Peter living what psychoanalyst Ken Corbett calls "a livable life."[9] I wondered now if Peter's literal difficulty breathing was a reflexive way to deny himself a livable life as a gay man, just as he had done as an adolescent.

Peter had organized his life by holding his breath so that other people could live. He played the role of Mr. Fix-It with the hope that he'd one day get a pat on the back, and finally get his own shot at life. This approach was how he had coped with abusive parents—by holding his breath as he cleaned the house and got good grades—with the hope that one day they would love him instead of beat him. This self-effacing posture was also how he coped with being gay back when homosexuality was still considered a mental illness—by holding his breath as he locked himself in "the closet" (which included marrying a woman) with the hope that he would one day turn happily straight. And this approach was how he coped with a wife who blamed him for her disappointments—by holding his breath as he paid off her excessive credit card debt while spending nothing on himself with the hope that she would one day say, "Thanks. I feel better. Your turn."

Though the Mr. Fix-It role served Peter well in some respects—it provided emotional and financial security for his wife and kids—it failed to make his lifelong wish to feel "good enough" come true. But that failure didn't stop him from trying. He pined endlessly for approval from his parents, his wife, his children, his coworkers, and even from me. And soon after the death of his wife, Peter's belief that he was not permitted to *live* a livable life only intensified—he held his breath.

"I need to figure this out," he concluded one day, in Mr. Fix-It mode. Over the years, we had explored his tendency to try to gain my approval by being the "good patient." In this case, to be "good" meant to have his own answers and solutions. His brow would tense at these times, like a shield, to deflect any potential criticism that might suggest he was not "good enough"—a message he often got from his parents and the society in which he grew up.

In the beginning of treatment, Peter would deploy his taut brow when he asked for my "expert" advice, which he planned to follow by rote. I would reflexively tense up myself, as if I was being forced into the spotlight prematurely, to give the "right" answer, under pressure. But on my better days, I would take a deep nourishing **breath** and give myself space to think before addressing my demanding "crowd." I would then remind Peter that his last therapist—back in the 1960s—had advised him to marry his wife: Did he really want to submit to another therapist's subjective prescription? My *super objective* there was to validate, empower, and liberate Peter, so that *he* could **breathe** and think. But my first mini-*objective* was to give myself space to breathe, so that I could not only **survive** Peter's taut brow—and the volumes of fear, self-loathing, and desperation that it contained and evoked—but also so I could **live** in the room with him, with a free and creative mind. This way, I didn't just feel what it's like to be forced to play Mr. Fix-It myself, without any time to rehearse, but was able to reflect on this predicament as well. I began to appreciate that this actor's nightmare I experienced was how Peter felt his entire life, and I shared this observation with him, empathically.

If I had reacted to Peter's provocation defensively, I would have furrowed my own brow, and held my breath as I forced out an answer to his questions like an uptight actor, terrified of disappointing his audience. But by finding my own breath, and my mind, I could help him to do the same—like an actor who, in creating space for herself to breathe and think, invites her scene partners and audience to join her. Peter began to use me as a collaborator rather than a punishing, authority figure.

But despite the considerable trust Peter developed over the years, for me and for himself, his brow shield returned with a vengeance when his wife died. He was pushed back into the spotlight abruptly. The opportunity to create a life on the empty stage before him overwhelmed him with guilt and fear.

I understood all this in theory; but as an actor, understanding the emotional stakes of a scene intellectually gets you nowhere if you don't breathe. As I shared my logical interpretation of why Peter was holding his breath, I could hear that my own voice sounded dull and flat. I delivered the lines like an actor relying too heavily on his script, telling his audience the story rather than showing them. And as with any performer, it took something more spontaneous and alive than my analytic skill or work ethic to get us back to the present. One day, Peter said, "Maybe the time has come for me to figure this out alone."

That statement woke me up! The idea of separation after ten years forced me to take a full breath, out of impulse, not technique. To apply the insightful observation of the client I invoked earlier, "It feels depressing sometimes to breathe." But, as we know, actors and therapists must go to places most of us would rather avoid, and that means being willing to breathe and to face all that we may lose in order to fully embrace all that we may gain. After all, we mustn't forget the second part of that client's thought: "[Breathing] reminds me that I'm not dead yet."

After a week of reflection, I entered our next session poised with breath as opposed to being defensive with tension. Peter started in, "I need to master this breathing thing…"

Typically, at a time like this, I would deploy a brow-shield of my own, and give off subtext of the *we've-been through-this-already* variety. But not today.

"Then what?…," I replied, with a warm half smile, tapping into our reserve of trust which we had cultivated over years. My voice was far more free and alive than the week before. This provocative line could have sounded glib if I had delivered it nervously or shallowly. It demanded a great deal of breath support not only to convey confidence and wisdom, but also sensitivity, empathy, and an edgy but authentic sense of humor.

He laughed (and breathed by default), clearly taken off guard. "Then I'll be perfect, I guess. For whatever time I've got left…" We both laughed.

The energy in the room shifted. This playful exchange between us was pivotal. By giving myself space to **breathe**, I could process the potential loss of working with Peter, as well as the thread of aggression underlying his threat of leaving—perhaps a way to express his anger and resentment at me for not giving him a solution to his breathing problem, just as the authority figures of his youth had denied him love and the freedom to live openly. Taking time to breathe also allowed me to share my feelings, including my own arguably aggressive reaction to him "leaving me," with ease and humor. This space invited him to respond in kind, to play (see Chapter 10: Play), and to feel safe enough to share more of his feelings with me—his fear, hope, loss, anger, and resentment.

In our subsequent sessions, we agreed that having taken good care of his loved ones for his whole life, Peter was now safe and stable enough to take care of himself. He could finally give himself permission to breathe. It was scary, depressing, and at times overwhelming for him to face his life. But breathing it in meant that he could laugh while also being able to grieve.

Like actors, therapists are often reminded of the need to breathe in new and surprising ways. And much like in my situation with Peter, this rediscovery happens spontaneously, when the unpredictable realness of life seizes our plans—e.g., cell phones going off during a performance, set pieces falling apart, forgotten lines or choreography, scene partners threatening to walk off set, and, of course, laughter when we least expect it.

Breath Capacity and Control: Do

Sometimes as a performer I need to **do** not just **be**. As a therapist, this means having to rise to a crisis, tolerate trauma or other intense emotions, or transition between different versions of myself with ease. To achieve this flexibility, I must be prepared to deepen my breathing beyond my everyday capacity, and also control the quality and timing of my inhalations and exhalations.

Breath capacity and control help me to survive as a therapist. Winnicott said that we must not be destroyed[10] by our clients if we are to help them heal, but he did not tell us how to do this, technically. My breathing practices have helped me to survive my clients, and to cultivate my capacity to live with them as well.

Breathing helped me to survive Peter's persistent tension, to understand and identify with his underlying fears, and to relate to him more authentically. Specifically, my breath capacity and control both helped me to make a deliberate shift from a tense, defensive version of myself—who resembled a critical parent to Peter—to a new character (see Chapter 11: Find the Characters). This new character was both strong enough to hold

Peter's decades of grief—despite being half his age—and buoyant enough to help him find the hope, desire, and mirth he had always craved and lacked, allowing him to truly *live*.

To increase my breath capacity, I practice an exercise (Exercise **V**) that entails breathing deeply to a count of ten until my ribs expand. I then keep them expanded and push on them with my hands as I slowly exhale, also to a count of ten. The greater my capacity—the wider my ribs get—the more emotional content I can tolerate. I can *stay in there* during confusing, disturbing, or otherwise challenging moments—in life, on stage, or in session—with a sense of centeredness and poise, but without tension.

To practice breath control (**Exercise VI**), I fill my lower ribs with air quickly, count to four, and then exhale, again a counting to four. I then repeat this, decreasing the in count and increasing the out count as I go. This exercise is particularly helpful when I need to maintain a sense of authority while remaining calm and collected.

I try to incorporate these exercises into my everyday life, while practicing being present, such as when I'm working out, on my way to work, walking between meetings, or waiting to meet a friend for lunch. I use my breath to not only ***survive*** my work, my performances, or any challenge throughout my day, but to *live* in those moments as well.

6   Embody

How do we *embody* the roles we need to play as therapists while remaining present and truthful? As psychoanalyst Paul Marcus notes, "roles are real parts of who we are, authentic facets of our self-identity, not, as some analysts may mistakenly believe, simply 'false masks that cover up some deeper self'."[1] To discover our potential roles, stage movement guru Lorna Marshall recommends we observe our specific "relations and reactions" through our bodies.[2]

In this chapter I share how I prepare my body for the various roles I play in session, looking at three clinical objectives: 1) To **frame** the treatment, 2) To empathically **join** my client (like an actor embodies their character), and 3) To empathically **relate** to my client (like an actor engages their scene partners). As I engage in these efforts, I am aligned with clinical psychologist Richard Schwartz who believes that "therapists must **embody** their own fullest Self, acting as a tuning fork to awaken the client's Self to its own resonance."[3]

Frame

Our first objective with each client is to create a treatment frame in which they feel safe, oriented to the nature and purpose of our scene work, and free to participate (see Chapter 9: Frame). My own sense of safety and freedom within the frame of my body helps me establish this environment.

But here's the trick: many therapists tend to live outside of our bodies, which is why we have the inclination to select our profession in the first place. Like actors, we want to get lost in another person's story, and can lose track of our own physical presence in the process. Acting training helped me find my sense of center so that I can *be* and *live* in my own body before getting lost in characters, and this continuously serves me well as a therapist.

Find your center: Our sense of center isn't "just there." As my yoga teacher Nancy says, we must "find center, again and again, in each moment of each day." This journey is not unlike the struggle towards *being present* (see Chapter 4), or how psychoanalyst and painter Marion Milner describes self realization, as a "continual development and process" as opposed to something "fixed."[4]

Our center can be found physically in the structure of our body, but also psychologically, energetically, and emotionally, as we adjust to each new unpredictable circumstance—e.g., during a bumpy train ride, through the loss of a loved one, or in an initial meeting with a client who defies our expectations.

Bodily center: When I have a sense of my physical center (**Exercise VII; Drawing 4**), I feel aligned, engaged in my core, and can breathe naturally. Remember, our instrument is all one interconnected system.

Now, it's one thing to find your center while in the sanctuary of home, but quite another during a stressful commute or when a scene partner throws us off guard with abrupt emotional demands. We need to adjust at those turbulent times and find our center anew—e.g., bend our knees slightly, engage our thighs, or lean a little to the left or right. I liken this to surfing on rough waves: you need to be responsive, flexible, and engaged as you find balance again and again. So whatever you do to be centered in your body, be prepared to adapt to the present circumstances throughout your day.

Energetic center: I learned to use the energy throughout my body creatively from a voice/acting teacher named Julia Carey, and this experience enlivens my clinical work. Julia taught a meditation (**Exercise VIII**) to access chakras—spiritual power centers throughout the body—and to work with the flow of energy between them. Having a sense of my bodily energy helps me find my center, groundedness, and aliveness—both internally and externally. In this case, what I'm calling my *center* is a state of presence beyond my *everyday self* (which for me can be somewhat slouchy, collapsed, and distracted when I'm unfocused). It is also not necessarily "neutral," which can imply being casual or disengaged. My energetic center is where I feel most present and true in my body, spirit, and self.

Julia's meditation includes an image exercise that walks me through images from childhood, and connects me to my emotional core (**Exercise VIII: B**). It also helps me to be physically poised, but without tension. As performers, we are often commanded to "relax," and although we want to be without physical strain, as acting teacher David Hlavasa says, "You don't want to be relaxed; you want to be poised. Not a jellyfish, but a panther."[5] This meditation helps me to find poise by locating and unlocking the energy blocks in my body, and allowing that energy to flow freely.

Empathic Embodiment

Energetic self states: Once I find my center, I can play with the energy in each of my chakras, (**Exercise VIII: D**) and explore my emotional versatility—my *total self*. From there I can observe where my clients live in their bodies and make empathic efforts to join their experience. In other words, my capacity to be and live in my own energy centers helps me to *embody* clients as I listen to them—the way actors embody characters—no matter how different from me they may seem on the surface. At the very least, I can better engage them in playful reverie as scene partners (see Chapter 10: Play)—and help awaken various parts of their total selves.

Here is a brief description of our chakras (**Drawing 5**):

Chakra #1, known as the Root Chakra, is located in our lower bodies, from tailbone to toes. The energy here is associated with stability and grounding, family of origin, sense of safety, and whether or not we feel supported and secure.

Chakra #2, known as the Sacral Chakra, is located in our lower abdominal and upper pelvic regions. The energy here is associated with emotions and sexuality, desire, pleasure, and control, as well as unresolved feelings of guilt or blame.

Chakra #3, known as the Solar Plexus Chakra, is located in our stomach/ diaphragm area. The energy here is associated with will and personal power, self-esteem, confidence, and anger.

Chakra #4, known as the Heart Chakra, is located in our chest. The energy here is associated with love, healing, generosity, group consciousness, communication, sense of oneness, as well as feelings of grief, fear, or resentment.

Chakra #5, known as the Throat Chakra, is located in the throat. The energy here is associated with creativity and perception, dreams, expression, as well as feelings of helplessness and denial of autonomy.

Chakra #6, known as the Third Eye Chakra, is located on our forehead. The energy here is associated with intuition and intellect, knowledge, clairvoyance, as well as fear of self reflection, paranoia and anxiety, and cerebral stubbornness.

Chakra #7, known as the Crown Chakra, is located on the top of our head. The energy here is associate with connection to higher power, inspiration, attitudes, values, ethics, our capacity to envision a larger pattern, and whether or not we have faith.[6]

Bodily Expression: The energy in our chakras corresponds to our idiomatic postures, movements, and gestures. As I said about our faces in Chapter 2, our bodies convey messages whether we are aware of them or not. So awareness of what my unique body wants to say, and from which chakra it wants to say it, helps me to communicate with clarity and confidence as opposed to forced or random movements.

In general, our physical performances as therapists demand only a small range of movements (our stage directions are to simply sit and listen). But every nuanced gesture has meaning—e.g., how we hold our head, what we do with our legs and hands. So if we practice using our bodies as truthfully and expansively as possible, we can get a sense of our full range of authentic expression (our *total selves*), which can then help us to move subtly, but with specific purpose in session (the way a great film actor tells a truthful story with emotional openness and impeccable precision, while seeming to do very little). To increase your capacity to connect to your body, and to use it clearly and authentically, I recommend you try any number of pilates, dance, tai chi, capoeira, or other movement classes. The more practice I have using my body, the more alive I feel as I work with clients, even when I appear to be sitting still. As theater innovator, Viola Spolin said of physical perform-ance, "reaching out is reaching in."[7]

Of course the more I know how my own body communicates, the more I can also imagine the range of desired expressiveness my client may harbor, no matter how subtle their physicality appears to be.

Something that helps me to embody my client (or "character")—to get a sense of life in their body—is to notice a particular gesture that reveals their specific essence, and explore how it feels to express myself through that ges-ture. I typically do this on my own time, though I might use it in session as I describe later in the chapter.

The gesture I identify in the client is similar to what Winnicott called a **spontaneous gesture**. Winnicott theorized that one's "True Self" did not become a "living reality" unless one's primary caretaker had "repeated success in meeting," or recognizing, their spontaneous, self-revealing gestures as infants, through a process of reverie (within a safe and "good enough" *holding environment*, or frame).[8] The great theater director Jerzy Grotowski described something similar in terms of the performer's impulse (i.e., inten-tion or flicker) to move:

> Before a small physical action there is an impulse. Therein lies the secret of something very difficult to grasp, because the impulse is a reaction that begins inside the body and which is visible only when it has already become a small action. The impulse is so complex that one cannot say that it is only of the corporeal domain.[9]

Winnicott believed that a therapist could work to recognize the client's **spontaneous gesture**(s) and help them to experience a sense of its inner impulse. He believed we could help reconnect the client to their True Self (or selves) no matter how much their primary caretakers had failed to do so, and despite the protective "False" selves the client developed to compensate for those failures.

In this vein, as part of my own therapeutic efforts to recognize and encourage my clients' sense of truth, I utilize an acting tool known as the **psychological gesture**, a concept created by the great acting teacher Michael Chekhov. The psychological gesture (PG), much like the spontaneous ges-ture, is a physical expression of the thoughts, feelings, and desires of a character embodied in one movement. According to Chekhov, the PG **awakens you to the emotional core of the character, and stirs, molds, and attunes "your whole inner life" to her truth, her will and objectives.**[10]

When I think of a PG for a client—e.g., the way they flail their arms, tense their shoulders, or widen their eyes—I explore what it is like to use that particular mode of expression (**Exercise IX**), and how it affects my whole being—mind, body, energy, and emotions. This exercise may give me a personal, visceral, and empathic sense of how my client guards herself, what she is protecting, what she desires, and what impedes those desires— as opposed to looking at her gestural tendencies from a cold, diagnostic distance.

My body awareness also helps me return to myself when the scene is over, the curtain falls, and it's time to go home. As movie star Natalie Portman has said, "It's important for me to return to myself at the end of the day. But it's nice…[during the process] to just stay in it."[11] And as Meryl Streep has likewise said of her characters, "[F]or the time that I embody them they feel like they are me."[12]

When I bring an embodied form of empathy and curiosity to session, I may implicitly give my scene partners permission to exist in my presence as well, or to, as Winnicott would say, "feel real."[13]

My physical preparation is most useful if it also keeps me feeling alive, curious, and focused at the same time. If the exercises I recommend here don't do that for you, then ignore them and do something else. Whatever you do, stay alive in your own mind and body. That decision alone may invite clients to increase their own mind/body connection.

To that end, all of my physical prep might amount to simply smiling at my client in a particular way to validate and encourage a flicker of life within them. Like the great psychoanalyst Dr. Edith Weigert writes:

> We must not underestimate the value of nonverbal, unconscious com- munication between therapist and patient…It may radiate warmth and kindle the light of sympathetic understanding, which has an evocative, creative influence on the patient, not only convincing the intellect, but transforming the heart.[14]

Getting in touch with my bodily energy sometimes helps me to recog- nize anger, sadness, or romantic desire that my client is palpably defending against. Or this process may help me listen carefully to a high-strung, tight- shouldered client, while I consciously and intentionally allow soft energy to radiate from my chest (my heart chakra), inviting them to open their bodies to vulnerable emotions they tend to block. Or it may even lead me to explicitly encourage the client to follow through with a tentative gesture that I intuit will reveal something they want to express. By completing their budding gesture, they can better connect with their own mind/body experi- ence, and may even increase their own self-observation.

Along these lines, I once worked with the wonderful theater director, Diego Arciniegas, who helped me find my entire performance as Shakespeare's Romeo by becoming attuned to my spontaneous/psychological gestures, however subtle and doubtful they were (and most of them were). When he observed my idiomatic impulse to move he'd say, "I agree," then suggest a physicalization that might fully express my budding intention with commitment.

I collaborate with my clients in a similar fashion. I might interject as they tell a story and say with a smile, "What was your hand trying to say?," or depending on my rapport with the client and the context of the moment, I may even mime the gesture (This is not unlike interventions in Gestalt therapy or psychodrama, in which a client is encouraged to give voice to their gestures). Over time, they can feel invited to tell their own stories with more freedom, clarity, and self-possession.

Sometimes this way of working also helps my clients to mentalize and share stories of traumas they have kept out of mind. As actress Viola Davis has said of the ways past traumas live in her body, "The big 'Aha!' moment is that the trauma never goes away." But now, through the practice of acting and storytelling, she has learned "to release the anguish" from her body "rather than hide it."[15] (I describe a clinical experience along these lines in Chapter 11: Find the Character).

Imagination: To effectively use my body to empathize with my clients, I must exercise my imagination. This exercise is how I approximate the client's experience of self, since of course I can never know exactly what it is like to live in their shoes. As psychoanalyst Paul Marcus explains, invoking the great acting teacher, Sanford Meisner, "It is through the imagination that one can access the instinctual aspects or "inner impulses" of one's personality."[16]

As Stanislavski, the founder of modern acting theory, writes:

> Our art demands that an actor's whole nature be actively involved… He must feel the challenge to action physically as well as intellectually because the *imagination*, which has no substance or body, can reflexively affect our physical nature and make it act. This faculty is of the greatest importance in our emotion-technique.[17]

And as my acting teacher Anne Scurria similarly argues:

> The **imagination** is our biggest tool. It's a muscle, it needs exercise. If it's not exercised it atrophies. We have to read books, we have to look at paintings, we have to listen to music. And when we bring all of those things to a scene and a character, we can learn how we feel about it. And where it lives in us.[18]

As per Anne's sage wisdom, we can exercise our imaginations and enhance our empathic understanding of our characters and scene partners by absorbing the various art, writing, media, culture, and life that surrounds us. This means our daily intake of novels, television, movies, music, YouTube clips, and random people on the street, can inspire us mentally, bodily, and emotionally. We can use all of this entertaining input to help us identify with characters who seem different than we are on the surface.

Observe how the various characters you encounter in art and life affect you. Daydream about them. Listen to your judgments about their quirks, choices, and relational styles. Consider how you judge yourself for those very same things. Observe how authors, actors, and painters help us to identify with people we might ordinarily dismiss by showing us their *total selves* (e.g., consider the wide spectrum of complex characters television has been offering us in recent years, drawings of all genders, colors, sexualities, sexual expressions, and facets of human experience). The appreciation I have developed for human complexity through various forms of art has expanded my own compassion for parts of myself I dislike, as well as enlarged my empathy for other people who exhibit similar qualities, including my clients.

Along these lines, Meryl Streep has spoken about versions of herself that she would often like to reject, but which she has learned to own. For example, she cites the deferential, high school cheerleader she once was, against her nature, in an effort to conform to the social scene of her adolescence. She has said of that time:

> I adjusted my natural temperament which tends to be slightly bossy, a little opinionated, loud...full of pronouncements and high spirits, and I willfully cultivated softness, agreeableness, a breezy, natural sort of sweetness, even shyness if you will, which was very, very, very effective on the boys.[19]

She made use of that "False Self" (if you will) in her Oscar nominated role in the film *The Deer Hunter*. Of that performance she commented:

> Often men my age, President Clinton, by the way, when I met him said, "Men my age, mention that character as their favorite of all the women I've played." And I have my own secret understanding of why that is and it confirms every decision I made in high school.[20]

But rather than dismiss this version of herself, Streep went on to poignantly observe:

> This is not to denigrate that girl by the way, or the men who are drawn to her in anyway because she's still part of me and I'm part of her. She wasn't acting. She was just behaving in a way that cowed girls, submissive girls, beaten up girls with very few ways out have behaved forever, and still do in many worlds.[21]

I share this self-reflective anecdote of Streep's with my clients to encourage them to have compassion and understanding for the arguably "false" parts of themselves that they want to disavow, (e.g., queer people who were once closeted, straight men who overcompensate with a "tough guy" persona, people who present with a contagiously fun-loving exterior to conceal despair). We may not want to be those versions of self on our best days, but we can own them as modes of expression we use to survive at challenging times in our lives—for worse or for better. And we can even use these "selves" creatively, like Streep did in her *Deer Hunter* role, and I did myself for a scene in a Farrelly Brothers film starring Alec Baldwin called *Outside Providence*[22]. Ironically, I was cast as a prep school sophomore who bullies a freshman—much like I myself was bullied as a teenager. To achieve this role, I allowed visceral memories of the nasty men from my high school to inhabit my body, and in so doing, I discovered a tough, Machiavellian, yet authentic part of myself (I thought the director was going to fire me when he saw me during a break on set being my nicer, sillier, less masculine, everyday self).

You can also use your imagination in non-literal ways to get in touch with your body, chakras, and total self with the help of music, paintings, and other inspiring stimuli. Along these lines, my conservatory acting teacher Annie would give each of us a specific, inspiring image and ask us to express it physically. We would refer to this as, "Taking it across the floor," because one at a time, we would move to the motivating flicker of our image, across the studio floor. Due to my tendency to collapse my torso (and my personal power along with it), I was often encouraged to play with images like "a volcano heart." You might try something like this at home—or at least allow yourself to daydream about and expand the palette of images and sounds that motivate you to live and move in your body.

All of these suggestions help prepare me to become the various characters the client may need me to be—whether that is a bad presence from their past, or a nurturing presence in their desired future, as I will discuss further in Chapter 11: Find the Characters.

Without feeding our imaginations in various ways, we are left with theoretical, categorical, dead ideas about who we and our clients are. But by utilizing our imagination, we invite playful participation in the discovery of new, authentic versions of self.

Sit Safely

Some roles have extreme physical demands and therefore require specific preparation to prevent bodily harm. The role of psychotherapist is one of them, as we must sit, every day, for hours at a time (and if you are unaware of how bad that can be for your body, Google "Sitting is the new smoking.")

In this sense, we are like the actors hired to play Richard III, whose bodies often suffer for their art. It's no accident that actors "who play Richard III on stage often end up with injuries themselves,"[23] as most of them are able-bodied and must hold themselves unnaturally to convey a hunchback every night, for weeks on end. But these days, many newcomers to the role consult their predecessors and creatively problem solve with their directors, costume designers, and choreographers, to ensure they are physically centered when they perform in the character's body.

Likewise, as therapists we can either throw ourselves into our scenes with abandon and risk the permanent pain of sciatica or other related back problems—like the actors who portray Richard III, or actor Bobby Cannavale, who is well known for injuring himself on the job[24]—or we can prepare ourselves to meet this physical challenge without getting hurt.

Practically speaking this means we can take yoga, pilates, Alexander, or any number of classes that can help us develop and maintain core strength, which will protect our backs when we sit. We can also invest in classes and equipment from the the MELT Method,[25] which promotes a balanced nervous system and healthy connective tissue, and minimizes pain throughout the body. And of course we can do little things here and there like type our notes standing up, take breaks during the workday to go for walks, or purchase an ergonomic chair.

But we can also prepare to inhabit our seated, therapist "characters" in ways that engage our core, protect our back, and keep us present with the client, all at the same time. To achieve this we need to use that mind/body connection we've been working on to find our sense of center (physically, energetically, and emotionally) while sitting down (**Exercise X; Drawing 6**).

To this end, **I think of my seated posture as active as opposed to passive. It is the physicality through which my "character" plays his main objective: namely, to listen** (not my chance to take a break and collapse into the sofa backstage). This thought helps me avoid slipping into deferential laziness, which not only clouds my focus and collapses my core, but ultimately hurts my back over time.

So, rather than dispense with my energy as I sit, I redistribute it, find my center and the capacity to actively engage within my physical limitations. As actress Mary McDonnell has said, "Great characters develop out of restricted situations. When people feel the limitations of life, something else takes over that's specific and colorful." In other words, don't just sit. Actively "take a seat," as yogi Nancy says. Embody the role of an active listener.

Sir Ian McKellen took this approach when he played Richard III on screen, focusing on the character's ability rather than his disability. He wore a "false hump" under his shirt, and accepted this as the character's physical limitation. But within that limitation, he found a center in this "new" body, and focused his energy on his "fully-functioning" parts. He has explained of the experience that, "The audience got the sense of someone who was fighting all the time against physical difficulties but successfully functioning," finally adding, "It also meant that I didn't put my back out."[26]

Similarly, we can take a seat in our scenes with clients *as if* we are physically active scene partners—as if our bodies *could* engage them in a variety of different ways, but for *this* scene we must be seated. As one door closes on our bodies, others open—particularly in our minds and imaginations, which allow us to find the "freedom of stillness,"[27] as psychoanalyst Stephen Stern has called it, and to listen with our whole body.

7 Speak

Ideally, we don't say much during a therapy session (Winnicott claimed he never used long sentences unless he was tired[1]). Most of our live "performances" are necessarily silent in order to serve our super objective: to listen to our clients in a way that invites *them* to speak (or at least to think and feel) freely. But sometimes our voice and speech can invite our clients to participate in the therapy process.

Playing Our Instrument

We have discussed how our instrument is a complex, interconnected system of mind, body, emotion, and imagination. If we liken it to a piano, we could say that we play only a small range of keys as our *everyday self*. Now we will explore our untapped keys, our *total self*, in terms of **voice** and **speech**.

All of the ideas I've offered so far—on self-awareness, being present, breathing, and using our bodies—are foundational to voice and speech work. In fact, many conservatory vocal teachers won't even ask students to make a sound for weeks, until they have sufficiently trained their mind/ body connection and breath control. "[F]irst we have to prime the body so that it can receive and transmit the imagination through words,"[2] says voice teacher Kristin Linklater. Without such preparation, the performer can end up with the "unwanted effort and eventual strain" that my Alexander Technique teacher Carol Gill Malik warns against (the large number of untrained singers who cancel concerts due to vocal injuries speaks to the long term effects of vocal effort and strain[3]). Obviously, as therapists we are not likely to injure our voices on the job (unless we regularly speak to large crowds in addition to our clinical work) as our scene partners are typically up close and personal. Nonetheless, a healthy and creative use of voice will broaden the range of roles we can embody.

Voice

> In the **vocal** process, all the parts of the body must vibrate.[4]
>
> (Director/ Acting Theorist, Jerzy Grotowski)

[T]he emotional states reflected in the therapist's **voice** is an important therapeutic factor.[5]

(Psychotherapist, Susan Lee Bady)

Traditionally, therapists have been advised to hold our tongues so that clients have the space to project onto us and their transference can emerge. But while silence often provides my clients and myself with powerful opportunities to connect with our own minds and bodies as we work, there are also times when my voice is an equally—if not more—effective clinical tool.

Along these lines, psychoanalysts Adrienne Harris and Virginia Goldner have invoked Lecourt's term "sonorous bath"[6] to describe the potentially nurturing, "primordial" sound of the therapist's voice. Psychoanalyst Susan Lee Bady also describes how the therapist's voice can aid in the therapeutic process:

> Sometimes I attempt through vocal tones to soothe an anxious, agitated patient. Other times I use my voice to stimulate a depressed and hopeless one. On still other occasions I talk to give the patient a human response and my words are less important than the vocal indication of my presence.[7]

Psychoanalyst Andre Green similarly believed that the voice reveals what he calls the "tonality,"[8] or coloring of one's inner life and "bodily states" even more deeply than the words one speaks. He writes, "The important thing is not to concentrate one's attention on words but rather to note those occasions when words fail or no longer perform their function."[9]

As useful as silence can be, I agree with psychiatrist Bella Van Bark who argues that, "[a]nalysts who use silence for long periods of time are unconsciously making it a cloak of authority."[10] Perhaps therapists would not reflexively hide behind this "cloak of authority," if more of us were trained to use our voices like actors. "For it is the therapist's manner, timing, physical presence, gaze and [also] *voice* that make a difference to the effect of what is actually said"[11] (or even what is not said), observes family therapist Sebastion Kraemer—invoking Stanislavski's call for every performer to find a truthful connection between mind and body.

My vocal preparation is most effective when I practice exercises that connect me to my body, my breath, and my sense of the present (**Exercise XI-A&B**; **Drawing 5**). I use the energy meditation and chakra work we discussed in the last chapter to find and explore various sounds in my respective energy centers. This connects my voice to emotions, and allows me to expand my vocal versatility—my capacity to express myself truthfully beyond the limited range of my *everyday self*—no matter what words I speak, if I even use words at all.

To practice my authentic use of voice, I will sometimes recite a poem or short bit of text while resonating in different chakras. As I do this, I both listen to and experience how the specific placement of vocal/emotional energy affects the meaning and expression of the piece: e.g., an intellectual, perhaps condescending reading from my head; an insightful offering from my throat; a warm invitation from my chest; a confident, willful sound from my stomach; an erotic, or otherwise self-possessed sound of pleasure from my pelvis; or a grounded, secure sound from my core down to my feet.

I also imagine myself using the text to talk to another person with intention. This connects me to "the action of the words,"[12] as theater director/vocal coach Cicely Berry writes, reminding us that words are not just words, but "acts,"[13] as psychoanalysts Harris and Aron have suggested. Sometimes I also think of an actor or someone in my life who tends to vocalize from each particular chakra, and imagine that person living in and speaking through my body as I vocalize. This exercise helps me to discover and play with unfamiliar roles that I find myself cast in during session, roles that are not within my immediate comfort zone—e.g., such as when I have to referee volatile family members; manage a crisis; respond to provocations with a cool, calm and collected exterior; or stay fully present with a client who is flooded with overwhelming grief.[14]

Clinical Application

The more I develop my vocal versatility, the more I can use my voice with intention on a case by case basis. Here are some basic suggestions for how you might vocalize as a therapist.

Set the Scene: When you first meet a client, you might intentionally speak with clear vibration from your head to help orient them to the work, along with vibrations from your throat and chest, to assure them that you understand them both intellectually and emotionally. As the work progresses, you might let them know you are listening and empathizing with their experiences by simply sharing some sounds of recognition, with resonance in your throat and/or chest.

Adjust: If your sound seems off-putting, cold, or harsh to the client, either because it is too distant or cerebral for them, or perhaps too intimate or invasive for them, you can always move into a different chakra to make them feel safer with you. Very often an adjustment of our vocal sound is more crucial to improving rapport with a client than the words we choose to say. This is an especially useful tool with clients who may have an extremely fragile sense of self, and who need our help to build ego strength. Our vocal tone can be a powerful tool we use to support and validate them as we work.

Find the Client's Voice in You: Obviously, our main objective is to help the client speak for herself. But once we get to know her well over time, we may begin to get a deep sense of what she's not saying and how she's not saying it. At those times, if we are confident in our own ability to tap into different chakras intentionally, we might offer some suggestions for what she may want to say (I always preface an intervention like this with a disclaimer, acknowledging that I'm "probably going to get this wrong"). For example, if you get a strong sense of a client's potential anger or desire from which they seem disconnected, as manifested in their exclusive use of head voice, you might speak from the willful energy of your solar plexus and say something like, "Of course that made you angry. It would have been quite reasonable for you to tell your brother, 'I feel unappreciated'." Or, with a client who is ambivalent about their erotic expressiveness, you might speak from your sacral chakra and say, "But it can be kind of fun to flirt, right?," or, "What's wrong with telling your husband you like physical affection?" Likewise, you might speak from your mask and head voice to a client who is used to being called "ditzy," and say something like, "It sounds like you knew exactly what you were thinking, you just didn't trust yourself."

This concept of helping the client find their *total self* through the voice reminds me of Nicole Kidman's portrayal of Virginia Woolf in the movie *The Hours*. Kidman has said that after listening to recordings of Woolf's voice for research, she decided not to imitate her exact sound because it would have been "comical."[15] Woolf's particular accent and vocal placement— mainly in the back of her throat—would not have been relatable for modern audiences, and more significantly, it would not have helped Kidman get to the heart of Woolf's complex and painful internal life, which was the central subject of the film. Instead of speaking with scholarly head and throat resonance like the recordings of Woolf, Kidman revealed deep will and conviction from her solar plexus, as well as a dark and ambivalent relationship to pleasure, eroticism, and creativity from her pelvis. And in a way, Kidman provided a sort of clinical intervention for Virginia Woolf, like a therapist to a client. She used herself to find an authentic emotional connection both to her own and to "Virginia's" body, that was not palpable in the reserved sound Woolf presented to the world as her *everyday self*.

Like Christopher Bollas says, there are times when the therapist "has a sense of a meaning that is present [in the client] and which requires [the therapist's] support in order to find its way toward articulation."[16] We can use our voices to provide such support.

Speech

> The **speech** of a character must bring to life the character itself.[17]
>
> (Voice teacher, Edith Skinner)

> [T]here are times when the music and prosody of **speech** illuminate more than the content or semantics…[18]
>
> (Psychoanalyst, Adrienne Harris)

Clear, distinguished, and articulate speech is certainly a great asset for any professional, but as with acting, in therapy, my facility with the spoken word serves me in a number of significant ways. For one, it helps me work collaboratively with clients to make meaning out of their experience of self through language. The process of choosing words, of creating spoken symbols, can be healing and transformative in itself. Speech making can help bring our curiosity, internal conflicts, confusion, and/or inextricable psychic pain into creative consciousness. It also helps us to symbolize our experience in a way that can be shared and recognized—what Freud referred to as a "dream language."[19] As Bollas writes, the therapist must help to "transform the [client's] inarticulate sense or feeling into some form of verbal representation that can be put to [them] for mutual consideration."[20] So, when I practice speech articulation exercises as part of my clinical preparation (**Exercises XII-A&B**), my aim is not necessarily to sound like Dame Judi Dench or Sir Ian McKellan. Instead, these activities help me to use language with intention, creativity, specificity, and connection between my mind, body, and imagination. This prepares me to not only express myself clearly and accessibly with each client, but also to invite them to participate in the creative act of speaking, to play with words and sounds, and to make meaning of their own experience.

When I practice expressing myself through consonants—even if I just repeat the sound of T or D or B—I find various ways to bring to life thoughts, stories, and images that can be playfully shared with other people. I then expand my practice to reciting poems, songs, or tongue twisters. And as I speak the words, I consider the specific thoughts I want to convey, the images I want to paint, the stories I hope to tell, and, most importantly, the connections I intend to make with each imagined listener. Thus, as I play with text and sound, I try to keep in mind Hamlet's advice to "suit the action to the word, the word to the action," which reminds me that "Language is action," one of my acting teacher Brian's favorite maxims.

Whenever I practice speech, I try to find a flicker of specific and personal intent, so that I don't just speak arbitrarily. This way, I connect to my own sense of interest, creativity, and pleasure. With each new intention and each new breath, I am mindful that in *this* moment I am transforming an internal experience into a symbolized sound, an action that will not only reveal an approximation of my subjective experience, but will also (hopefully) invite my scene partner to share in that experience as well, and to respond with an expression of their own.

Clinical Application

Connect: Speech exercises help me to find what Bollas calls the "meaningful representational potential"[21] of language. This experience prepares me to use words as a therapist not only to make sense, but to make connections with my clients—to talk *with* them rather than *at* them. Yet again, we find another example of being in *two places at once*, as the discipline of my voice and speech practices in private frees up my capacity for spontaneous expression on stage or in session. As Grotowski has suggested, "An inarticulate voice cannot confess. One cannot achieve spontaneity in art without structure of detail."[22] So while the idea of "speech exercises" may seem solipsistic and stilted, my intention in doing them is always to prepare for opportunities to engage with my scene partners freely and creatively.

Create: The act of speech can be a significant clinical intervention in itself. My efforts to find words that express my client's subjective experience—as well as my own—invite us both to participate in a dynamic, creative process. Sometimes I am able to successfully transform their "inarticulate sense or feeling into some form of verbal representation" that we can mutually consider.[23] Many other times, my word choices completely miss the mark. But either way, I share with them my interest in the act of making speech, and the process of creating a self-driven narrative. When we invite the consulting room to be a creative laboratory in this way—creating a third potential space, a rehearsal studio—we forge a sense of safety between therapist and client. We are able to reach an understanding that we will never perfectly read each other's minds, but as a much more freeing and productive alternative, we can each play with words without any pressure to land on the "right" ones. As Andre Green writes, through the interaction of language between therapist and client, we can create a *tertiary structure*[24] (or third[25] space) that constitutes a sign of recognition between us both.

Don't Speak: Again, everything true about acting and therapy is also untrue. So, as helpful as speaking in session can be, it can also get in the way. I have learned to look forward to moments when a client rejects my vocal and/or verbal contributions. As much as I dislike the sting of rejection, the experience helps the therapeutic process immensely when I can recognize the particular ways I have tried and failed to reach the client by talking when I should be listening. As an artist in general, I am always instructed by obvious indications that my ego has in some way intruded upon the character, the painting, the piece of writing, or my scene partner. I have learned to see these empathic failures and narcissistic injuries as gifts and opportunities. They are invitations from the client for me to feel, or at least better imagine, what it's like to be them. The pang of rejection gets me out of my own way, activates my sense of a third space between us, and emboldens me to ask rather than impose. To "*ask this way and ask that way, ask again, wait… receive*[26]," as actress Robin Weigert describes her own creative process. I can then shut up and listen to my scene partner with a more attuned and specific sense of what they want to say.

Ironically, my speech practices help prepare me for these necessary moments of silence, in two crucial ways.

1)   **Subtext:** When I practice using language with personal connection, I do much more than produce sound. I actively **engage my mind in the creative process of translating emotion, thought, imagery,**

and ideas, into words. So even when I choose not to open my mouth as I listen to a client, I formulate specific thoughts *as if* I *could* speak, *as if* I *could* ask the questions, or offer all the specific reflections and validations that are present in my mind. This internal action keeps me energetically engaged with my scene partner even if I don't utter a word or even make a noise. In this sense, speech exercises help me to sharpen my *subtext*, and therefore my ability to engage in focused, non-verbal, *relational events* with clients, as we discussed in Chapter 2.

2) **Listen More Carefully:** Speech practices remind me of the space and time I require to connect to my internal life and to external expression, and to grant that same space and time to my client. This approach is particularly helpful when my clients indicate in some way that they want me to turn down the volume on my voice (which happens more often than I would like to admit…) and help them increase the volume on theirs.

This way, I'm not just getting out of my clients' way in session in order to hide behind "the cloak of authority" because I believe it is the "right" way to do psychotherapy, or because I feel the need to fully submit to their voice at the complete expense of my own. Instead, by surrendering to their voice for the moment, I can receive their specific request for space, and become actively attuned to their process of making speech.

From there, I can also find ways to encourage their process without having to speak myself. I can listen to the poetry they create, react to what feels true and specific, and encourage them to find more such genuine emotions.

I learned this approach to therapeutic listening primarily from Ken Corbett when I was in clinical supervision with him. He showed more than told me how to adopt this practice. He would listen to me talk and talk (bless him), and react genuinely, especially when something I said sounded to him like my authentic voice (very much the way Diego Arciniegas directed me as Romeo, as I discussed in the last chapter). He would laugh or indicate in some way that he recognized me in those moments, and occasionally he might even say a few words like, "You could say that to your client," or "That could be the opening line of your next article." He understood and appreciated how deceptively tricky it can be to find one's own voice through words, and very delicately encouraged mine to come through.

I find I am better equipped to help my clients the more I practice the creative, spontaneous act of making speech.

8 Warm Up

Much like actors, musicians, dancers, athletes, and all performers, therapists must *warm up* our instruments before show time.

From the genesis of our profession, we have been encouraged to prepare for the unknown and for paradox[1]—to enter each session "without memory or desire," as Bion famously suggested, while also poised to recognize and respond to the client's emotional needs.[2] But there are very few technical suggestions for what a therapist can actually *do* to achieve this seemingly oxymoronic state of prepared openness. I am fortunate that the paradoxes I need to anticipate as an actor are very similar to those I face as a therapist; therefore, I find it extremely helpful to do an actor-like *warm up* before sessions.

For me, a *warm up* is whatever I need to do to be: 1) **Grounded** enough to create a clear and safe frame for me and my scene partner, 2) **Relaxed** enough to be emotionally and mentally accessible, to absorb new information, and to have the capacity to adapt when necessary, 3) **Poised** enough to receive and respond, 4) **Focused** enough to maintain a clear intention and purpose, and 5) **Open** enough to run with any and all possibilities.

To prepare myself in this way, I perform variations on all the exercises I've shared so far, depending on what the particular client and particular scene requires of me. As an actor, Nicole Kidman has said, "I'm willing to use whatever is needed to get to the place."[3] Here are some *warm ups* I use to get to each new "place" as a therapist.

Research

As performers, we constantly research ways to improve ourselves artistically and professionally. But there are specific forms of research I do to warm up for each scene.

As an actor, my research may include: **1) Reading** and re-reading the given script to make sure all of my creative contributions are in service to *this* particular story. I might also read about the time period and place where the story is set, and about the character's profession and other details of their life that are different from mine. **2) Talking** to people like the character, those who know/knew the character (if the performance is based on a real person), who work in the same field or who understand something significant about the character's life is also a strategy I've used. **3) Watching and/or Listening** to recordings of people like the character, who talk like him, move like him, or who face similar challenges can be useful as well. **4) Writing** a character biography, which gives me the opportunity to conceptualize and personalize the specifics of the character's life—both those included in the script and those that are not—is yet another potentially helpful warm up. The great actress/acting teacher Uta Hagen suggests guiding questions for character biographies, such as: **Who are you and where did you come from? What are your given circumstances? What are your relationships like? What do you want?** (Both the super objective and immediate objective), **What are your obstacles?** and **What can you do to get what you want?**[4]

Our research as therapists is similar. We study the "script," the presenting circumstances each new client brings. We read about their identities, relationships, and challenges. We talk to experts who work with people like them, or who are more knowledgeable about their circumstances than we are. We may even watch videos and listen to podcasts to gain a more intuitive sense of them. And of course we write psychosocials, genograms, and treatment plans in an attempt to personally understand their unique lives.

I'm sure you already apply many of these research methods to your clinical work. What I propose here is that thinking of this preparation like a performing artist—not just a mental health professional—helps us to use the aspects of our research that forge a live connection between us and our scene partners, and to let the rest go—which is not necessarily how we are trained. The clinics, hospitals, and other bureaucratic settings in which we grow our clinical wings encourage us to prioritize treatment plans over the people they are intended to help. But as actors, we are very explicitly and specifically taught to use any groundwork we do to explore the highly specific, spontaneous, visceral life of our character on stage.

The efforts we make to embody our character or client, inside and out, orients us to each new scene. This approach keeps us grounded, relaxed, poised, focused, and open to possibilities, as any good *warm up* does. As the great acting teacher Stella Adler has said, "[r]elaxation [on stage] comes from the truthfulness of the circumstances the actor creates."[5] That truthfulness comes from the performer's research, which is not to say that we will show up for rehearsals with all the answers no matter how much research we've done, but at least we will be armed with guiding questions. Our research provides an initial launching pad from which we can take our first leap. From there, we can navigate each scene, moment to moment. And when we are suddenly at a loss, our research gives us something to fall back on, to inform our next question so we do not fall completely flat.

According to actress Viola Davis, "They tell you in acting school, 'Arm yourself with as much information as you can.'"[6] For Davis, writing a character bio is particularly helpful, especially when she has little time on stage or screen to establish her character's whole life. Her preparation gives her a specific point of focus so that she doesn't "overplay the scene." Which is what we all tend to do, in art and life, when our intentions and motivations are vague. As my acting mentor Brian always reminded me, "You can be as big or small as you like on stage, **as long as you're specific**." To prepare myself to be specific, truthful, focused, and not "overplay" as I approach a character or client, I use the research methods I describe above. And the more visceral the information I gather, the more opportunities I can find to relate to each unique client/character without overdoing it.

As with any warm up, my research is only useful if it helps me create a frame, within which my client and I can generate new life together, spontaneously and freely, one scene at a time. Again, in the words of theater innovator Jerzy Grotowski, "One cannot achieve spontaneity in art without structure of detail."[7] And as screen actor Jake Gyllenhaal has said of his artistic process, "Freedom is on the other side of discipline."[8]

Coco

Coco was the first child of a wealthy family, and like many privileged teenagers, she was living faster than her caregiving adults could keep pace with (Her previous therapist described her as a "moving target"). My main dilemma in treating her was therefore to maintain an open connection while keeping a keen and responsible eye on her.

My primary concern was her sexual health, which from a physiological perspective was not an intuitive conversation for us to have. Coco talked to me freely, albeit superficially, about her regular sexual activity, which was a plus in the "openness" column of our treatment goals. But as a man who grew up with brothers, I did not know how to talk with her about sexual safety in specific terms, which was a big minus in the "responsible care" column, as I was unable to offer more than general concerns about her self care, like a vague, anxious, out-of-touch parent (e.g., "Are you using condoms?" "Have you been tested?" "Be safe."). I felt strongly that in addition to our emotional work, she needed someone with whom to discuss sexual health and safety more intuitively and practically than she could with me. She claimed she did not talk about sex with her pediatrician, and that her mother would not allow her to see a gynecologist—ironically, fearing that such access would only encourage her to have sex. Coco also insisted that I not meet with her mother about this subject because she feared such a conversation would make her mother even more worried, and consequently, more strict. This impasse made me increasingly anxious each week. I struggled to share my concerns with Coco without shutting down our spontaneous rapport. As a performer, I was stuck. How could I encourage her to take care of her body without anxiously "overplaying" the scene?

Not only did I need to understand appropriate sexual health care for a teenage girl, but also what it was like to be Coco (and her mother), and how I could best encourage her to establish that care.

Fortunately, I have a large number of good friends who are women. I asked them not only about their health care as teens, but also about their emotional experiences of that care. They also gave me detailed accounts of their conversations (and lack of conversations) with their mothers and/or women caregivers during that period. What seemed most consistent and relevant to Coco's case was that the mother/daughter relationships tended to work better on the topic of sexual health when there was both enough trust and enough space between them. But more than getting practical tips from the women I spoke to, I absorbed personalized accounts of their visceral experiences. This prepared me to empathize with Coco and her mother, and to actively seek specific opportunities to connect emotionally with both of them on this topic without overplaying my concerns. This research, in addition to various forms of clinical support and reading—from medical websites, as well as psychotherapy journals—warmed me up to talk *with* Coco and her mother about her sexual care, rather than *at* them.

I entered my next scene with Coco feeling focused, grounded, relaxed, poised, and open. As I listened to her, I found an opening to share my recommendation in a way she could receive. She was frustrated with her mother for not letting her attend a party: "She's afraid I'll have sex…Which is stupid because I'm having sex anyway." Without preparation, I would have felt the compulsion to *do* something big in this moment, to overact in order to express my concerns—but really more to allay my own anxieties of feeling unprepared. But instead, I gave a clear, relaxed, and focused performance. I replied, "I've got an idea. If you want to build trust with her, ask her to bring you to a gynecologist. That way, you can talk to a pro about birth control and safe sex. Show her how responsible you are." Coco shot back, defeated, "No. I told you. She won't let me see a gynecologist…" "Well," I responded, calmly introducing a solution, "Maybe I could meet with her and your father and convince them to take you." Coco suddenly seemed interested, and I believe the change in her attitude was in part due to the confident ease of my delivery. "You think that would work?" she asked. "We can try," I said, with a casual smile, suggesting I was not overly attached to the outcome (Bion might say I played this moment "without desire" or too much of my own idiosyncrasies getting in the way). My research/warm up prepared me to be in this scene clearly and subtly, without the interference of my anxieties.

I was also now able to enter the next scene, which featured Coco's mother and father, equally confident. I did not have to wait long for her mother to express her worries: "I try to lay down the law: Curfews; no parties. But the truth is, I don't know what she's up to or how to protect her anymore… From drugs, from sex…" I looked at her with calm, reassuring warmth and said, "Maybe it's time she see a gynecologist. At least that way she'd have a medical professional she could trust and talk to in case she becomes sexually active. Would that alleviate some of your concerns?" Without preparation, I would have likely overplayed this moment. My vague anxiety could have manifested in a strident tone, which would not have opened up connection with Coco's mother. Instead I might have triggered her own anxiety, causing her to double down in her resistance to the gynecologist. But she responded to my warmth and clarity with openness. "Well, I don't want to encourage anything …," I nodded and replied, "I understand. It must be hard to let go as your first child grows up. But if you're worried she might have sex anyway…won't she be better off with a doctor she can trust?"

Within a few weeks, Coco had a gynecologist. This extinguished not only my anxiety, but ultimately Coco's and her mother's as well. This development also created a safe frame within which we could play our subsequent scenes together with mental and emotional freedom.

To be clear: this is by no means a universal instruction on how to provide mental health care for teenage girls. Nor do I mean to insult your intelligence with an obviously pedestrian lesson along the lines of "If you're lost, ask for help or read a book." With this vignette, I specifically intend to show not only how actorly research gave me access to characters who partially eluded me—Coco and her mom. More significantly, I wish to show how this specific form of warm up helped me to perform necessary clinical interventions with focus, groundedness, relaxation, poise, and openness.

Intend

"Before you move into the pose, have an **intention**," my yogi Nancy has often said. "Ask yourself what your personal **intention** is for *this* performance," my acting guru, Brian, has similarly instructed. And as psychiatrist Howard E. Gorman has said, all psychotherapists begin each treatment with **intention**.[9] I agree. We always start with an intention that we will inevitably need to adapt along the way. As Gorman puts it, our overall intention (or super objective) is always to collaborate with our clients in an effort to make meaning out of our exchanges—both consciously and unconsciously, textually, and subtextually. At the same time, we also want to help them expand their sense of *self*. But each scene along the way presents its own challenges, and therefore, calls for its own specific intention (or objective).

Identifying my intention before each session is a highly effective warm up in itself. But as I emphasize throughout this book, I also try to practice being intentional whenever I do any kind of preparatory exercise. Whether I'm warming up my mind, body, or voice, running, practicing yoga, or doing research, I always aim to find that *flicker* of personal motivation. Here are a few intentions I have set before entering specific scenes.

Meet a New Client: My intention with a first meeting is typically to make the client feel safe and invited to talk. I will generally do a grounding energy warm up and an exercise to find my center and breath, and imagine specific people, bodies, and voices that personally make me feel safe and welcome as I do it. I'll notice what might be blocking sound from vibrating in my head or my chest and use imagery to help open those areas up with each new breath and each new vibration. Even if I'm sick or tired, I can find the best possible way to physicalize and vocalize my intention within those limitations. By specifying my intention as I warm up, I also give myself something tangible to rely on when the client defies my expectations— either because they are new to therapy, are slow to warm, or are distractingly uncomfortable for some other reason. If I have warmed up my chest/heart chakra with energy and sound and images, I can maintain and even adapt my intention to welcome the client without getting thrown off guard.

Make an Adjustment: If a client seems to experience my two cents as an intrusion, I might warm up before our next session with a very clear intention to receive and follow their every move (which is not the same thing as simply shutting up, or negating my voice, as I discussed in the last chapter). To prepare, I might think of my intention *to receive and follow* as I do the "Take a Seat" exercise for example (**Exercise X; Drawing 6**), so that I find a personal, physical connection to my action. I might also practice opening my throat to allow myself to make intentional soft and open sounds to support and encourage the client's voice as opposed to interrupting them abruptly with my own. In this manner, I find a way to remain actively present with them, even as I get out of their way.

Meet with a Couple or Family: To prepare to meet with multiple clients at once, I tend to warm up my voice and body with the intention to facilitate, guide, and/or coach. This means doing an energy meditation to get grounded as well as the "Fly in Place" exercise (**Exercise III; Drawing 2**) to use my whole body to breathe. I will then use various vocal exercises to get in touch with sounds of authority within myself. However, I also want to prepare to empathize with each of the voices in the room that will want to be heard. To that end, I will practice oscillating from a commanding sound located in my lower body to a more welcoming and/or intimate sound emanating from my chest and throat.

Resist an Enactment: We all know what it's like to get caught in an enactment with clients, both reacting to each other at light speed, before we even know what is happening. At these times, we both feel attacked, and neither knows how to break the cycle of blame—creating what Jessica Benjamin calls doer/done to dilemmas.[10] As Benjamin and others have pointed out, we rarely, if ever, understand what is happening in the moment, but only later on when we've the chance to reflect.[11] For me, when this happens with a client (e.g., If I feel blamed for not helping them and I'm tempted to blame them in turn for resisting the help I have given), I might warm up for our next session with the intention to hear and be heard without being reactive or defensive. I might allow my breath to deepen while I practice plank pose, while doing push-ups, or performing the "Take a Seat" exercise so that I'm prepared to breathe and think under pressure. Connection to my breath will be necessary as the client and I unpack what happened between us. These exercises will help keep me from submitting to their blame—or, conversely, blaming them—and instead allow me to surrender to the multiple perspectives at play with a sense of curiosity.

Crisis Intervention: Sometimes we need to warm up for highly technical performances or interventions. For the actor, this would be a *fight call*, *dance call*, or *singing call* to practice choreography or a song. As a therapist, this is the immediate prep I do to meet with client(s) in crisis—e.g., couples in a domestic violence situation, a teenager who has made a suicidal gesture, or a family processing a severe boundary violation. In these cases, the intention of my warm up will be highly technical and specific: to promote safety for all involved. The exercises I do will be geared toward performing my interventions with a combination of mental clarity, grounded strength, and emotional warmth—whether it's establishing a safety plan with a couple or family, or recommending a higher level and/or more specialized form of treatment for a client. I will want to be able to breathe deeply and expansively, to simultaneously have a commanding voice resonating deeply in my body and a logical voice resonating in my head, as well as crystal clear speech. In these cases, I will rehearse exactly what I plan to say to the client(s) as I warm up my body and voice.

Give

My acting mentor Brian says that before you enter a scene, you should always "[r]emind yourself that you are there to give a gift to the audience." This was enduring advice for me throughout drama school. It woke me up from moments of lethargy or laziness. It freed me from stage fright, from my inhibiting self-consciousness, and from the pestering of my inner critic. It shifted my focus from, "Do I really have to do *that* again?" or "What if they don't like me?" to "How can I help them?" It transformed the energy in my body from static fear to dynamic generosity. Similarly, as a therapist, I remind myself before each session that no matter how challenging it may be, the client has chosen to show up for help, and I have something to give them—even if it's simply the gift of listening.

Act II

Rehearse

Whereas the first period of work on a role was only one of preparation, this second period is one of creation. If the first period could be compared to the early courtship between two lovers, the second represents the consummation of their love, the conception and the formation of the fruit of their union.

(Constantin Stanislavski, *Creating a Role*, 1946b, p. 46)

9 Frame

Once we decide to cast each other as client and therapist—following an initial consultation (see Chapter 18: Audition)—the psychotherapy rehearsal process begins. And as with any performing art, the first step of rehearsal is to establish a *frame*, to find our footing and to create safe, stable, and clear (enough) parameters, within which we can explore the unknown.

Since my super objective in any rehearsal process is to invite participation, I find the treatment frame (or contract) to be more sturdy if my scene partner and I create it together over time, rather than if I impose it on them at the outset.

Sometimes we hand the client a literal contract that includes technical aspects like the terms of service, a cancellation policy, or an explanation of confidentiality. But beyond the basics—i.e., safety, scheduling, and payment—I prefer to co-create the treatment frame with each new scene partner as we go. Just as I want to help clients find creative freedom in their lives, I also want them to find their own way into our scene work, beginning with our first objective: to set the frame.

The first few weeks, even months, are like trust-building exercises. We test each other to see how safe and/or comfortable we feel speaking, sitting together in silence, being vulnerable, and sharing humor in order to get a sense of whether we trust the other to catch us if we fall. Obviously, as the therapist, I don't lean on my clients in quite the same ways they lean on me (I have my own therapy, supervision, and support networks for this purpose). But I can get a sense of how much room there is for me to "fail" my clients in some way—which is inevitable—and, more importantly, how much they allow me to recover from those stumbles. From this period of exploration and creativity, I find that we formulate more meaningful and useful treatment goals than either one of us could possibly articulate alone on the first day of *rehearsal*. As Jessica Benjamin says of this process, "To the question who discovered this pattern you or I the paradoxical answer is 'both and neither.'"[1]

Below are a few of the actions I perform in order to establish a safe, inviting, and mutually created therapeutic *frame*. The particular way I play each of these actions depends on the particular scene partner with whom I am working, and our particular rapport.

Hold

It's powerful to be held by nothing more than someone else's listening, and this realization is easy to forget.

When my listener makes me feel safe and expresses (implicitly or explicitly) endless curiosity about me—and that they are sturdy and non-judgmental enough to hear what I want to say—I feel securely held in a healing chrysalis, within which self expansion is possible. Over the years, I have discovered that it's much simpler to create such a holding environment than I used to think. To best customize a mode of listening that holds each unique client, I must simply, but deeply, trust that I am enough. I must have faith that simply being present with them for the hour is entirely productive, whether or not we speak.

As a young actor, I often struggled to feel I was enough. I would rummage outside of myself in search of big voices, accents, and gestures, so I could feel like the character, often forgetting that my most effective tool is my own belief that I *am* the character. At the very least, the realization that everything I need to discover about the character is somewhere within me is a vital step in the process.

Likewise, you already have everything it takes to successfully play the part of the client's chrysalis. You already have the capacity to make them feel safe and to be endlessly curious about them—and this can come across in how you simply but truly listen—as I have described in the opening chapters.

But, again, don't take it from me; see your listening face for yourself (as per Chapter 2). From there, you can sense what it might be like to talk to a therapist like you. You can remind yourself how little it actually takes to *hold* your client—to make them feel secure enough to want to take risks and to grow.

I for one have often felt amateurish and inadequate in countless sessions when I did nothing more than listen, especially at the beginning of a new treatment. *That's all you got?*, my inner critic would say. I imagined clients saw me as a kid playing in grown-up clothes—inadequate, unprepared. *I better do something, say something, sound smart*, I'd think. That's when I'd interrupt my natural flow of listening by spouting platitudes they could get from bumper stickers: e.g., "Use 'I' statements," "Set boundaries"… "Look both ways before crossing the street."

To my surprise, I learned that even the *consumer clients*—the ones who explicitly demand "practical feedback" at the outset—seemed rebuffed when I would interrupt their thought process with clunky aphorisms, even though I was literally giving them what they had requested. It was like those cringe-worthy moments when Charlie Rose would interrupt luminous guests on his show—like Viola Davis or Kate Winslet—before they could complete their interesting thoughts. I still find myself *Charlie-Rose-ing* my clients on occasion, but now I'm more aware of such moments and, again, awareness is one of our most crucial tools as performers. I have learned that whatever words I throw around at the early stages of rehearsal are really only useful if they hold the client, and none of them are as important as intentional listening.

Most—if not all—clients really just want to be heard and seen in a safe environment, especially at the beginning of therapy. Though few, if any, articulate this simple desire to us (or, very likely, even to themselves) directly. I understand this complex dynamic better now that I have worked in this profession for a number of years. Having seen myself in video sessions from time to time made this particularly clear.

Oh that's what I look like when I do nothing but listen, I said to myself, the first few times I watched my eyes follow the client's every thought. To my surprise, I looked like a professional making an effort to understand his clients, and not like a clueless amateur. *If I were the client*, I thought, *I would not need more from the therapist right now.* In fact, I conveyed more strength, groundedness, and wisdom in quiet stillness than I did when I spoke— which I noticed I only did in order to prove myself worthy to the client. But I realized that if I were the client, I would feel more held and less anxious by talking to the version of me who is comfortable in the stillness of his body and mind—the guy who has gotten out of his own way and can actually *listen*, rather than the one who responds to his own anxious need to have an answer for everything.

Seeing my own face in the role of therapist reminds me that we are all in the client's position at times. We all have a deep, human yearning to be held, emotionally and mentally, by another person. This observation reminds me of my own experience receiving therapy, and what a luxury it is to be looked at with eyes that are interested and capable of absorbing every idiosyncratic aspect of me that I present. Such a feeling of security and closeness also very specifically reminds me of being held by my father, literally, when I was about five. I had run to his arms, upset, because I didn't want to play ball with boys in my neighborhood who had made fun of me (Like the famous children's book character Ferdinand in *Ferdinand the Bull*, I wished to smell the flowers instead). By picking me up and holding me, my dad let me know that my preference was ok. Within the safety of his embrace, I could expand not only my immediate choices, but also my sense of self.

I have learned how little it takes to convey a similar warm holding environment to that which my father provided for me. If my intention to hold the client is clear, this desire can simply show through my eyes.

Keep the Ball in the Air

Therapy works best if both scene partners can keep our minds engaged, if we both keep the scene alive—or, as theater people say, *keep the ball in the air.*

This engagement means that even if I don't know what is happening at any given moment, even if I don't speak, even if the energy is low, and even if my scene partner and I are not looking at each other, whatever they throw my way I will somehow catch, hold, and return to them in a new form. *Keeping the ball* in the air is a conceptual yet specific tool I use to *hold* my client and to *be in the present* with them (as per Chapter 4).

As a listener, one of the most effective ways I *keep the ball in the air* is to have something to say but not say it (see *subtext* in Chapter 2 and Chapter 7). I try to let my mind come up with a response to what my client has said, and stay engaged with them as if I might speak the thought—but I don't. Even if the response would just be a momentary bit of validation or a question. They often notice how awake, alert, and attuned my mind is, and sometimes even respond as if I've actually spoken. And when my silence makes them anxious, I do actually speak the thought to see if that vocalization makes a difference. This way, I let my scene partner know I am, in fact, following their every word, if they need to be reassured of my attention, and make clear that my frequent silences are choices I have made to give them space to talk.

There may even be times when I use my eyebrows or make noises of recognition that suggest I understand the gravity of something the client has said. And though these subtle gestures may seem insignificant, they are indicators that I am catching the ball and returning it, which may encourage them to keep the game in play—to keep thinking, feeling, and talking.

Actors sometimes practice this form of engagement by playing catch with an invisible ball. Or by practicing the classic improvisation game called, "Yes, and." In this game, you must respond to whatever your scene partner says or does with either, "**Yes, and**," (finishing the sentence however you choose) or "**Yes, but**….". The only thing you can't do in response to your partner is say, "No." "No," means that you dropped the ball, the game is over, and the scene has simply died (see Chapter 10: Play).

So, in this vein, even if I am presented with something ridiculous, dull, or uninspiring, I always try to begin with (at least the attitude of) "Yes" to validate what I have heard. From there, we can take the scene wherever we like. I can say "Yes, and…" or "Yes, but…," with my listening, without having to open my mouth. But I do my best to avoid saying "No"—which is effectively what I would be saying if my silence were accompanied by complete blankness behind my eyes. When I began working as a therapist, I actually thought I was supposed to deploy blank eyes, and was encouraged by teachers and supervisors to "be quiet" and "let the client talk." I now know that silence is not mutually exclusive with *keeping the ball in the air*.

Be Curious

The most reliable method I have found to **hold** my clients and to **keep the ball in the air** at the same time is by being actively **curious**.

Curiosity is much more than being interested; it is a wholehearted commitment to not knowing, to not settling on answers, and thereby to allowing my client to bloom perpetually before me. Curiosity keeps the therapy car running, which is why I don't necessarily notice I need it until we stall. In those moments, when both the client and I are at a complete loss for words or thoughts—especially when they look to me for answers or solutions—I put in an emergency call to my curiosity to jumpstart the engine.

Clients often cast us in the role of *the fixer*, and we like to accept and to play that part by suggesting solutions—if we can. But most of the time we are just as lost as they are. That's when my curiosity becomes my safety net, and helps me to do the following without having to speak: 1) Let the client know that though I do not have a way out of their dilemma, I will join them in moving through it, 2) Model a way for them to navigate dilemmas on their own, and, most importantly, 3) Hold them steady in the moment.

I learned how powerful the performance of genuine curiosity can be from several of my therapists and mentors. In addition to being highly accomplished analysts, scholars, teachers, and writers, whether they know it or not, they are all great performers. I learned as much, if not more, from their simple acts of quiet curiosity than I did from their sage advice. As I shared myself with them, their eyes were not full of answers, but of endless questions. The wonderful sparkle of their curiosity put me at ease and made me feel safe to talk freely without fearing my voice would be stunted.

Their method as performers (even unwittingly) is actually not unlike that of Meryl Streep, who says, "I'm curious about everything and everybody. I do not limit myself with a certain kind of acting."[2] I'm sure your unyielding curiosity also helps keep your therapy car in motion. And that regardless of your clinical orientation, the genuine, searching look in your eyes is enough to *hold* and inspire your clients to be actively *curious* about themselves.

In certain circumstances, I even fake it before I make it. Just thinking specific, open-ended thoughts—really, just thinking them—conveys my curiosity and genuine intention to understand my scene partner before I truly get what they are saying; e.g., *I'm following…tell me more. No, really, tell me more.* To keep them feeling held by my "silent movie acting," I might throw in some comforting and stabilizing thoughts like: *That makes a lot of sense, I think I understand. I can't imagine what that must have been like. Let's keep exploring this together.* By simply having such thoughts as I listen, my own, intuitive, curiosity eventually kicks in and becomes second nature.

We must also remain aware of our unintended subtext, or we can easily send unwitting messages to clients that suggest we are not curious about them at all: e.g., *Get OUT of that relationship, I don't understand why that's hard for you,* or *What do you want me to do about it? Get a grip.* Those reactions could be read in our eyes if we do not transform them consciously into open-ended questions. As a result, clients may refrain from telling us more about themselves. Of course there may be critical times when certain clients need me to step into the role of a take-charge parent or coach, and explicitly tell them what to do (see Chapter 14: Direct); typically, however, this final step is not necessary.

Look Away

I'm sure you don't need me to tell you to make eye contact with your clients, but we can always be reminded to look away. Sometimes, eye contact can be too much. We can feel that our listener is too interested in us—that we are too in the spotlight, too exposed and vulnerable. As my eye doctor friend, Drew, says, "people don't like being stared at for too long because it makes us feel like prey." Similarly, the pioneer of improv theater, Keith Johnstone observes, we feel the loss of power and status in situations when we can't see submission in our scene partner's eyes.[3] Our minds tend to go blank at such times, out of self protection, and we can't truly engage until we press pause on "the scene" and regain our bearings. Remember this as you listen to your client, and look away from her or him when it seems like your gaze is obstructing their process in some way.

Looking away serves a similar function to the clients' posture assumed in the classic psychoanalytic tradition—in which the patient lies on a couch, facing away from the analyst—granting them space to possess their own mind.[4] You can help clients to have this kind of space even as you are seated face to face by simply looking away when you sense they need to gather their thoughts. You can then look back when they seem ready to re-engage. This way, they can learn to participate in an equitable relationship in which power is shared, rather than feel scrutinized by an authority figure who assesses them with a "mysterious stillness"—which is how Keith Johnstone describes a scene partner who conveys "high-status."[5] Looking away can convey to clients that they are equal participants in the rehearsal process of therapy. This simple gesture can send the message that you're interested in them, but also that you're not overly attached to every word they speak or move they make—like a prying reporter or strategic lawyer.

In my experience, looking away with intent conveys to clients that: 1) I respect their privacy and space, 2) The interesting and complex thoughts they've shared with me warrant taking space to reflect on them, and 3) I can hold them in my mind, even when I'm not faced with them directly (and who doesn't want to be thought of?).

The simple act of looking away can emphasize that you and your client are separate, and that separateness is ok. You let them know that you are available to absorb them with your curiosity whenever they are ready, and that you are prepared to give them space when they want or need it. This action may also model a way for your scene partner to be present with you, and in all of their relationships, without feeling pressured to perform at full capacity in the spotlight, at all times.

Link

One of the subtlest, yet transformative acts of listening we can do is to help people link[6] their thoughts together—to help them find coherence and meaning in their natural flow of mind. We can help them to do this by simply listening—actively, curiously, and empathically—from the very beginning of our work together.

Of course we hope to listen like this all the time, but let's face it, sometimes it's hard. Clients may be jumbled, staticky, relentlessly vague, anxious, dissociative, or unfocused. At such times, it is challenging to make sense of what they tell us, which can be frustrating if not overwhelming. Moments like these are when performers must rely on technique.

Professional actors certainly prefer to use their natural instincts to play a scene; but when they are in an amphitheater, without mics, in the middle of a hailstorm, they can't just phone it in. Dire situations require them to use skills—e.g., vocally and physically—that they have practiced, and which they can consciously deploy, all while making their work seem effortless. Here's how I have been able to achieve this when my clients don't make sense to me.

Before I do anything, of course, I am always curious about the range of possibilities. Is the client merely anxious because therapy is unfamiliar to them, or are they like this all the time? Do they get flustered talking to people in general, do they have ADHD, or do they perhaps even suffer from psychosis? At first, we often just don't know, so we want to begin with the mindset that any of those explanations are possible. But if I discover that after getting a medical and psychiatric history there doesn't seem to be any glaring indicators of something more serious, I give them the benefit of the doubt, and listen **as if** they are making sense (I can always refer them to a psychiatrist if my efforts repeatedly fail to help them to be coherent).

The concept of *as if* is one of the most basic and engaging tools an actor has at their disposal. Like the phrase sounds, it just means to simply play our action *as if* we are in the character's shoes—e.g., as if we just won the lottery, or as if we just lost a family member. For our purposes here, we want to listen to the client *as if* they are making sense.

A technical move I sometimes make in the spirit of *as if* is to anticipate and accept their thoughts as they try explaining them to me whether I understand what they are saying or not. What do I mean by this?—I mean I slightly nod, smile, and widen my eyes as if what they've said makes perfect sense to me. Again, it doesn't have to actually make perfect sense, at least not intellectually. This action is aspirational. But what's more important is that it signals to the client that I accept them, whatever they say and however they say it, and that even if I don't understand what they mean at first, I have faith that we will eventually make meaning out of it together. Then, I observe where this signal takes us.

I am not lying, necessarily, or being disingenuous, but am instead anticipating and accepting their thoughts. I can be quite genuine in my attempt to give the scene what it needs to stay open and connected. To this end, I might say something with my face like, *I completely accept that this is your reality, and I want to join you in it even though it's a place I've never been.*

I've had therapists who would smile and nod and anticipate and accept all of my unformed thoughts; their acceptance validated me, and helped me to trust my own process. Like a painter throwing drops on a canvas here and there, I began to trust that the picture I was crafting would eventually take shape—if I stayed engaged and reflective. And that powerful belief in myself came just from my scene partner's, warm, accepting nod as I spoke, as if she was saying, *Whatever you have to say I can take it, I will try to understand, and we will discover what you are intending to express together.*

Also, as previously mentioned, listening does not just mean silence. When the warm, welcoming, subtext gleaming through your eyes is not enough for your clients, especially in the beginning, you can give them a little more to hold onto by briefly telling them what you heard and how you understand it. This way, you assure them that there is a thread that you can follow in all of their free associations, and that you are in fact following it. I try to keep in mind that being a client is very hard for most, if not all of us, and for those who have suffered severe relational traumas, it's especially anxiety-provoking. Some clients enter therapy feeling like Sandra Bullock's character in *Gravity*, torn from the mothership abruptly, floating in space, crying out, "Tell me what to do, tell me what to do…" I do not necessarily tell them what to do, but I can at least let them know I hear and understand them.

I once had a client whom I initially thought might be psychotic because his thoughts were so disorganized. However, he did not report any history of mental illness in his family, or any severe traumatic events in his past, and he had never been hospitalized or prescribed psychotropic medications. He denied having ever hallucinated or wanting to hurt himself or anyone else, and he wasn't paranoid. Therefore, I gave him the benefit of the doubt. And even though the first few sessions were like the beginning of a rough and surprising roller coaster, I anticipated and accepted his thoughts as if they made sense. This response represented a deliberate adjustment on my part. If I had listened instinctively as I normally do, I would have been as completely confounded and bothered as he seemed to be. Fortunately, the challenge paid off. When he asked me if he was making sense, I didn't just say, "Ugh…what do you think, buddy?!!" Instead I told him what I understood of his plot-twisty narrative—a fragmented, jumbled story about a boss who gave him promotions but never a raise, a mother's gambling problems, needy siblings, and suspicions of a cheating boyfriend whom he was too afraid to confront because it might cause the boyfriend more stress than he was already under with his demanding job. The client would share bits and pieces of this saga with me each week, with wide eyes, heightened affect, and fragmented sentences, and my immediate reaction was always, "What's happening?…" But I learned to give myself space to breathe, reflect, and practice anticipating and accepting all of it. I began to smile and nod and answer him with something like, "It sounds like everyone in your life always depends on you to manage their chaos. How overwhelming. Who manages yours?"

After sharing what I heard and how I understood the links between all of his associations, he seemed validated and awakened to the fact that he actually did have a point. As we moved forward, he asked me less what I was hearing because he trusted that I was listening. More importantly, he trusted that he was making sense, or at least that he would eventually make sense. Once he got the drops of paint out of his mind and onto the canvas (within our mutually created frame), he began to make coherent shapes. In time, he was palpably more calm, centered, and coherent in his presentation, and it became very clear that he was not psychotic.

Of course, as I noted earlier, if your empathic efforts do not help the client to link his thoughts more successfully, you may need to refer him to a psychiatrist for an evaluation. But even if he and his psychiatrist decide that medication is necessary, the practice of helping him to link his thoughts together as you continue talk therapy is of great value nonetheless.

To deploy this linking technique, I have to assume a position that I repeatedly describe throughout this book, which is to be in *two places at once*. In this case, that means performing my confidence that everything the client says will eventually make sense, while also allowing my mind to gather footage, play and replay it, analyze it, and make efforts to link her disparate associations together the best I can.

10 Play

Plato's maxim, "[y]ou can discover more about a person in an hour of *play* than a year of conversation," is key for performing artists. We can try to apply theory, research, and "script analysis" as we engage in scene work, but it's not until we *play* with our scene partners that the characters come alive. As Brian, my acting mentor, would often say, "Great work, but you forgot to *play*."

Psychoanalyst and painter Marion Milner describes how critical play is to the art of therapy:

> In our childhood we are allowed to act, move, behave, under the influence of illusions, to play 'pretend' games and even get lost in our play… In adult life it is less easy to find settings where this is possible (we get other people to do the pretending, on the films and the stage), although we do find it within the framework of the analytic session as patients.[1]

As a therapist, I remind myself to "play" in some of the following ways:

Pleasure

"[There is a] virgin pleasure I always try to have when I'm acting,"[2] says actress Audrey Tatou. I too seek pleasure when I perform—as both an actor and a clinician. This goal helps me to transform the energy I would otherwise spend on fear, nerves, or stress into desire, discovery, and creativity.

Also, if I'm genuinely enjoying myself, my scene partner is more likely to do the same. And if she doesn't, then I get curious and learn something significant about her—e.g., she may feel left out of my "good time" or that I'm teasing, minimizing, or dominating her in some way. By recognizing and acknowledging this potential issue, we can find better, more informed ways to exist together.

The paths we take to reach each client are complex and untrodden; pleasure can be like a compass to lead us to them. For me, the innate pleasure I get from learning about other people is an especially illuminating guide—and part of what inspired me to become both an actor and a therapist in the first place.

Every unique detail about people fascinates me: our voices, tics, preferences, favorite movies, cherished poems, daydreams, vices, heartbreaks, worries, and the random sound bites that capture our attention. Clients occasionally tell me they fear I might get bored if they talk freely about what's actually on their mind. And I always respond with the truth—as long as their revelations are true, I'll never get bored. The only thing I ever find boring—in art or in life—is when someone blocks their authentic expression. Boredom is usually my first clue that something true has been contorted. And even then, I'm interested in the fact that something's boring me, and I want to know what's happening within me and the other person to produce such a response. When I connect with that curiosity—about a character, a client, or a striking moment in a scene—and the pleasure I take in the discovery process, I not only increase my investment in the performance, but I invite my scene partner to invest in it as well.

I realize that these suggestions can initially sound rather simple. I belly laughed once with friends as we received similarly basic advice in a 1980s video on how to improve our wardrobe; a former soap star enlightened us with the keen observation that: "Your eye will be drawn to the things you like." We thought, "Hmm, really? And we needed *you* to tell us that?..."

But the truth is when I am simply given permission to pursue "the things I like"—to be a child at play—it is quite effective. The entire field of psychotherapy as we know it began with Freud helping people to free themselves from debilitating anxiety by way of accessing pleasure.[3] While training to be an actor and a therapist, I had my entire world change when mentors simply gave me permission to *like* what I was doing—to take up space and *enjoy* my work.

To reference Freud again, therapists can get overly *reality principled* about our work, and defer taking pleasure in it, as if for the greater good of the client/the process/"the work." But I continue to find that the pleasure I take in the therapy process opens up more possibilities to reach my scene partners than would otherwise be available to me.

For example, my active pursuit of pleasure comes in handy when clients enter the rehearsal room and simply stare at me with insinuating intent. At such confusing and unnerving moments, rather than submit to their cryptic demand for me to DO something, or get frustrated that they are making the scene more about me than about them, I might take a breath and find a way for us both to take pleasure in this confounding, inchoate communication. This could perhaps be accomplished by "Yes And-ing" them with a line like, "I suppose you're wondering why I called you here today"—which often induces laughter, followed by thoughtful reflection. This way, my scene partner is invited to talk playfully and openly about their choice to implicate me, without feeling criticized or put on the spot.

My own sense of pleasure proved to be particularly crucial in my work with an extremely depressed and disturbingly quiet adolescent client. Huge events were happening in his life (offstage), such as getting bad grades, sleeping poorly, and posting online that he wanted to "disappear." While in session (onstage), we could only hear crickets. Needless to say, his parents, school counselor, and I responded to these signals and helped to keep him safe and alive—helped him to *survive*. But helping him to *live* was another story. Living requires liking. And there was nothing he seemed to like, at least not that he expressed in my company.

He always showed up for "rehearsal" diligently, but our scenes together were lifeless. Neither of us could find anything we liked about being together. I said all the "right" lines—"How are you? What's new? How's school?"—I even inquired about the things he purportedly liked, asking, "How was the movie? The beach? The new video game?" But his responses would always end the scene before it even started. "Fine," he would say, then look away.

We sat in excruciating silence for weeks upon months; some clinicians would say this was exactly what we should have done until he was ready to speak, while others would insist I was remiss in not coaxing something—anything!—out of him sooner. But regardless of how much time it took or what I said or didn't say, the scene didn't spring to life until I decided to bring my own pleasure into the room.

One day, after reading comparisons in the news between Donald Trump (who was then beginning his campaign for president of the United States) and Hitler, I became aware of the gaps in my knowledge about World War II, and was hungry for information. I just so happened to be meeting with my adolescent client that day; while he was stubbornly quiet, as usual, when I asked about school, he did tell me he was studying World War II in his history class. I instantly abandoned our professional (boring) weekly "script," and instead asked him to tell me about the events leading up to World War II, my eyes flickering with genuine interest. His eyes lit up in response, and he began to share specific things he had been taught that interested him—e.g., the propaganda posters, music, and short films that had helped bring Hitler to power. This exchange led to conversations about the role of the media in elections, which led to conversations about *him*. I sat on the edge of my seat and listened with interest, asking questions only occasionally as he took the stage. He spoke more freely in my company than ever before.

Over the next few weeks, I allowed myself to stay "off script," and followed my childlike interest in the obscure movies and computer games he liked. This openness spurred him to voluntarily share his hopes for the future, and the perceived obstacles in his way. Through our playful rehearsals, he learned to trust me—and to trust himself with me.

In some cases, mutual pleasure with our scene partners can divert us from our purpose, the client may feel pressure to be entertaining, or they may feel we like the process better than they do. This potential obstacle is not unlike when an actor indulges in his own feelings—laughs at his own jokes and cries for the sake of his own catharsis—rather than allowing his scene partners and audience their own emotional experiences. To me, this is all part of the rehearsal process, as long as we remain aware, curious, and willing to explore with our scene partner. Like any rupture in therapy, such moments don't necessarily constitute irreversible[4] mistakes, but can represent great opportunities—windows through which we can see our clients and ourselves more clearly.

When I permit myself to take pleasure in my clients, I invite them to take pleasure in themselves. This permission can encourage them to share a broader range of their desires and, as a result, to make room for their vulner-abilities, dreads, disappointments, frustrations, and resentments as well—to expand their capacity to grieve, to feel resentment, to express anger, and to laugh. If they can own the experiences and emotions they like, they may also own those that they don't.[5] Approaching therapy with a sense of pleasure helps us to enjoy the process of constructing a self narrative, or autobiographical[6] mosaic that integrates all the various shards of our often fragmented experience.

Try

Everything I do or don't do as a performing artist is a choice. I first learned this as a nine-year-old in a production of *The Music Man*. My first rehearsal was the "library scene" in which Harold Hill tries to woo Marion, the librarian. My job was to do "library things" in the background. But I was so fascinated by the action between the two leads that I just sat and watched. And although I felt invisible, the director viewed me as a huge eyesore. "Mark! Don't watch them," she shouted, instructing me to "Look for a book! Read! Be a kid in the library!" She offered me various choices to *try* to help tell the story—which was about a guy trying to pick up a lady, and not about a quiet boy watching them.

Making no choice is still a choice, both on stage and in session. When I enter each scene with this in mind, I take responsibility for the choices I make, even by default, and encourage my clients to do the same.

As casting director Michael Shurtleff advises, "You must make a choice. But it's not important if you're right or wrong."[7] According to Shurtleff (and I agree with him), what is important is that we *try* something to lead us toward the emotional truth of the character. In making a choice, we try to bring the scene to life, and get the ball in *play* with the other actors. In therapy terms, Winnicott suggested we try to get our client "from a state of not being able to play into a state of being able to play."[8]

The various suggestions I introduced in the last section prepare me to try a wide variety of choices in session. But the most important aspect of my performance prep—whether I'm breathing, speaking, or going for a run—is to practice being *present*, and to find that flicker of playful motivation that I keep mentioning. Because even if we choose our objective ahead of time— e.g., to listen compassionately, to speak with authority, or to validate—we never know exactly how we will execute it until we enter the present with our scene partners. Only then can we discover a choice in the moment that will allow us to connect to them through play.

As a therapist, my primary objective is most often to *invite* participation. How I play that objective varies depending on the chemistry between me and the particular client on the particular day. Maybe I will first try a smile, a few welcoming words, or a look of warm, genuine curiosity. With someone who struggles to take the spotlight, I might validate for them how unusual the therapy situation is with a short impromptu monologue—a gradual effort to make them feel safe enough to play at their own pace. Whatever I try, I see it as a choice that will affect our relationship in some uncertain way. We can always reflect on that choice later, whether or not it was deliberate, and from there make more effective choices as we continue to play. But whether or not our choice is "right" or "wrong," we must try something to get the party started—as I learned to do in that production of *The Music Man*, and with my relentlessly quiet adolescent client, when I enthusiastically asked him to tell me about World War II.

When I make reference to "choices," I not only mean those choices we initiate, but also our responses to scene partners—including the involuntary ones. These responses are arguably our most important actions as therapists, since our main task is to listen. I can't know exactly how I will respond until I receive the "ball" my client throws to me. But as part of my practice to stay present, I can follow the first rule of improvisation, which is to return the ball in the spirit of "Yes, and…" or "Yes, but…", but never with "No." This doesn't mean I have to literally say "Yes" or to speak at all, but I can choose to receive whatever my clients send me in a way that invites openness, participation, and play. Or at least I can *try*.

Psychotherapists from various theoretical backgrounds have written about the similarities between improvisation and therapy.[9] "Success in both requires an expertise in process rather than a depth of reified knowledge or an ability to skilfully re-apply the already known,"[10] says psychologist Matt Sellman. In other words, both art forms require participants to enter the unknown through play. "The goal of improv," writes psychoanalyst Paul Marcus, "is to increase the player's capacity to enter a playful state at will and to broaden his or her capacity to think, feel, and act beyond his or her habitual ways of being in the world."[11] Along these lines, I try to find spontaneity in all of my choices in the therapy room. Whether I throw the ball or receive it, my ultimate intention is to help my clients discover their *total selves*. As Winnicott said, "It is in playing and only in playing that the individual child or adult is able to be creative and to use the whole personality, and it is only in being creative that the individual discovers the self."[12]

Psychoanalyst and couples therapist Phil Ringstrom has also written on the effectiveness of "improvisational modes of engagement" in therapy. He emphasizes that if therapist and client (or any scene partners in life) can find an "openness to playing with one another," we can begin to imagine new possible ways of relating, which can then literally be played with interpersonally.[13] Again, it doesn't matter if the choices I try are "right" or "wrong," what matters is that they encourage openness and the possibility for my clients to exist and to envision new ways of relating—with me and with other people in their lives. In this sense, Ringstrom suggests that by "improvisationally playing-off-of-and-with each other," we can create a quality of psychotherapeutic "thirdness" with our clients, thereby contributing to the cultivation of the relationship having an open/creative "mind of its own."[14] Acting teacher Richard Hornby describes an ideal rehearsal process in a similar way. He believes scene partners must try, "[t]o achieve that feeling in which the performance is moving of its own accord rather than the actor's."[15] Hornby says, "It is not a matter of saying [or doing] something, but of creating something, which takes on a life of its own."[16]

Ringstrom effectively describes how both client and therapist tend to cling tightly to our "scripts," and to the rigid expectations of our *everyday selves*. But our capacity to play together—or at least to *try*—can lead to the "spontaneous co-creativity of improvisation"[17] (that third/potential/ rehearsal space that is greater than either of us), which allows us to find more of our *total selves*.

In terms of acting, this description makes me think of Meryl Streep's performances as Julia Child and Margaret Thatcher. Playing such iconic people presents obvious pitfalls. One can so easily stay "on script" and simply mimic the person's well-known voice and mannerisms—e.g., Child's bubbliness, or Thatcher's steeliness. But through a playful process with her scene partners, Streep discovers a lusty, angst-fueled passion in Child, and a fragile yearning for love within Thatcher, which not only defies our surface expectations of these women, but makes both performances magnetic, relatable, and inspiring. As the audience, we witness not necessarily an absolute version of Julia Child, Margaret Thatcher—or Meryl Streep, for that matter—but entirely new ways of being and relating that have a life of their own.

When I am in session, I try to encourage a process that similarly allows my clients to drop their scripts and become new versions of themselves. But it is the playing together, the improvisational process that I hope for them to take away most of all, not necessarily the exact technical steps we took, or the performative outcomes we achieved. The choices we tried were only a means for us to play—a process they can hopefully find opportunities to create again and again throughout their lives.

Fail

"Try again. Fail again. Fail better."[18] My favorite quote from Samuel Beckett also speaks to the challenges of this aspect of therapy. Just as we occasionally fail when we attempt to breathe deeply, speak with proper diction, or stand with poise, we can and must allow ourselves to fall short of our treatment goals in session. Our first try is never as important as our more informed subsequent attempt or the one after that. The more we allow ourselves to fail, and the more present we can be with our scene partners, the more present they are encouraged to become with us (again, in the words of my acting teacher Annie, "Just because you start a scene badly, doesn't mean it has to end badly.").

When we expect and invite failure as an inevitable part of our process, we can commit to our objectives truthfully, thoroughly, and without fear. We can also play with our scene partners openly and without censoring or curating ourselves self consciously. As with contemporary acting (in most cases), the performance of therapy is not an Olympic tightrope act in which we must execute our moves with technical precision or else fall flat. If a choice we try makes the client uncomfortable, offends them, or just clearly misses the mark that is not necessarily the end of the story. We can get back up, acknowledge what happened, and continue playing together with even more awareness and freedom than before. We can offer our clients a process of creative freedom as opposed to a fixed outcome that will irreversibly define either one of us or the work we do together.

The word "fail" can sound rather harsh, but I'm using the term here in the way I discuss "loss" in Chapter 4 on being present, and the way Jessica Benjamin (and psychoanalyst Manuel Ghent before her) uses the word "surrender"[19]—in the spirit of giving ourselves over to a creative process (to third/potential/transitional space) that is bigger than either scene partner involved. In contrast to *surrender*, Ghent uses the word *submission* to connote the experience of bowing entirely to another person's will and point of view. But by using *surrender*, he wrote that, "rather than carrying a connotation of defeat, the term will convey a quality of liberation and expansion of the self as a corollary to the letting down of defensive barriers."[20] In my own creative process, I think of my scene partner and myself both finding a way to surrender to the third space between us. And in that spirit, I say "Yes, and…" in my exchanges with them, not as a means of submitting to them, but as an invitation for both of us to be changed by our process of play. I find it easier to make this leap of faith as an artist when I am prepared to feel some degree of loss and failure as we go. What finally happens is never exactly what I originally intended,[21] as Milner would say, but the point is to be willing to give up my first idea as soon as the play between me and my scene partner yields something else.

Acclaimed actress Olympia Dukakis had a revelation along these lines while working with her husband on a production of *Long Day's Journey Into Night*, which they had performed together on two prior occasions. "You'd think, *what is there to unearth?*"[22] she initially observed. But during one rehearsal, she became blocked. She complained to the director (who was her brother) that she did not know what to *do* since her husband was not making the *right* choices—thus, she could not do the scene *right*. Her brother replied that he too was at a loss, not knowing how to help when she clearly "wanted to control the stage." Hard as this was to hear, Olympia allowed herself to say "Yes" to her husband's choices, risked feeling the loss of her expectations, and surrendered to the process. She later said, "What I had rejected was exactly what I needed to see. I had to stop trying to win. I had to start *playing* again. Which is of course a great *pleasure*. Never mind that the best work comes from it, but it's a great *pleasure* [emphasis added]."[23] Being open to playing with her husband in that third/potential space between them—and risking the failure of a "perfect" performance—helped Olympia discover something new in a play she had initially decided was old hat.

Stanislavski might say that Dukakis learned to "love the art in yourself, not yourself in the art."[24] And legendary actor/teacher Uta Hagen might add that she was reminded that "we must serve the play by serving each other; an ego-maniacal 'star' attitude is only self-serving and hurts everyone, including the 'star.'"[25] Hagen referred to this idea as her moral and ethical sense of performance, and it reminds me of Jessica Benjamin's concept of *moral thirdness*, "which entails a mutual shouldering of responsibility for the co-creative activity of psycho[therapeutic] enactments."[26] Philip Ringstrom also refers to this therapeutic process as "scene work," and he finds that each participant's willingness to fail, to feel loss, to surrender to a process of improvisational play, leads to "heightened moments of relational authenticity."[27]

This dynamic is especially true in the heat of the moment, when performances do not go as planned (like an actor dropping a prop on stage, a therapist saying something that clearly offends the client, or a client saying something that provokes and confounds the therapist). Rather than gloss over and move past the incident, we must acknowledge it in some way in order to maintain an open and authentic connection between every participant.

Dorian

My client Dorian, a man in his early twenties, sought perfection in everything from his hair to his grammar. I would always feel self conscious and physically tense whenever he would ask me to confirm facts I did not know—e.g., dates of historical events, names of authors, famous quotes, or other details that seemed irrelevant to what he really wanted to say. His eyes would widen with penetrating inquisitiveness, and my anxiety would rise as my mind went blank. It wasn't until I let myself feel the pang of failing him that we were able to live in the room together. I learned to have faith in our creative process and surrender to the third space between us—as opposed to submitting to the idea that I was an inadequate therapist for not having the facts he demanded, or to the idea that he was making the "wrong" choice for asking me questions rather than free associating like a "good" patient. This pivotal shift happened for us spontaneously, in a moment of improvisational play. While sharing a story about having dropped something, he accidentally said the word "breaked" instead of "broke." His face dropped with cold mortification: "Oh gosh, what did I just say?" Rather than correcting him or pretending it didn't happen (in other words, responding to him with, "No!") I responded with a warm, accepting look of "Yes," and said, "'I like the word 'breaked.' 'Breaked' is fun" (The colorful, upbeat energy with which I pronounced the word—and effectively returned the ball to him—was an extension of the playful preparation I do with my voice and speech, as I described in Chapter 7). We both shared a laugh of relief, and we were able to move—and to breathe (as per Chapter 5)—through this unexpected moment of "failure" together, playfully. As scene partners we each surrendered to the other's "spontaneously suggested versions of reality." I accepted his malapropism, and he, in kind, was able to accept my implicit suggestion that it's ok to speak without "perfection"—in fact, it can even be fun! Both of us could now imagine relating to each other off script—more openly, and with a greater range of our true selves. As master improv teacher Viola Spolin writes, the whole effort of spontaneous play "is to bring you, the individual player close to or back to your own persona, own ground of being, resources, treasure house, intuition, x-area, fresh, open, alive!"[28]

Reflect and Adapt

Our "scene work" is only as good as our capacity to *reflect* on the choices we've made, and to *adapt* accordingly. Sometimes I can assess and adjust in the moment, like a skilled improviser. Most other times, I need to take the week between sessions to reflect—and I often use my time while running, meditating, or commuting to do that. But either way, my consecutive choices always come from a place of reflection.

Ringstrom describes this aspect of the therapy process as a "private" improvisational state of reflectivity, a state of reverie.[29] This is when I ask myself what happened spontaneously between me and my scene partner last time. Then, I try to discern why it happened, to extrapolate meaning out of it, and to decide on my next direction—hopefully toward our potential to play beyond our expected scripts.

I love what trailblazing theater director Anne Bogart says about reflection and adjustment:

> The Taoists describe the art of life as the art of constant adjustment to the current surroundings. Similarly, nothing could be more central to a successful creative process than the ability to adjust to what is happening in the moment. A painter continually adjusts to the previous strokes on the canvas. A musician adapts to the room and to the choices of other musicians. A theater artist is sensitized to the constant spatial and temporal changes that are taking place from moment to moment. Clearly, the practice of adjustment is essential to artistic training.[30]

This includes the art of therapy. During our process of reflection, Bogart suggests we ask if it is possible to make space within ourselves as well as in the rehearsal spaces we share with our scene partners, so that they can join us in play (along the lines of Stanislavski's idea that "[o]ur first duty is to *adapt* yourself to your partner"[31]). Bogart says, "It helps to understand that what most matters is the space created by the situation rather than the situation itself."[32] In other words, if our current situation is one of conflict, confusion, or some other form of stagnation, our process of *reflection* helps us to better recognize our scene partners and their subjective viewpoints—no matter how foreign or challenging they are to us. And through that recognition, we can find and create opportunities for us both to live.

However, the process of reflection and adaptation is easier said than done. It requires a great deal of humility to playback the memories (the dailies, if you will) of my choices, and to face how they actually affected my scene partners (my practice of *staying in there* with challenging feelings, as I describe in Chapter 4—particularly in terms of keeping my mind awake during strenuous exercise—helps me to tolerate this uncomfortable process of self examination).

For example, maybe my client seemed comforted by my choices. Great. But then I must ask myself if that outcome gave them more or less room to play than they had before. Did I dominate the stage? And if so, did that help them to be present, exploratory, and creative in the rehearsal room with me? Maybe so—I might have inspired them to express themselves like they never have before. Or maybe I gave a divo monologue that foreclosed their capacity to try choices of their own. Or perhaps my choice seemed judgmental and took the wind out of their creative sails.

It feels great to "nail it," to get it "right" the first time, and to avoid the humiliation of failing (to cross the finish line quickly and without pain). But it is always better to reflect, adjust, and make more room for our scene partners to participate in the journey. The ruptures in therapy—as with any collaborative process—are not as significant as the repairs.[33] In fact, the ruptures are necessary, as they are opportunities to acknowledge[34] each of our individual contributions to the scene, and to establish a process of rocking back and forth between similarity and difference. This process becomes the reliable frame/structure/container within which my client and I can safely engage in spontaneous play. And in the wise words of Viola Spolin, "True playing will produce trust."[35]

Emily

Emily did not like my quiet, curious approach to our first few sessions, and though she never said this, I intuited it through her subtext and adjusted—spontaneously, without much reflection. I *tried* to validate her feelings verbally, took *pleasure* in her genuinely funny jokes, and even threw in some jokes of my own to make her feel less alone (this was, of course, motivated by the voice of a commercial casting assistant, ringing in my head, who would bark at me just before I entered auditions, "Don't leave 'em alone in there!"). My new approach worked—in a way; she seemed less nervous. And although this dynamic we established and relied on each week was arguably collaborative and playful, on a deeper level, it felt precarious—*What happens when we stop laughing?* I'd think. She would enter sessions with wide, nervous eyes, and then ritualistically get on-script, settle in, and recount her week with witty humor, while I laughed. My adjustments gave Emily a temporarily comfortable frame, but they also foreclosed opportunities for less curated versions of her to emerge—as though I was an actor who said "Yes" to his scene partner's tried-and-true commercial choices, but "No," to her ambivalent yet palpable desire to take artistic risks. We were both too afraid to explore discomfort in the rehearsal room—hers or mine.

But our co-created routine did serve a purpose: it provided a holding environment for a few years, during which she was able to improve her finances, career, and love life. And as our relationship evolved, I would gradually variegate my choices, albeit coyly. Not yet brave enough to *not* laugh at her jokes, I at least drew attention to our "comfortable" yet tenuous rapport, in a meta way, so that we could both observe and acknowledge our process from above—a step toward finding third/potential/rehearsal space between us. I even wrote an article[36] on how our meta communications[37] opened up her sense of possibility and led her to seek and effectively land a good job outside of her comfort zone. The article—which I invited her to read—symbolized my intent to get the scene right; to call "cut" and "print" on the Emily story, and then sit back to collect my Academy Award.

As our work continued, though, I **reflected** on my short-sighted temptation to have it all "figured out." I acknowledged to myself how my "casting" of Emily, which was intended to liberate her, kept her confined to my script. Both of us **fail**ed to conjure the latent, unsung versions of her, which only faintly shone in her consistently nervous stare at the beginning of sessions, and her increasingly sporadic dips into despair, despite successfully getting many of the things she wanted on the surface—salary, job, boyfriend. Any deliberate attempts to invite off-script versions of herself into the room were "like pursuing a thief hiding in the forest by loudly banging a drum,"[38] or, as Stanislavski would call it, an assault to the subconscious.[39] Her standard response to any advice I gave was simply, "I don't know how to do that." I would have to wait and be ready for her to make a bold choice of her own free will, to which I could say, "Yes, and…"

One day, after weeks and weeks of describing a stressful situation at work, she sat in silence and deep despair. Where I ordinarily would have interjected with some comforting words—and stolen the scene from her by default—instead, I said "Yes" (without speaking) to her raw feelings, and joined her silence. This lasted for twenty minutes or so; the experience was difficult for both of us. But I *stayed in there* with her emotional pain and my own guilt for not being able to soothe it. We both left this scene open, without forcing a tidy ending.

Several weeks later, Emily **tried** an even bolder choice: "I think I should take a break from therapy," she said. Even as I felt the blow of rejection and failure, I responded with the spirit of, "Yes, and …," and tried to surrender to this deepening of our process (the way I *stay in there* and breathe, during push-ups or an uphill run; see Chapter 4). The unexpected timing and delivery of her choice was, as Stanislavski would say, a surprisingly effective lever in our creative work.[40] She said she'd been feeling this way for a few weeks, but she wanted to discuss what to do. We agreed to take the next month to determine if terminating was indeed what she wanted, or if this was a pivotal opportunity for our work to expand.

Once again, I was tempted to cut and print, having it all "figured out." Here was an opportunity for the spontaneous versions of herself to enter stage right. Perhaps now she could share what she did not like about our sessions in words, not just looks. But when I presented this scripted idea to her, she replied with her scripted line, "I don't know how to do that." Brilliant as I thought my clinical formulation to be, it did not reach her emotionally. This was, admittedly, frustrating for me. Like Olympia Dukakis in her rehearsal with her husband, I was sure I was making the "right" choices, and all my scene partner had to do was agree with me. As I *reflected* between sessions, I realized I needed a new approach. I did *research*, consulted with peers and mentors, and read articles (as per Chapter 8). But more than anything, in order to take our process to the next level, I needed to adapt to her. And though I thought I was doing that in our meta-communications, I began to realize that was only one small part of our continuous creative process. In order to truly make more room for her in our spotlight at center stage, I had to first join her in the darkness of the wings. In other words, I needed to genuinely acknowledge my *fail*ures, including my hubris in *try*ing to be "right" with my article about her. As I discussed this with her, and felt the red hot tingle of guilt and shame in my face, I also acknowledged the other times in our sessions when I imposed self-congratulatory inter-pretations of her, and how that left her no room to take the stage in her own way.[41] The tension between us released ever so slightly, and we agreed to continue working together, week by week, checking in as we go.

Our sessions continue to be improvisational. Sometimes I'll catch myself trying too hard to soothe her pain, and remind myself that if I truly want to invite her to participate unencumbered, I need to *stay in* her feelings, not be above them (as my acting mentor Brian would say). And on occasion, I commit to a spontaneous, playful, choice as a way to invite us both to exist more freely together.

For example, one day she entered with familiar feelings of hopelessness and defeat after being denied a much-coveted job. I could feel the chill of failure, hers and mine, tingle up my legs as she retreated in punishing silence. I realized that for all the times we had been in this scene, I never acknowledged exactly how it affected me. "Not to be too new-agey," I said playfully, "but I feel a chill in my body. Like I've failed you. And, I know this sounds crazy, but I keep hearing in my head, 'You can't give her what she needs!' And, I feel like you're…angry? But don't know how to express it?"

"I'm not angry," she retorted, like an improv partner saying, "No," "Just sad."

"Hm. But I sense anger," I replied, risking confrontation as I picked the ball off the floor and kept it in play. "Does that resonate at all?"

"Yeah. People are always angry with me for being down. Because there's nothing they can say to make it better."

"Right," I said. "That's the bind you and I get in together at these times. But the anger…Could it be coming from you, on some level? Maybe you don't think you're allowed to be angry, so you give the anger to me? I mean, I feel like you…hate me. Yes. Hate." I relished saying the word, inviting her to participate in the **pleasure** of expressing potentially provocative feelings. "You hate me because I can't give you the job you want. But you don't say that, because you know it sounds irrational. So you stay silent, and sad, and push the anger into me." I said all of this not from on high, or with blame, but with a sense of wonder and play. Like I was trying a fun new choice in our work together, and inviting her to participate.

She shrugged and continued, "Well… Sure. But again, I don't know what to do with that. I can't go around telling people I hate them for not giving me what I want."

"Maybe not. But at least we can talk about it. How much you hate me." We both smiled. The energy between us was more open and free. We didn't avoid her pain, or get defeated by it, but found a way to process it together—with all of its contradictions—through play.

Even as I write this, I realize my temptation to summarize Emily's story with another tidy Shakespearean ending. Then I remind myself to reflect and acknowledge that what I describe here is just one more stop on our train. The real Emily transcends my ability to "get" her—in session, or in this clinical musing. It is our live rehearsal process, our playful willingness to try, fail, reflect, and adapt that hopefully continues to generate greater possibilities for her and for me.

11 Find the Characters

Actress Robin Weigert explains that one of the great values of comparing acting to therapy is that in acting there is a name for the mystical (third) element that steps into a scene when invited, this "child that is born of our listening. We call it a *character*." Weigert emphasizes that:

> It is not your character that enters the scene when invited, it is the other actor's character. You believe in her character, she has become manifest through your listening, your belief has sparked belief inside your scene partner and now that your scene partner believes in herself, she is able to listen your character into existence as well.[1]

This reciprocal process also occurs between client and therapist. As we listen to our clients, they observe themselves and discover various versions of who they can be. Meanwhile, in turn, we become "characters" by how they listen to us. We embody (as per Chapters 7 and 8) people from their past, especially those with whom they are in some form of conflict, what psychoanalyst Frank Lachman has called the trailing edge of their transference.[2] We also become characters born of their hope, as we follow the leading edge of their transference.[3] At the same time, we discover that these characters are authentic (though perhaps unfamiliar) versions of our*selves*.

My hope is that each client will continue to listen, embody, and expand the characters in their repertoire, not only throughout our work, but for their entire lives, with a variety of scene partners. This way, our time together can be seen as a rehearsal for a dynamic, creative, and liberated life.

The Ideal Listener

The idea of sharing our inner lives with a mysterious stranger can ignite the hope of being truly recognized. This hope often motivates us to enter the therapy stage no matter how much "stage fright" we have. I try to locate that hope in each client by observing how they want me to listen to them—which helps me embody a character I call the *ideal listener*: the mystical person who lives in each of our minds and has an abundant capacity to hold, validate, and encourage us.

Obviously it is impossible to bring that role to life exactly as each client dreams, but like Marlon Brando once said about audiences, they "often do much of the acting themselves..."[4] Brando is suggesting that we project onto the characters we watch on stage and screen, regardless of what the performer does or doesn't do—similar to Freud's ideas about transference in therapy.[5] With this dynamic in mind, my main job is to receive the ways clients relate to me, and let that inform how I listen to them.

My first clues about a client's *ideal listener* typically appear when I try too hard to validate them, and fail. For example, my attempt to let them know I "get it," may be experienced as a crude interruption (what I call a *Charlie-Rose*; see Chapter 9). If so, I get out of their way, and pay closer attention to how they seem to dream me into their very own Wizard of Oz.

This idea is similar to the psychoanalytic "blank screen" in that I make room for the client's projections; however, I try not to be blank. I think of myself as "the man in front of the curtain," not behind it, and I collaborate with them as they construct their "wizard." I try not to impede their imaginations, but also try to stay present and allow the ways I receive them to register in my face and body. And as I gradually grasp how they want me to listen, I make subtle adjustments to help facilitate their creative process (which may mean sitting closer or further away, widening or contracting my eyes, or concentrating energy in my root, chest, or head chakras, depending on the client). But no matter how much or little I do, I am always their scene partner, not a blank screen or a prop.

For example, if my attempt to validate a client comes across as patronizing, my adjustment might be to sit back, move the energy from my head to my chest, and listen to them with an open, naive, curiosity. This way, I let them see how genuinely moved and changed I am by their unique discoveries, rather than imply that I already know everything. In other words, I listen like a parent who wants to be led endlessly by his "child's" thoughts, as opposed to a teacher who can't learn anything new. Conversely, another client's *ideal listener* may be more like a supportive professor, and for that person, I might try to focus energy in my forehead to follow, encourage, and consider their every thought.

But even as I try to describe how I strive to embody the *ideal listener*, my examples fall short. The process is too interpersonally specific and of the moment to be captured in schematic illustrations. This elusive character emerges from our sense of collaborative thirdness, of something greater than either scene partner alone. We find it together in an improvisational dance (what I take Jessica Benjamin to mean by the "rhythmic third"[6]). This interaction requires us not only to tune in to what our client needs from us in the here and now, but also to our own spiritual sense of wonder and possibility.

We all know what it is to sit in a dark theater just before the curtain rises or the movie fades in. No matter how good the show turns out to be, it can never live up to that anticipation born of our own imagination. Similarly, we know how it feels just before we enter our own therapist's office, when we hope and trust that our inner lives will be witnessed by our great and powerful listener. I keep all of this in mind as I try to embody each client's *ideal listener*—which is typically at the beginning of a treatment, at the start of most sessions, and various other times when the client's thought process is embryonic and in need of unadulterated support. Who knows exactly what I will do to encourage their imaginations in those moments, but I trust that the clues for what to do will be there as long as I listen closely to how they want to be held by someone all-powerful, all-curious, and all-loving.

One beneficial aspect of the *ideal listener* is that it frees me from self-consciousness more than any other role I play as a therapist because of its mystical, larger-than-life nature. When I greet a client in the waiting room, for example, I remember that it's not *me* they anticipate talking to, it's *him*. It doesn't really matter how I walk or talk or smile as long as I make room for the client to bring *him* to life (which is a relief, because as Helen Mirren says, the most difficult thing to do as a performer is "to walk as yourself"[7]). Playing this character also removes the pressure I put on myself to be the "good doctor" and to understand everything my clients tell me right away, because part of the *ideal listener*'s job is to make room for process, to be cool, calm, and confident that all will make sense in time.

When it's hard to get out of my own way and let the client access *him*, I think of images that inspire me to transcend my *everyday self*. These images might come from a reference the client has made to an intriguing listener in their life—such as a robed shaman one client described encountering at a retreat, a kind stranger on a bench another client mentioned, or the celebrity idol another client met who smiled at her generously and with "genuine interest." If I'm really at a loss, I might think of Wallace Shawn in *My Dinner with Andre*, whose warm, endlessly curious embodiment of his scene partner, Andre Gregory's *ideal listener*, gives me a flicker of inspiration.

The Client's "True" Selves

As I listen to each client, I ask myself how I can help them embrace more of their true selves. This question can lead me to be a more active scene partner, akin to an acting coach or a highly attuned parent engaged with their child.

I deliberately use "selves" in the plural to emphasize that our truth takes many forms and is "always embedded in social context and relationship."[8] It's easy to get caught up in the idea that we have one true self hiding within, and that our mission in therapy is to reveal it like a detective at the end of a whodunnit, but I find that approach problematic. Clients sense our overdetermined sleuthing for their repressed "real" self beneath what we may presume to be their defensive, "fake" one—a presumption which then makes them self conscious and even more likely to hide their vulnerability and truth. This can lead to a cycle of forced, mechanical performances between us—what actors call "acting tricks"—which keep our interactions defensive and on the surface.

Alternatively, I often find openness with my clients when I approach our clinical scenes with the notion that we all embody various selves for different reasons, at different times, and with different people. Some of those selves feel more true than others, and some are more necessarily "false"—such as the closeted characters many queer people need to portray to survive in our communities, or the "affable" cheerleader Meryl Streep was compelled to portray to survive in High School (as referenced in Chapter 6). But all of these characters are us. They are part of our *total selves*, and among the wide range of keys that make up our instrument.

Psychotherapists and actors tend to agree that "each of us is a company of many,"[9] as seminal psychoanalyst Joan Riviere has said, or as Meryl Streep noted, quoting the great classical actress Sybil Thorndike, "we all have the germ of every other person inside of us."[10] Psychoanalyst Philip Bromberg also believes that the "...human capacity for creative living is based on the intrinsic multiplicity of the self" and the "ability to feel like one self while being many."[11] He finds inspiration in the words of voice teacher/theater guru Kristin Linklater, who says:

> ...the idea of **finding the character** in myself suggests that I am multi-faceted and illimitable, and that each character I play finds the roots of its truth in the fact that I am All as well as One; that from my wholeness I can create multiplicity; that I have the capacity to understand the natures of all people and can become any of them by expanding the seed of my understanding until it dislodges and rearranges the ingredients of my personality and a different part of me dominates.[12]

Building on Linklater's conception, Bromberg says that when we embody one version of self—not just as actors but as people—our multiple other selves are still within us. They haven't gone anywhere, they are simply "kept from interfering with what is going on at the moment...," which he says, "is a normal part of everyday mental functioning."[13] I agree, and in playing both a scene partner and an "acting coach" at various times in session, I try to help my clients to own all of the characters they inhabit.

When I work this way, I am particularly inspired by psychoanalyst Claire Winnicott, who writes beautifully about a client who brought a photograph of herself to session hoping "that someone would help her to join up with that bit of herself which she had lost and could not recognize." Winnicott observes that, "[s]he needed my help to do this."[14] Here are a few ways I have similarly tried to help my clients join up with themselves.

Embody Their Power: Clients who have obvious masochistic tendencies can induce anger, desire, or some other passion within me on their behalf, and in some cases I may discuss that with them. I might simply describe how their behavioral patterns affect me, or I might speak a few words on their behalf that approximate what I perceive to be their repressed feelings. Hearing me give voice to their lost self—e.g., with resonance in my will-power chakra—can gradually inspire them to find their own assertive voices (as per Chapter 7). Sometimes, we may enact a debate between two parts of their mind in which I take on the part of their conviction or power while they perform their doubt or sense of defeat. When this occurs, I first do my best to recognize that it is happening, why it is happening, and how it is happening, and then I share this awareness with my scene partner. Following interventions like these, some clients are better able to tell dominant and/ or bullying partners or family members how they feel and what they need. More importantly, our scene work helps them to consciously identify and claim their emotional experience.

Validate Their "False" Selves: One of my clients, an accomplished CBT-oriented therapist, was concerned that he had spent most of his life "winging it," and that the "real" *him* had been deferred. Not only did he often get by without preparation, but he was even rewarded for this behavior. He had earned impressive degrees and jobs without much effort. But life started to catch up with him as career and family goals became priorities, and his hap-hazard whimsy—which resulted in late nights, racking up debt, and falling behind at work—no longer served him well. He needed to organize and make plans. "It's so annoying," he would say, doubtful of his capacity to change, observing, "I know where it comes from. My family. We're all ambi-tious but disorganized. We have prestigious jobs, but our homes are a mess and we can't get anywhere on time."

When I would play the "doctor" as per his casting and prescribe CBT-style exercises (such as simple meditations), he would only disparage himself for not doing them. I came to understand this pattern to mean that he did not need my help to judge or attempt to exorcise his fly-by-the-seat-of-his-pants persona; he was able to punish himself for this well enough on his own. What he needed was for me to love, validate, and accept that part of him. No other clinical intervention—e.g., symptom management, behavioral modification, family separation and individuation—was going to help until this happened. In this sense, I thought of myself as an acting coach helping an actor protect his character, no matter how problematic their behavior. This way, he could better understand his motivations and drop deeper into his truth.

Through this lens, I began to observe the positive side of his avoidant/ negligent behaviors—such as the contagious zest he had for concerts, dan-cing, and travel. He would bubble over with a euphoric enthusiasm when he talked about the passions that took him away from responsibilities. He would also take deep breaths periodically as he spoke, as if his body needed to catch up to his mind. I tried to join him on these narrative journeys, and to embody his energy, which was mostly concentrated in his head. Joining him in this state actually felt delightful, like dancing or parasailing. This experience helped me to validate how wonderfully rich his mind is, and what fun it is to live there (why wouldn't he want to dance the night away?). I suggested that his periodic deep breaths might indicate his body wanted to join the party too, but had a hard time getting past the bouncer. "That makes me sad," he replied, "and I don't know why."

After exploring this "sadness" for many sessions, he eventually discovered that he was afraid of connecting to the slower, calmer versions of himself, deeper in his body—which he associated with loss and the fear of missing out. He now continues to work on connecting with his body, which increases his capacity to be present, to feel loss, and to organize and plan. All this can be accomplished without him having to disavow his ebullient *everyday self.*

Use Their Imagery: A client whose identity tends to be that of "provider" was frustrated with his boyfriend: "I've told him that I need him to meet me halfway, but he just responds by promising to do more chores. That misses the point. I want him to *think* about me." After an incident when his boyfriend completely dropped the ball on their plans, my client looked at me blankly and said, "I'm at a loss. I'm like the woman in a movie who says 'I trusted you!' to her husband." He then continued to express fatalistic frustrations about his boyfriend—but I was stuck on his movie image. It evoked something more true to his experience than his text alone. I also noticed that he hadn't shared his feelings of frustration with his boyfriend. Was it too hard to be vulnerable with him? Did his feelings conflict with his role as "provider?"

As I let the "I trusted you!"-movie-moment replay in my mind, I sensed a mix of emotions, including betrayal, anger, sadness, and disappointment. (Clearly, I imagined a layered performance by a Viola Davis-calibre actress, as opposed to a one-note Lifetime-movie-of-the-week starlet). I then asked him why he had not told his boyfriend how he felt. "He's fragile," he responded, explaining, "I'm afraid he'll shut down if I'm too emotional. I have to be the strong one." I asked, "You would not be strong if you shared your feelings?" He thought about it, and answered, "I guess I'm afraid I'd fall apart?…" That's when I went back to the woman in the movie (as I imagined her). "The way you described that character…the fire in your eye, makes me feel like she wouldn't fall apart," I said. "She's grounded. And very disappointed. But not broken. She wanted a companion, an equal, and she was let down. There is strength in owning those feelings." This landed. He was better able to connect to his vulnerability, and could envision a way to talk to his boyfriend openly and directly, inspired by his own image.

Hold Their Trauma: A successful young actor, whose life and career were derailed by a severe accident, started working with me a year after that event. His superobjective with our scene work was to get his life back on track. After months of physical therapy, he was still not ready to go back to work, especially since his job requires him to be physically and emotionally vulnerable. The accident had left his body scarred, and the necessary period of sequestered healing left him with a great loss of physical fitness—which, in addition to the isolation, exacerbated feelings of inadequacy, depression, and social anxiety. But he quickly moved off of that topic, and talked each week about his dating life (a topic which wasn't completely out of left field, because he chose to work with me in part because of my writing on sexuality and relationships). He'd describe his latest efforts to increase his social and sexual confidence with men. We had created a safe enough rapport for him to share this aspect of his life openly, and though he rarely referred back to the accident after the first few sessions, it never left my mind.

Different therapists would advise different interventions with a case like this, but the most salient guide for me was our chemistry as scene partners. I felt it best to receive his idiomatic bids to play together, using the part of himself that was currently most alive—romance and sexuality—while also being prepared to welcome his depressed, frightened, and traumatized selves when the opportunity arose. And, of course, it did.

"I wonder sometimes…should I be talking about the accident?" he would muse, explaining, "I mean, I guess that's what brought me here. I enjoy talking to you about guys, but lately I'm wondering…should I see a trauma specialist too?…" I nodded to validate his questions, and asked, "Do you feel you can't talk to me about the accident?" "I guess I just don't know how this works," he answered back. "Of course," I said, affirmingly, continuing, "I'll tell you how I've been thinking of our work. I've been following your lead, and it seems that talking about dating has been a way for you to find your way back into your life, which was one of your goals. But I assure you, even when you don't bring up the accident, it's always on my mind. I'm ready to hear more about it whenever you are. If it turns out that you don't feel safe talking about it with me, then I can definitely make recommendations for good therapists who practice specialized trauma interventions." "Thank you for explaining that," he said, "I would like to talk about it, I think." "Take your time," I replied, adding, "we can check in as you go. Sometimes people are afraid to go too far because they are afraid of traumatizing the listener. I want you to know that I am trained and prepared to hear it, however it comes out. But it's also up to you how much you want to share, and when you want to share it."

As he narrated the accident in horrific detail, I did a version of the grounding meditation (**Exercise VIII**), and allowed myself to breathe deeply. At the same time, I imagined versions of my own *ideal listener*—some combination of my best therapists, mentors, and my father holding me as I described in Chapter 9—watching over me as I listened. This exercise helped me to stabilize so that I would be palpably strong enough to hold and survive whatever he told me. Psychotherapy, like all performing arts, is an apprenticeship profession. And a great benefit of having a clinical supervisor and our own therapist is that—like an acting mentor—in addition to sharing their expertise, we can internalize their ineffable strengths, and bring them into the *rehearsal* room with us.

I also shared the appropriate meditation and breathing exercises with the client so that he could use them to help stabilize himself outside the "rehearsal room," on his own. We also discussed ways he could use his creativity to hold and work through the gamut of feelings that surfaced as he discussed the event—including journaling, painting, and practicing his acting.

This client continued to share more about the accident intermittently over the next few weeks, and I continued to validate his tendency to dip in and out of memory. "This is how our minds work, especially when we experience trauma," I explained, "we activate the parts of our minds that make the most sense, and put the other parts on hold. We all do it to survive." This explanation suggested to him that I too dissociate and/or let versions of myself wait backstage while others take the spotlight, and that this is not only common, but serves a vital purpose. He then felt permission to continue to participate in our work on his own terms. Gradually, he metabolized more of the traumatic memories that had been waiting in the wings, and was able to talk about them interchangeably with his erotic life—which became increasingly more adventurous.

At one point, he wanted to attend a party at which everyone would be "mostly naked," but first felt the need to process what it would be like to show his scarred body to multiple people at once. As we discussed his feelings about the scar, he asked me if I wanted to see it. "Sure," I replied, calmly and without hesitation.

I surprised myself by the confident way I responded with, "Yes, and…" at such a potentially uncomfortable moment. But the innate faith I had that we could both think clearly as he showed me his physical vulnerability was not only supported by the trust we had cultivated together, but also inspired by observing another clinical performer, years before. I once had the privilege to watch psychoanalyst, Helene Kafka present her paper, "The Man Who Could Not Cry and the Psychoanalyst who Could,"[15] a work focused on her scene work with a client with severe bodily disfigurement. Kafka showed in the live performance of this case—beyond the text of her "script"—the significance of truly looking at her scene partner's body, even utilizing mirror exercises from acting teacher Sanford Meisner in order to help him feel held and recognized. This exercise also helped her client connect to feelings of mourning about his physical self, and to connect with a range of other experiences—e.g., rage, compassion, love.

As my client lifted his shirt and showed me his scar, I took it in like a parent observing his child's body. He seemed to recognize my capacity to hold him—including his scars—in my mind, and he was at ease as he pulled his shirt back down and took a seat. The exposed, vulnerable version of himself was just as present as the clothed, sequestered one.

He continues to process the traumatic disruption to his life, while he explores his dating life, and has found new and exciting professional opportunities as an artist—not only as an actor.

The Client's Internalized Objects

I typically do not realize I have been cast as a character by my client until the scene is over. I'm like an actor on a haphazard film set, with no idea who I'm playing until days or weeks later when I get to see the edited footage: "Oh, *that's* how the filmmaker used me?", I would think, "....Wow, that's not what I intended; I guess I had less control over my performance than I thought."

This is why I take time alone to reflect on each session. I replay all the exchanges between me and my scene partner—the choices I've made, reactions I had, and their responses to those reactions. This reflection helps me understand not only how I have been cast, but also how I have unwittingly cast them (my countertransference), and how that has affected our interactions. I then get curious about the conflicts the client is working through with the character I have become to them, and what they may want the other side of that conflict to look like.

To offer an extreme example, while working at a community mental health clinic years ago, I could have won an Oscar for my portrayal of a client's lifelong tormenter. My scene partner was a man in his fifties, who had lived through countless abuses since early childhood, and was always denied validation of this trauma: e.g., "That didn't happen," his mother said after his father beat him when he was only five. Granted, as a middle aged man obsessed with 9/11 conspiracies and the arrival of extraterrestrials, it was easy to dismiss him as merely "paranoid." But there were significant truths buried beneath his ridiculous-sounding suspicions. Some of that truth broke through the surface on August 23, 2011, when we both felt a quick tremble in my office. "That's an earthquake," he said with certainty. "No," I responded with equal certainty, assuming it was just the lights flickering. He moved on to another topic, reflecting on how he had recently been stopped by police officers who suspected he had illegal drugs on his person, though he did not. As soon as the session ended, I was of course mortified to discover that what we felt was indeed an earthquake. Guilt does not begin to describe what I felt having reenacted the gaslighting that pervaded his entire life. But dark as this was to recognize, on the bright side, I also now had the opportunity to play a version of his tormentor that he had never experienced before. The following week, I apologized profusely, and acknowledged how similar my egregious mistake was to those of his parents, among many others, who denied his sense of truth. Fortunately, our rapport was strong enough to survive this, and he found this moment to be healing, but it easily could have gone another way, as it so often does with clients who are unable to survive ruptures in the therapeutic relationship.

As I did with this client, after I have reflected on "the dailies" from each scene, I try to enter the next one informed and armed—not only with the intent to listen for more clues about the character I have become, but to find unexpected layers within that character that can help my client to heal from their past and grow toward their future.

Peter

Peter—my client from Chapter 4 who came out as gay later in life—chose to work with me because I am gay. The leading edge of his transference cast me as *the good gay therapist* who would help him to live free (as opposed to the bad straight one he saw in the 1960s, when homosexuality was considered to be a disorder, who advised him to marry a woman). But neither of us could know how complex the role of *good gay therapist* would be to play, or how long it would take to fully realize this character through our scene work.

Peter had just come out to his wife of fifty years, and he needed a safe and supportive psychological space to process his intention to separate from her. Not only had their relationship become toxic, but she had abused him physically. Since safety always comes first, I connected Peter with the Anti-Violence Project (which provides counseling and advocacy specifically for the LGBT communities), and discussed options for him to move out. This, I thought, was certainly what the *good gay therapist* would do. But he did not agree. Though he met with an AVP counselor, he did not intend to see her for long as he was "not comfortable depending on other people." Dependency threatened his self concept, his role as the *good husband*, the loyal provider who could solve everything on his own. As for moving out of the apartment, he was not at all ready to sleep anywhere but the bed he shared with his wife. His eyebrows would furrow, as if I meant him harm, when I'd supportively encourage him to relocate. "You're like my ex-boyfriends," he'd say, explaining, "All they ever did was nag me to leave my wife. They were insensitive." *How is telling him to run from violence "insensitive?"* I thought. I became frustrated that I could not offer help without being cast as the *bossy boyfriend*.

It took months of listening, trying, failing, and listening more for me to recognize that when I urged him to break free of his violent partnership, I threatened to take away his role of *good husband*—a role he had spent his adult life trying to get right. He had assumed this role after a childhood of striving to play *the good son*, and worked extra hard around the house and in school in order to maintain it; as he grew older, he strived to be masculine, straight, and married to a woman, all so he could win the Oscar for *Best Son*. But his parents never presented him with that honor. He was now repeating the same pattern with his wife, hoping that if he was hard-working and loyal enough, she would eventually honor him with the trophy for *Best Husband*. I was standing in the way of that.

Ironically, he had come to me for help escaping from this debilitating cycle. How could I aid him in achieving this goal and validate his wish to stay with his abusive wife at the same time? Certainly his ex-boyfriends never cracked that code.

But one advantage of approaching my therapeutic work as an actor is that I can take time to reflect on the role in which I've been cast, and then use my sense of foresight to explore the character in multiple directions.

In other words, as Peter and I continued to *stay in there* with our scene work, I gradually began to discover nuanced ways to expand the character of *bossy boyfriend*. One day, after I offered what I believed to be a supportive suggestion, he responded with, "All I hear is you telling me I'm not good enough." Something clicked for me, and I said something his boyfriends never did. "I get it. You feel you're not good enough for any of us: parents, wife, boyfriends, counselors." By acknowledging this feeling, I came closer to playing the *good gay therapist* that Peter felt he needed.

This was a pivotal moment in our process, but it still took years of listening and expanding our characters for Peter to feel worthy enough—as the adult gay man that he is—to move into his own apartment. And it would be years after that before the characters in his dreams would transform from abusive to supportive. He used to have a recurring dream in which his grandfather would glare at him with disgust; but when he last dreamed of his grandfather, he was smiling lovingly.

Tara

We can't always be the good guy or girl. Sometimes it is necessary to embody flawed characters in order to allow more of our scene partner's true selves to emerge. As psychoanalyst Howard Searles has said:

> Most therapists are [eager] to help patients in ways in which the therapist can enjoy being regarded as kindly, helpful and so on and staying a million miles away from the patient's need to perceive him as hateful, terrifying and so on. And yet if the patient is ever to get free of her own most terrifying internal contents, she needs help with that [sic] kind of feelings.[16]

Our scene partners especially need such help when they have less social power than we do—e.g., in situations involving disparities resulting from gender, race, sexual orientation, physical ability, religion, etc.

For instance, I have what feels like a very good relationship with my longtime client, Tara. We share a lot in common: e.g., we are both actors who are self reflective and endlessly curious about people. Listening to her explore the challenges of her career, relationships, and talking to her peers about race is always a pleasure. Oh, right...Tara is black; I am white.

Sometimes, as I reflect on our work, I wonder why our scenes rarely have much conflict around this issue (my experience as an actor has taught me that *every* scene has conflict). "If everything is always so pleasant," I ask myself, "what are we missing?"

These questions arise not only from our sessions, but also from my engagement on the topic of race in my life, specifically as a friend to many people of color, and as an artist who advocates for inclusion in entertainment. For years, I ran a theater company[17] with the mission to cast against type and tell stories about people we rarely see on stage and screen, and I continue to write articles about the need for this in art and life. But no matter how "woke"/socially aware I'd like to think I am, I—like all those who are placed in systemic or cultural positions of privilege—nonetheless must reflect on the less conscious ways I may contribute to white supremacy. There are, of course, times when I fail to check my power and privileges as a white man which, ironically, can include my wish to be cast as *the good "woke" therapist*, a role that is not unlike one of those impossibly "good" white characters from movies like *The Help* or *Hidden Figures*, who function mainly to relieve white audiences of their white guilt without having to confront the complicated power imbalances inherent in American race relations. So even as I allow myself to take pleasure in my sessions with Tara, I also use my *foresight* as an actor to imagine all the possible ways our scenes could go, and ask myself why we don't go there.

One day, Tara discussed incidents in her life that she felt were "random" and unrelated. These involved a Facebook friend who posted about her need for emotional support, along with her airbrushed naked selfies ("Does she actually want my help?…"), a coworker whose religion dictated that black people should not date white people and that Tara was making a mistake dating a white man ("It's impossible to talk to her"), and a conversation with her boyfriend in which he pleaded with her to share more about her day with him after work ("He thinks I'm too quiet. Maybe I am?").

When Tara introduces topics like these, she tends to elicit my feedback in a "What should I do?" sort of way. I'm tempted to receive her invitation to play the character of *wise sage* at these times, to help her process her reactions, and to let her know I *get it*. On a certain level, this interaction works for us both—or at least makes us comfortable. But it also keeps us in the status quo, within predetermined hierarchical roles—e.g., teacher and student, doctor and patient—and forecloses the opportunity for more of me or of Tara to come through. To challenge the characters with which we are familiar, I finally let my imagination play while she shared these recent episodes, and envisioned a variety of ways our scene could go. What would happen, for example, if I somehow offended her? What if I wasn't careful in my choice of words and betrayed my inadequacies as a therapist, my privileges as a white man, or my blind spots related to race and how it functions between us? How would she react if I lost the veneer of *the "woke" sage*, and was just another ignorant white dude? As I envisioned the potential, unfamiliar versions of Tara that were yet to emerge if this happened—e.g., reactive, angry, biting—I realized how much work she typically does to accommodate me, how responsible she is for the calm enjoyment of our sessions. She had been protecting us both from facing some of the messy possibilities that our racial differences inevitably would bring to our scene work.

"I wonder what would happen if you told the Facebook friend that she seems to want attention more than your help, or your coworker that your love life is none of her business, or if you told your boyfriend that you need space when you get home from work?…Or if you told me to stop mansplaining to you…" Her face squinched in discomfort as she thought about this:"I guess I'm afraid people will be too fragile to hear what I actually have to say," she replied.

We both listened to her words and I observed Tara observe me as I heard and held what she had to say. She then connected her insight to her childhood. Her parents both struggled with addiction and employment, and she perceived them to be "fragile," often worrying they would "break" if she offered advice or expressed too much of her point of view to them. She explained that as she grew up, acting helped her find her voice, her *total self*, and to "push back" against her learned instinct to "shrink" and accommodate other people when she was in the role of her *everyday self*.

We continue to explore how she protects me from assertive versions of herself by maintaining her role as *student* to my *wise sage*. But now we also discuss how I contribute to this dynamic by wanting to be the *good guy*.

Each day, I practice allowing inevitable enactments to play out between us, including scenes in which I am an unlikable character. For example, in discussing the Oscar-nominated movie *Get Out*—which effectively uses the horror genre to illustrate the internal experience of being black in America—Tara was able to tell me how dehumanizing it can feel for her when white people speak with perceived "authority" about "the artistic merits of movies by black people, about black people, and primarily for black people." Ashamed as I felt, having been that very white person in that very session, I acknowledged this to Tara, along with my feelings of embarrassment, having flaunted my white privilege so ignorantly, but also noting that I appreciated how safe she felt sharing these feelings with me, which was ultimately the point of our work.

Even now, I have to remind myself to resist the temptation to wrap up this case example like *the good "woke" therapist* I reflexively wish to be. I know that there is much more to mine between us than I have summarized here. Each week, I look for ways to maximize the roles that Tara and I can play together in order to promote mindfulness and growth for us both.

Surrogate Roles

We all know what it is like to have an absence of close relationships at different points in life—due to deaths, losing touch with family, or not having family who share crucial aspects of our identity. Here are some examples of surrogate roles I have played for people at such times.

Parental Guide for Couples: When the couples therapist my husband and I once saw told us sincerely that, "Your families don't realize how cool you are and how lucky they are to have you," her observation marked an extremely powerful moment for us. We needed to hear this because we were without parental recognition to help us embrace the distinct family we had created together.

Like our couples therapist, I sometimes offer recognition and guidance, the way a parent might, for my couple clients who do not have someone to play that role in their lives. This particularly applies to same-sex couples who may not only lack supportive parents, but who are more specifically lacking gay parental figures who have experienced long-term relationships. Filling this role does not mean that I call them on the weekend, visit them at home, or do anything drastically outside of what a typical therapist does. But through the action of recognizing their strengths, contextualizing and normalizing for them the typical challenges that long-term couples face—and queer couples in particular—and maybe even offering them practical shorthand advice, I allow myself to be used as more than a service provider. I lend myself as a surrogate parent who has been through similar challenges, has wisdom to share, and who cares about them.

For example, one of my straight couples with very little extended family have been meeting with me once a week for five years, mostly because they felt held by the surrogate parent role I have played for them. As a result of the safety and recognition they received from me regularly over time, they are now able to address their communication patterns more deeply and committedly.

Mentor: Along the same lines, I occasionally offer practical shorthand advice to my individual clients who share a significant characteristic with me, especially those who are queer. Most of my clients are gay men who are looking for a kindred connection in addition to therapeutic support—a relationship which, for a lot of queer people, is very hard to come by in a meaningful way. Granted, any advice I give comes from the idea that as queer people we have the freedom to create our own identities and families, and each of us must do this in our own way. But I can sometimes help people (especially gay men) navigate some of the specific challenges to piecing together an identity with self-awareness, relatedness, and without shame—such as family of origin conflicts, romantic conflicts, sexual concerns, and social pressures. I'm sure therapists of various specialties and focuses play similar roles for clients who have chosen them because they share crucial aspects of self experience with them.

Primary Emotional Contact: Every now and then, there is a short period of time during which I am the most trusted and intimate connection in a client's life. I have not yet experienced this in a way that feels outside the scope of clinical boundaries; in such cases, this temporary relationship is always acknowledged explicitly between me and the client, and it is noted that it is not a permanent solution. But the temporary surrogate role of *primary emotional contact* has proven to be a great catalyst for healing and growth for some of my clients.

For example, a client I had worked with for six years moved to another city with his fiancé with whom he had worked through communication difficulties with the help of our individual sessions. One year later, he contacted me with the horrific news that his fiancé had abruptly died. He wanted to do remote sessions for a few weeks while he processed his shock and grief, and made plans to move his life in a new direction. I was, of course, shocked myself and felt incredibly inadequate to help him through this unimaginable nightmare. But as we entered these scenes, I realized that all I needed to do was to be present. He just needed me to be me; we had already done the "work." He reminded me of this on our last call. I reflected back to him how much I appreciated his capacity to take care of himself during this crisis. He said, "Well, I have to give you some credit, Mark. Over the years, you always encouraged me to be on my own side."

Another significant primary contact I played was for a client who was doing relief work in a war-torn country when we began working together via video. She was an only child who had lost most of her relatives. The nature of her work kept her traveling around the world in very intense circumstances, and did not allow her to focus on intimate relationships. As her current position was coming to an end, she was contemplating several jobs, most of them involving more relief work in dangerous locations. One of them was a teaching job in New York, where she grew up. As we processed her feelings about these options, she said that she would feel too guilty to take the teaching job: "I am needed elsewhere. I don't know if I, or anyone, really deserves to enjoy the safety and comfort of New York." She didn't want me to challenge her perspective: "I'm pretty confident this isn't coming from a lack of self worth," she insisted. But she did ask me what I thought she should do. I chuckled and preempted my answer with the disclaimer that my opinion is completely subjective and not nearly as important as hers. I then told her what I thought, based on my reverie, and intuitive sense of the role I felt was missing in her life at the moment: "I think you should come back to New York. It's safer here. You've done great work, and I think you have a lot to offer as a teacher." She did exactly that, and has since gradually grown into her life here. She even acknowledges now that she was too traumatized by her circumstances to admit, even to herself, how much she wanted to put down some roots and start a relationship and family.

The role I played helped her to find more of her *total self*, and to *act* more productively and creatively in the world than she could as the *everyday self* to which she had grown accustomed.

12 Love

I love my clients. And when I don't, I ask myself why I don't—and then find a way to love them. Similarly, actors find a way to love their characters, scene partners, and audiences, no matter how different, unlikable, horrible, inscrutable, or unresponsive they may seem. As actress Glenn Close says, "[i]f you're judging them, that separation will show."[1]

Theater director Jerzy Grotowski believed that to achieve great acting, "[o]ne must give oneself totally, in one's deepest intimacy, with confidence as when one gives oneself in love."[2] Likewise, acting teacher Stella Adler has said that "[t]he actor must above everything be generous,"[3] because their capacity to love helps our collective "soulfulness to emerge,"[4] and offers "people something that will change them."[5] And psychoanalyst W. W. Meissner made a similar point about the scene work of therapy, observing that "it is through love that [one] grows, becomes more human, and achieves self-fulfilment"[6]–which falls in line with Freud's belief that "[t]he secret of therapy is to cure through **love**."[7]

Surely, the skeptical reader will insist, I don't *love* my clients who are mean, who insist I've done nothing to help them and that I've wasted their time and money—or those who refuse to pay, remind me of relatives who gaslight me, or, have repulsive hygiene?

No, I would answer honestly, I do not love those clients initially, and I may even hate[8] them at times. But as Winnicott pointed out, our hate[9] must be surfaced and understood before we can find a way to truly love. Like actors, I believe one of the great, necessary, and ultimately rewarding challenges of our work is to find a way to love each and every one of our clients, no matter how challenging that may be. "[T]hat is the work," says actress Charlize Theron on approaching characters, "to try and find those things that you can't just kind of go, 'Easy, easy, easy.' It's the stuff that scares you a little bit that makes you go: 'What if I find something about that guy that I can actually have empathy with? Fuck!'"[10]

Just as Theron finds empathy, kindredness, and love for even her most challenging characters, we can attempt the same with our clients—if we feel safe enough to go there with them.

Boundaries Set You Free

Therapy and acting both require a foundation of safety for all parties involved. In art, however, safety is a tricky word. The great theater innovator Antonin Artaud insisted that theater should not be safe but "dangerous"[11] in order to wake us up, "nerves and heart,"[12] from the artistically deadening trappings of "culture."[13] Just as Freud believed analysis should free our erotic unconscious from civilized repression,[14] Winnicott believed therapy should allow us to take emotional risks in order to feel "I AM, I am alive, I am myself."[15] As social psychologist George Goethals put it, "[i]f one will only experience that which is safe and secure how can one mature, develop… take the risks that are imperative in any human being's evolution of personality?"[16] But as Grotowski reminds us, emotional freedom is "impossible without structure."[17] And as psychoanalyst Jody Davies has written, in order for both client and therapist to optimize "the rich efflorescence" of our creative exploration, we both need to feel contained within a safe clinical frame.[18]

For me, safety as a therapist and as an actor means finding boundaries that allow me and my scene partner to think, feel, and explore together, as freely as possible. As Tony Award-nominated director, Moritz Von Steulpnagel observed, performers "must be safe and in control while projecting a real sense of fear, anger, passion"[19]—or love. Here are some structural boundaries that make me feel safe enough to love my scene partners.

Professional Boundaries: Before I can open up emotionally and generously as a performer, I need to nail down a basic treatment contract—including an agreed upon fee, a standard procedure for payment, an established meeting time, and a cancellation policy (see Chapter 9: Frame). Otherwise my energy will be too consumed with anxiety and/or resentment about being exploited. Actress Kelli Barrett makes a similar, incisive point, noting that "[a]s actors we want to feel thoroughly used up, but there's a difference in what you give to your art and what's stolen from you. When cultivating flowers, you must address the weeds."[20] The same is true for clinicians, whether we're talking about getting paid reasonably for our services or having our time respected. The more these boundaries are acknowledged, the more I am able to invest emotionally in my clients.

Physical Boundaries: Most of my clients have an intuitive sense of the parameters needed to do our work with a free mind, but when I am asked about clinical boundaries, I typically say something like, "We can't have sex, we can't be violent, and we can't socialize outside the office, but everything else is fair game." I get right to the point, but I also try to keep my answer playful, alive, and slightly ambiguous. I don't want to throw out the baby (the creative potential of our intimate scene work) with the bathwater (any contact that would make us feel too crowded, invaded, or engulfed, to be mentally and emotionally free in each other's presence).

Aside from the basics, physical boundaries are not useful to me as static rules to follow slavishly, eyes wide shut. They work better when I ask myself in each new situation what specific parameters are needed to keep the scene open and dynamic for each actor. Like my yoga teacher Nancy says, "As you do each pose, find stability in the physical boundaries so you can open your mind and heart."

Scene work that involves dance or fight choreography provides an illustration of how physical boundaries open up the minds and hearts of actors. Actors need to rehearse complex technical movements before each performance—a ritual known as dance or fight call—not only to prevent injury, but also to make everyone involved secure enough to be emotionally and creatively free as they perform (I cringe as I recall missing a step during a combat scene in a professional production in which I wielded an axe at another actor's head. On a good day, fight call made us secure enough in the moves to play the scene with spontaneity and ardor. On *that* day, however, my scene partner twisted his ankle, fearing I would actually strike him with the axe, which left him on crutches for the remainder of the play's run).

Each situation requires specific boundaries to ensure enough safety to open up our minds and hearts. And to that end, physical touch is sometimes (though rarely in my clinical experience) actually necessary.

While working in a community mental health clinic years ago, I had a five-year-old client who would physically act out, sometimes violently. Often the only scene work we could achieve involved him making a scene by kicking and throwing toys while I tried to manage him. If I set a boundary by ending the session early, he would occasionally cooperate, but this approach eventually stopped working. One day, in a fit of fury, he attempted to climb a very tall bookcase in my office. Before it fell on top of us, I reflexively grabbed him and held him in my arms, as if in a straight jacket. He kicked and wriggled and screamed, "Get off." And then I let the straight jacket become a hug, called him gently by his name, and said, "Stop. It's ok. Calm down." And he did.

The palpable danger in that moment propelled me to do something most adults who work with children are understandably afraid to do: put their hands on a kid. But this particular move was necessary to ensure safety for us both. Fortunately, I had opened my door before things got too wild, and the entire event was witnessed by a colleague—another way to ensure safety during a risky performance. I discussed this incident at length with the boy's mother, and with the clinical director, and we all came to understand his behavior as a reaction to the absence of his father—who was in jail. As I continued to work with him, he would act out occasionally in order to get me to hug him again; and after I did, he would typically calm down and share vulnerable emotions, which had previously been hiding underneath his rage. When I left the clinic, I was heartbroken to separate from him, and gave his mother the address of my new office so he could send me cards (of construction paper and crayon), at his request. He sent them for a few months before moving on. To this day, I hope he found other attachments with adults who made him feel safe. And I like to think that even the short time I spent with him will live in his memory and remind him that it is possible to be held safely enough to express a range of emotions, just as the memory of my father holding me as a child lives in my mind and heart decades after his death.

I have also worked with adult clients for whom touch was necessary to create safety between us. In one instance, I treated a man in his early thirties who had been severely abandoned throughout his life. Not only did both of his parents die of drug overdoses when he was twelve, but his aunt and uncle who took him in threw him out five years later when he came out as gay. Normally, I don't initiate sessions with a new client with a hand-shake, preferring to welcome them with a warm but open-ended greeting that includes a smile, a few words, and a gesture that invites them to sit down—allowing them to find their own way into the scene. But this man made a beeline for my hand at the start of every session. I strongly sensed he would be too fragile to process my observation about this ritual. So instead of asking him about it, I reflected on my own, and discussed it with peers. But I kept coming back to my initial instinct, which was that it was better not to address it with him, as I didn't want to threaten his capacity to *stay in there* with me. Something about touching my hand made him feel safe enough to reveal the abyss of emotions inside of him. **What's key here is that at the same time I did not feel compromised in any way by granting him the handshake (probably due to my years of experi-ence as an actor, during which time I grew comfortable with phys-ical contact, and learned to discern the difference between touch that allows me to be present and touch that does not). Otherwise we would have had to explore another course of action.** After about a year and a half of working together, we eventually found a way to talk about the handshake. I observed that it perhaps stabilized him enough to open up to me, which made sense given his relational history. I wondered if without that initial touch before sessions he might feel like Sandra Bullock's character in the movie *Gravity*, floating chaotically in space, crying out to her scene partner via headset, "Tell me what to do, tell me what to do." He seemed to appreciate my recognition of his internal experience. And though the handshakes continued, the acknowledgment of their significance enhanced the safety between us, and helped him to reveal even more vul-nerable emotions throughout our rehearsal process.

With most of my clients, finding enough space between us is typically a more effective way to open up our emotions than close proximity or phys-ical touch would allow. The paradox here is that I intend the boundary of the physical space to make them feel just as safely held as the man who needed a handshake and the boy who needed a hug. The goal is the same: to find a way for us both to surrender to our scene work, without submitting to our scene partner. And though I intend for my energy to invite and encourage their participation *as if* I held them in my arms, I don't actually touch them (as per Chapter 5: Embody).

To get an evocative sense of this concept, we can consider the physical boundaries that are necessary for actors to be emotionally, or even literally, naked on stage or screen. Actress Maggie Gyllenhaal, for example, has made a career of playing characters who find agency in extremely vulnerable circumstances. From her breakout role in the movie *Secretary*—in which she played a woman in a sadomasochistic relationship with her boss—to her acclaimed performance as a prostitute-turned-porn-director on the HBO series *The Deuce*, Gyllenhaal always manages to reveal her most bare emotions while conveying a sense of center, groundedness, and self possession. Even as she performs scenes in which she is physically naked, she somehow never seems objectified or exploited, but instead comes across as an active agent in a creative collaboration, empowered by her own gaze, curiosity, and point of view. Gyllenhaal has credited her capacity to share herself so openly and generously not just to a strong connection to her own body,[21] but also with the safety and trust she establishes with her directors and scene partners.[22] (By contrast, Gyllenhaal's description calls to mind the legions of actresses who, are continuously exploited by the lack of safe and equitable boundaries in Hollywood.) One significant boundary that allowed Gyllenhaal to be artistically free in her work on *The Deuce*, for example, was her insistence on becoming a producer, which meant she could collaborate on the script. This additional role yielded a scene in which her character masturbates in private, giving the audience a window into her own subjective desire, allowing her to see while being seen. With this in mind, we could say that as a performing artist, Gyllenhaal finds enough physical, mental, and emotional space to be both agent and participant in even her most vulnerable scene work.[23]

I try to keep this concept in mind when considering how much space each new client needs to think and feel freely as we collaborate. I ask myself in each new scene how we can be as emotionally generous as Maggie Gyllenhaal (keeping our clothes on, of course), while also being as secure in our own minds and skins as she always seems to be. This entails staying present with each scene partner and negotiating space so that we both can have agency in our creative process.

For instance, there are occasional clients who sit extremely close to me, seeming to devour me with wide, hungry, and/or anxious eyes, sometimes making me feel physically invaded. I am unable to offer love freely and generously when I feel engulfed by another person like this. Instead, I become reactive, frustrated, and shut down until I can wriggle myself free—and become a co-producer of our scene work, as opposed to a mere object to be exploited, used up, and discarded.

One particular client who sat very close to me and whose stare made me feel like prey in her crosshairs was also a heavy smoker, and the smell of cigarettes on her stifled my capacity to breathe, think, or feel freely or generously in her presence. The dilemma was therefore in finding a physical boundary to make myself feel safe while also preventing *her* from feeling rejected and emotionally unsafe as a result. She would stare me down suspiciously and penetratingly if I listened to her silently, and when I spoke (which I would often feel coerced to do), she would squint in discomfort, as though she were being scrutinized under a microscope by a cold, critical analyst; the situation seemed lose/lose. I felt intuitively that retreating from her physically would only make her feel more judged.

Preparation (as per Act I of this book) was key in this case. Between sessions, I reflected on how little room there was between us to breathe or think or feel. As I engaged in this reverie, I *embodied* her physicality and facial expressions, to get a visceral sense of her need to smother/consume me, so I could think beyond my reflex to retract and protect myself, and find a way to empathize with her. I began to appreciate that the literal smokescreen she laid between us indicated how emotionally fragile she was underneath it. I also replayed our scenes in my mind, and practiced ways to *stay in there* with her without compromising myself. I tried out various listening approaches so I could be actively curious while conveying warmth, but also energetically grounded and able to *breathe*. Rather than being thrown off guard by her, I could then turn to these technical actions in the moment. This way, even if I needed to back my chair away, I would do it confidently, with the clear intention to gather enough space to hold her—generously, with the warmth of my curiosity. This boundary invited her participation as opposed to pushing her away.

Most importantly, the space and security I found in these technical adjustments allowed me to *listen* to her better. I was able to take in the anecdotes she shared about men in her life for whom she felt love, and therefore—as a defense mechanism—felt the need to "make smaller" than her in some way (This dynamic may also explain my feeling devoured by her). This way, she could "have them" without the emotional risk of losing them. This helped me appreciate how the death of her father when she was a child impacted her—a fact she shared during our first session. It also helped me understand how irritated she would get when I'd offer anything that sounded remotely like an interpretation, as it reminded her of the therapist she was forced to see shortly after her father's death who smothered her with analytic interpretations at the most powerless and disorienting time in her life. Rather than repeat this trauma of analyzing her under a microscope, I learned to join her by saying things like, "If only that therapist gave you enough space to explain how you felt in your own way, at your own pace," and "Of course you want to make those men smaller than you. It must be hard to trust that they care about you as much as you care about them. I can appreciate that." She gradually felt safe enough to back away from me and engage in her own thought process silently (what Winnicott would call her capacity to be alone), while granting me enough space to collaborate in my own way as well. This understanding allowed me to *love* the little girl who lost her dad rather than be repelled by the adult shielded by smoke.

Environmental Boundaries: Performers need to trust that the environment in which we work is safe enough for us to play. For instance, Romeo and Juliet won't be able to lose themselves in romantic ecstasy if their balcony is at risk of collapse (sadly this is no joke, as at least one artist has been paralyzed for life due to a faulty "Juliet Balcony"[24]). I can't say that the condition of my office has ever threatened injury, but I do pay attention to how the temperature affects my scene partners, and whether or not clients advocate for themselves and ask me to adjust the thermostat. I also observe how their interaction with my office decor affects me.

For example, while I may find it endearing to see a client settle into the couch and get cozy with a pillow, I will likely be distracted and feel disrespected if they pull apart the embroidery on that pillow (I use this mostly as a hypothetical illustration, as the integrity of my pillows have only been compromised in this way exactly three times). There is no telling how a client will respond when I set an environmental boundary (such as, "Hands off my pillows"), but it is important for me to know my baseline (I like my pillows to be intact). Once when I playfully said to a client who plucked my pillow's threads, "If I were that pillow, I'd say 'ouch,'" she left my office and never came back. Another client, who had done the exact same thing and with whom I used the same line, immediately apologized and proceeded to reflect on a pattern of boundaryless, entitled behavior in her life, and her desire to change that—which certainly helped me to *love* her better.

The most extreme example of my office being compromised was by a severely socially impaired forty-something man. I did not initially recognize the level of help he needed when I agreed to work with him. Having spoken to him and his previous therapist, and considering that he held down a respectable job for a decade, I optimistically thought that talking in an emotionally safe environment would be enough to build his relational skills. I was wrong. After a year, his symptoms seemed to get increasingly severe—including dishevelled hair and clothes, and poor hygiene—and though this apparent neglect was arguably due to his feeling safe enough to regress through his work with me, I did not possess an environment that could absorb (so to speak) such regressions. As he got up to go one day, I noticed a wet spot on my couch, and asked him if he was alright. He assured me he was, and that the wetness was from his umbrella. A couple weeks later, he entered my office smelling so intensely of urine that my nostrils literally burned. I reflexively asked if he had an accident, to which he replied, "Oh, yes, on the train. But…I cleaned up afterward…" Horrified, confounded, and utterly disgusted, I spoke from deep in my solar plexus and insisted he go home to clean up properly. I could barely hold back my anger, resentment, and disdain as I explained that he had soiled my couch, which I would have to have professionally cleaned before meeting with other clients. I then asked if he was planning to go to work that day in that condition, to which he replied, "Yes." Words cannot describe my reaction to this revelation. Fortunately, I was able to move the rest of my clients that day (and I had been planning to replace the couch anyway), but I would have to terminate treatment with him as I could not risk anything like this happening again. At the same time, I would have to find a higher level of treatment for him, and somehow discuss all of this with him in a way that made him feel cared for and not despised. When I regained my bearings, I emailed him my thoughts, along with links to DBT clinics that had been highly recommended where he could receive social skills coaching and support. I suggested that we do phone sessions for the next few weeks so that we could process what happened and discuss next steps for his continued care while maintaining some form of safe connection, even as we experienced this unimaginable rupture. He agreed to these terms. During these sessions, the boundary of the phone helped my empathy and **love** for him to emerge from the repulsion that had been a natural response when he was last in my office. On our last call, he told me he had never felt more rejected by a "doctor" while at the same time being the recipient of such compassion.

Cultural Boundaries: We can't truly love another person if we don't offer them continuous empathic curiosity about their sociocultural experience. Without this, it is impossible to master what clinician's call *cultural competency*, as one's cultural experience is highly specific, dynamic, and fluid. But we can increase our *cultural fluency* by approaching every person with an open, curious mind, with empathy, with research we do on our own, and with the willingness to be corrected, to take responsibility for our ignorance, and to own our power and privilege. My clients who have significant sociocultural differences from me seem to most appreciate my efforts to love them when I try to validate them and fail, but then recognize my failure and keep trying, while also making room for their disappointment in my failures. When they see that my intention is to understand and appreciate *them* and not simply to cast myself as the "good therapist," they often feel safe enough to open up to me.

Love Means Never Having To Work With Everyone: Actors sometimes turn down roles that would be too much of an uphill battle for them to play freely or generously—especially when they know another actor who could do it with ease (I, for one, would probably turn down the chance to play an uber-masculine, super-muscular, action hero in a big-budget movie if the producers were counting on my performance to yield instant box office success—especially since The Rock could meet their distinct demands in his sleep). And the same is true for therapists. We too have the option not to work with clients who feel like a bad fit. I like to think of this as yet one more boundary that helps me to open up my mind and heart to anyone who contacts me. By reserving the right to tell a prospective client we are not a good match, I free myself up to *love* them by offering referrals to colleagues whom I think would be better cast in the role of their therapist.

Showmance: Explore Erotic Transference and Countertransference

"It is more important to explore erotic transference than to interpret it,"[25] says psychoanalyst Mark Blechner—and I agree. The same is true for our erotic countertransference. When we keep the frisson of our chemistry with scene partners alive—without letting it become too much—it can lead us not only to a greater understanding of our (and, consequently, their) love needs, but it also helps both of us to maximize our creative potentials. This is possible as long as we feel safe enough to explore these feelings in the context of our scene work (Actors refer to a similar process of falling in love with each other's characters during their rehearsal process as a *showmance*).

I feel safe enough to explore erotic aspects of myself as a professional performing artist when I acknowledge and take care of my needs for eroticism, romance, and sex in my personal life. Much like I consider yoga, running, and the mindfulness exercises I do in private to be part of my job as a clinical performer (as per Act I: Prepare), I consider my efforts to care for my emotional, relational, and sexual needs to be just as crucial. When I feel secure in my personal life I have more capacity to dive deep into intimate emotions with my professional scene partners without needing them to satisfy me, and without ever feeling confused about our purpose in going there together. I believe this is an example of what Stanislavski meant in his directive to "Love the art in yourself, not yourself in the art."[26] I never forget that my relationship with my clients (our showmance, if you will) exists only in the context of our work.

The best wisdom I ever received along these lines was when I played Romeo at a regional theater. Our director took me and Juliet aside one day and said, "Let's break this down: I'm gay and married. You're gay and married [meaning me], you're straight and married [meaning her]. We all know that our job here is to tell a story. With that in mind, you can give yourselves to each other, deeply and intimately. Go for it." This reminded us how safe we were to explore the love between our characters, without the fear of boundaries being crossed. We weren't going to have sex or violate each other, but within those boundaries we could find ways to be in love. And as it turned out, both of our husbands responded to our performances emphatically. Neither of them was jealous; rather, they were impressed with our ability to find the characters within ourselves, and to explore their journeys passionately and with full commitment.

As in my work with Juliet, I always look for the best possible boundaries to make my collaboration with each scene partner safe enough to explore a wide range of feelings and playful interactions, including those that are erotic.

These explorations demand that I be present with each individual and that I observe the chemistry that forms between us, as well as the often subtle and implicit ways it finds expression. If our exchanges feel like flirtations, I explore the nature of them in my mind. I observe the roles we tend to play in our scene work, and ask what feels exciting (or not) about these particular roles—for me and for them. I try to be honest with myself about my own idiosyncratic erotic desires and fantasies, and how they contribute to our unique chemistry. And I ask myself if the playfulness between us invites us both to participate in the process or if it inhibits us somehow. Social context is also important to consider whenever eroticism and sexuality enter the therapy stage, as psychoanalyst Galit Atlas has incisively observed (We mustn't forget that psychotherapy originated with men in power soliciting erotic and sexual details from women, and that social power related to gender continues to play a significant role in our scene work.[27] As I write this, I recognize that being an out gay man informs the shared power I often find with many of my scene partners, especially those who are gay men and women, even as erotic feelings and sexuality enter our playing area).

Through a process of playing, daydreaming, and reflecting I often get a sense of what my client may want emotionally underneath the erotic surface. I also wonder about the particular ways our rapport and chemistry may or may not gratify them. From there, I can work to help them feel safe enough to surface, recognize, and express their wants and needs in a more conscious form. Their desire may initially manifest as flirtation, but through our rehearsal process, it may transform into a meaningful verbal description of their emotional needs.

After years of clinical experience, I've learned not to be afraid of flirtatious exchanges with clients as they are usually a playful way to express something deeper. Thinking of myself as a performing artist has helped me transform my former fears of "breaking the rules" into curiosity about how erotic play transpires between scene partners—in life, in art, and in therapy.

Different scene partners conjure different aspects of ourselves—different keys on our instruments—and the unique chemistry and reverie that develops in clinical and/or creative encounters would not manifest the same way outside the boundaries of the therapeutic or artistic situation. Consider actors who discover a genuine erotic love for each other in the context of their scene work, but who would likely never find a comparable chemistry together in their everyday lives. The most stark examples of this are straight actors who play same-sex lovers on screen, passionately and effectively, such as in the award-winning films *Moonlight*, *Call Me By Your Name*, and *Brokeback Mountain*. Likewise, even though the version of me that comes alive in my scene work with each client may be genuine, it is not necessarily reflective of who I am as an erotic/romantic/sexual being in my everyday life.

For instance, when I am playful with someone like my client Harry—the energetic man I described in Chapter 4, who always seems to be in a rush—I may find myself pulled along by his charm in a way that turns me into a coy dance partner. My posture shrinks, my smile widens, and my feet become ungrounded. While with a client like Wade—whom I also described in Chapter 4, as someone I always seem to be ahead of—I may find myself in the role of dominant partner. My heels root into the ground, my energy and voice drop into my core, and my whole body widens.

I see these implicit erotic exchanges as just one of the various ways the intersubjective dynamics between me and a particular scene partner take form. For instance, playful flirtations between us may mimic the dynamics I have described in which Harry always feels ahead of me while Wade feels behind me. The particular chemistry between each partnering may correspond with the specific characters in which each of them casts me—e.g., for Harry, I sometimes feel like an authority figure from his past whom he "successfully seduced"—a relationship about which he still feels ambivalent; and for Wade, I am often cast as any number of familiars in his life who put demands on him. When I step away, reflect, and recognize the dance in which I am participating—including my own feelings and fantasies that contribute to it—I can then use our flirtatious play as a conscious opportunity to invite them to discover a greater range of relational experience (their *total selves*).

For Harry, this may mean consciously getting ahead of him in our playfulness, grounding myself, reversing our roles, and giving him the opportunity to engage with a dominant partner. For Wade, it means not only following his lead as far as the content he wishes to discuss, but also, in terms of his erotic impulses to engage with me playfully, to encourage his erotically dominant versions of self to emerge by diluting the energy in my body and becoming affably passive. All of this can happen on the implicit level of play—in the micro erotic exchanges between us—which can contribute to new ways of being "while bypassing the head-on confrontation that may evoke anxiety and shame."[28] At the same time, we also have the option to discuss our chemistry explicitly in order to secure safe boundaries around it, but in a way that keeps it open and playful. For Harry, this may mean talking about the ways our relationship mimics the one he had with the authority figure from his past in some ways, but also the opportunity we now have for such a relationship to be different; to explore our chemistry within safe bounds; to give him the chance to feel the pleasure of being "held" by an older man who does not respond to his flirtations by acting on sexual impulse, but who instead offers him responsible care. This way, we allow ourselves to be conscious and open about our playful exchanges, and find a purpose to them that expands his (and my) sense of self. For Wade, this may mean discussing how our chemistry can be a default escape from relationships in his life that smother his autonomy, and from there we can consider ways he might follow through with his own agentic impulses (including those that are erotic) more frequently, both in and out of the *rehearsal room*.

When I acknowledge erotic chemistry in a therapy situation, and reflect honestly on my own fantasies as they emerge, I invite a process of reverie that can ultimately bring me closer to the client's relational needs. I also mitigate the fear and stigma of sexuality (mine and theirs) being present in our work, which can otherwise easily obstruct our collaborative, creative process, and yield unnecessary tension and conflict.

Screen actress Winona Ryder has described how the stigma of sexuality—particularly female sexuality—warped the erotic impulses of her character Abigail Williams in the film adaptation of Arthur Miller's *The Crucible*. Williams' resulting actions, of course, spurred the destructive Salem "witch" trials on which Miller's play is based. Abigail is often dismissed as a "bitch" or "femme fatale" due to her seductive and vengeful behaviors, but Ryder says she found a way to understand her: "She's a very young girl having an affair with an older married man. So, when he says, 'Go away!' she is obviously devastated and hurt and confused."[29] Ryder does not necessarily justify Abigail's lethal accusations against her innocent neighbors, but she does attribute the devastating crucible of events that ensue in the play to fear of the unknown—particularly in terms of sexuality, love, and desire.

Similarly, an insightful teenage client of mine who was working on the role of Martha in Edward Albee's *Who's Afraid of Virginia Woolf?* for an acting class explained to me that, "people see Martha as this emasculating flirt, but deep down, she really just wanted her husband to hold her, to love her."

When we reflect on our erotic dynamics with clients the way actors explore the erotic lives of their characters, we can better empathize with their underlying emotional positions. This is true for all clients, but especially with those who feel "seductive" to us.

Jake

Jake, a twenty-something client—who, like me, is a gay male actor with a lean build—always seemed to enter our scenes along with a high voltage of sexual tension. Unlike the cases I described above, the energy in the room did not feel like a flirtatious exchange but more like an intense seduction. This created a palpable sheath between us because Jake did not seem to be asking for my active participation, but instead seemed to push me away from his underlying emotions with his bedroom eyes. This continued for many months, and I realize now this situation was in part because I enjoyed it at times, and also because I was afraid of enjoying it, and therefore didn't give myself enough private mental space to process it effectively. Over the course of two years, I became more consciously aware of the fantasies our dynamic evoked in me, and reflected on how an actual sexual encounter between us might go. It always began with Jake as the alluring seducer luring me inside of him (An example of a moment in session that would evoke such a fantasy are times he'd move close to me, open his eyes wide, and say, "Enough about me, tell me about you…"). As I played out the erotic fantasy in my mind, I discovered that the key to unlock the door between us was not necessarily apparent in the sexual part of the imagined encounter, but in what might come later, if our impulses were followed to completion. I imagined him post-sex, seeming sad, broken, ashamed, and alone. This conjured a warm fatherly character in me who could hold and *love* him for exactly who he is, not merely for his slinky seductiveness. I learned to embody this father-like character in session, and to hold the sad, frightened little boy inside the tantalizingly sexualized adult. Sometimes, I did this simply in the way I listened, by grounding myself and opening up my heart energy to him in a safe and nurturing way. Other times, I talked explicitly about his seductive defenses, not necessarily in terms of us (as I felt that could induce too much embarrassment or shame for him to think clearly), but in reference to the anecdotes he'd share about sexual encounters with men that paralleled our dynamic. I found ways to address his emotional guardedness with me, especially given our similar identities and his fear of being judged by me. And I acknowledged that for gay men in particular, we have practically no opportunities—especially as developing children—to explore our romantic feelings openly, playfully, appropriately, and without shame or fear—with adults who make us feel safe enough to do so (e.g., We never talk about "Daddy's Little Boy," yet we always hear about "Daddy's Little Girl."[30])

My work with Jake reminds me that at the end of the day, we're all just human beings playing various roles in an effort to help each other heal, grow, and *love* as freely as possible.

Receive

> To love another person is to see the face of God.[31]
>
> (Victor Hugo, *Les Misérables*)

We help our scene partners heal and grow not only by giving them love, but also by allowing them to love us in return. As Jessica Benjamin writes, the client comes to therapy "to find her own love as much as to be or feel loved."[32] Through this process of "reciprocal responsiveness"[33] and mutual caring, the third/transitional/rehearsal space between us truly comes to life.

Eve

A primary theme that my not-yet-thirty-year-old client Eve and I have explored over the years is her challenging relationship with her mother. Eve rarely felt recognized emotionally by her mother, especially since her parents' divorce when Eve was only nine. Despite the fact that she is an independent adult with a successful career, which she has worked hard to achieve, and a relationship that makes her happy, Eve continues to feel the sting of not being held in her mother's mind. She has described her mother as self-focused, impulsive, "extremely moody," and "inconsolable." "She's like Humpty Dumpty. She takes and takes love and attention from other people, but it's never enough to put her back together again," she explained, noting, "She can rarely see past herself. She only sees me if I'm sick or something. When she can take care of me like a baby." Having struggled myself with a mother who was incredibly loving and present in crucial ways when I was a child, but who continuously fails to recognize me as a subjective adult who is separate from her, I am able to validate Eve's experience, and even offer some practical advice. Namely, we have focused on acknowledging, understanding, and accepting her mother's limitations, and creating boundaries so that Eve can feel emotionally safe enough to love her mother without feeling frustrated, disappointed, or compromised by her lack of reciprocity.

Recently, just before the holidays, Eve thanked me for the years of attention I have given her, particularly with regard to her mother. She also wanted to share her latest creative solution for them to spend quality time together. Eve's mom is an eye doctor, and when she learned that Eve wanted laser surgery to improve her vision, she made an offer Eve did not refuse:

> She wants to do it for me, for free. All I have to do is pay for a plane ticket…and fly across the country. Which is not the most convenient thing, but I figure, that's one way she can give me something I actually need. And on her end, she gets to take care of me like a baby (Truly, like a baby. I mean, for a few hours she'll see me without me being able to see her. For a change). If this is how she needs to love me, and I can give it to her, why not do it? You've helped me see that I'm the bigger one emotionally. And even though I have to protect myself, I can also find ways to love her and let her love me, however possible.

When I was greener, I would have likely been demure and blown off Eve's suggestion that I had helped her. But as I validated her considerable work, I also tried to embody a version of myself who could receive her gratitude—inspired by mentors of mine who have received my love and appreciation graciously. But that's not all I received from Eve. I also received her creative strategy to spend time with her mother in a way that allowed each of them to love and be loved—which invited me to explore an untapped version of myself.

I was about to see my mother for Christmas, and had no idea what to get her, if anything at all. She hadn't given me or my husband a gift in years, and the gifts I gave to her always seemed to disappear—including my efforts to improve her mood. My generosity was at an all-time low with her until I received the gift of inspiration from Eve, which catalyzed me to search for and find a photograph of my mother I had taken when I was a teenager. This picture captured the version of my mother that always comforted me most: warm and full of care, but grounded and self possessed (At the time, she was

enlivened by her career as a school psychologist, which gave her the opportunity to make other people feel seen). *Surely she wouldn't fail to recognize an
attractive photo of herself*, I thought. I framed, wrapped, and happily gave her a
form of my love I thought she could receive. And she did.

I believe love guides our work, every day with every client, whether we
realize it or not. As with acting, we don't have to force it, and it's often best if
we don't. As psychotherapist Irvin Yalom says, our love can manifest simply
as concern "for the life and the growth of another."[34]

A scene from one of my favorite movies describes love similarly. A student who has been complaining about her hometown—and her mother—
for most of the story, meets with a teacher for feedback on an essay about
her hometown. The teacher observes that the student clearly *loves* the
town. Taken aback, the student adamantly denies this, and says she merely
chronicled the town accurately because she pays attention. In response, the
teacher asks her if they aren't the same thing: attention and love.

Act III

Perform

How can I strengthen and make the most of the slight contact between us?
(Constantin Stanislavski, *An Actor Prepares*, 1946a, p. 194)

13 Narrate

To "narrate" is to provide a spoken commentary to accompany a perform-ance.[1] According to that definition, all therapists perform the act of narration at various points in our scene work. As psychoanalyst, Jessica Benjamin has said, "[T]he dramatic art of [psychotherapy] requires **narrative**…"[2]

If you're a psychoanalyst, you might call your narrative performances "interpretations," which illuminate hidden meanings in your client's sub-conscious, "mirroring," which helps them to develop a cohesive sense of self, or "metacommunications," which allow you to talk about your communica-tion process. If you're a Jungian analyst, you might narrate your client's story in terms of archetypes and myths. If you're a rational emotive behaviorist, you might use narration to "dispute"[3] your clients' irrational beliefs; or, if you are a cognitive behaviorist, your narration might take the form of "sum-marizing" or "problem solving"[4] to help them relieve their symptoms. For couples or family therapists, narrative action helps your clients hear, acknow-ledge, and validate each other's perspectives. In group therapy, narration can challenge each member's instincts, and increase their awareness and related-ness. As a psychodrama or Gestalt therapist, you might encourage your clients to perform "monologues" of their inner thoughts to help them be aware of the stories they tell themselves. If you work with children, your narration of their play helps them to bring inner conflicts and worries to the surface. And of course you might simply call yourself a "narrative therapist," which means you help clients to be the expert narrators of their own lives.[5]

We often emphasize the theoretical differences in clinical work, much the same way actors contrast performance techniques—like Lee Strasberg's inside-out "Method Acting,"[6] Vsevolod Meyerhold's outside-in "Biomechanics,"[7] Anne Bogart's kinesthetic "Viewpoints,"[8] or David Mamet's no frills "Practical Aesthetics."[9] But just as all actors share the same core mission to effectively perform stories about lives, all therapists share the same ultimate goal to help our clients effectively perform their own lives. And no matter how we are trained, what professional title or "modality" we use, or what we call the actions we perform in session, at times we all *narrate* each client's experience to aid them in their creative process.

The great theater innovator and playwright Bertolt Brecht believed actors should use narration much like we do as therapists: to step outside of the emotions of the characters, and engage the story with a sense of "astonishment and curiosity."[10] Brecht wanted audiences to *think* about his plays and not be emotionally manipulated by the characters. However, the problem with Brecht's prescription as I see it is his insistence that *all* performance be detached from emotional mimesis.[11] Like the therapist who believes *all* therapy should engage the mind over the heart—or vice versa—such a rigid position denies the full dialectic potential of a play (or play in general) to engage multiple perspectives at once.

I think Brecht may have even adapted his uncompromising statements about acting had he been alive to see Meryl Streep play the title role in his play *Mother Courage and Her Children*. Using her sharp intellect, empathic heart, finely tuned body and fertile imagination, Streep skillfully and effectively realized Brecht's wish for actors to step out of the play's action and address the audience directly. But she achieved this without ever disavowing her character's complex inner life. As she narrated the play's themes to us— explicitly and bawdily through song—we never forgot the specific woman she embodied. And when she returned to the world of the play, she dropped back into her character's given circumstances in a way that would make Stanislavski proud. Much of Streep's success was due in large part to her staying present with each scene partner in each moment, whether that was another actor or a member of the audience. As clinical performers, we too can stay present with each of our scene partners, and help them to think and feel at the same time.

Mirror

As a therapeutic action, *mirroring* is often described as a neutral echoing of the client to help validate and strengthen their sense of self.[12] However, when I perform my version of *mirroring*, I acknowledge that no matter how "neutral" I attempt to be, the way I narrate my client's experience will be filtered through my subjective and creative point of view. Therefore, the intention behind my choice to *mirror* my scene partner is to invite them to participate in a collaborative narrative process. As Brecht might say, I not only attempt to hold up a mirror to their reality, but I also give them "a hammer with which to shape it."[13]

For the first few weeks, months, or years of a psychotherapy *rehearsal*—of trying, failing, and playing—we do not really know where we are going, but instead lend ourselves to a process that churns unformulated actions into a "performance that creates meaning,"[14] as Jessica Benjamin has put it. Along these lines, when I choose to mirror my client's experience, I hope to galvanize them to actively create their own meaning out of our scene work.

For example, I might say to a client who repeatedly refuses to assert her needs to her emotionally enmeshed family, "It's hard to imagine having yourself and your family too, huh?" In performing this narrative, I do not intend to be "right" or have the final word. In fact, the client could respond with, "No that's not it," as easily as "Yes, that's right." Either way, they have accepted my invitation to collaborate in the process of making a cohesive story out of our rehearsal. This is much like long-form improv, which begins from a place of playful not knowing but eventually becomes a clear narrative that can continue to be adapted, again and again, through a collaboration of choices made by the performers (If you are not familiar with long-form improv, I highly recommend that you experience the work performers like TJ & Dave, who have mastered the art of entering a stage without characters, dialogue, or a plot, and creating an engaging, thought provoking, one-hour play[15]).

I also liken the act of mirroring in the therapy process to press junkets in which actors are forced to describe their characters as opposed to simply play them. Such interviews are performances in themselves, as the actor gets to put the character's journey into an objective context for an audience in real time. This is especially beneficial to the actor if they get the opportunity to return to the set and continue to embody the character after the interview, with a more conscious sense of purpose than before. Clients and therapists similarly get to dive back into our clinical scene work, informed and guided by the narrative observations we make along the way.

Mirroring is a particularly helpful form of narration with clients who share a marginalized identity with me. Many of my clients choose to work with me in order to feel recognized by someone kindred to them in significant ways—a dynamic that I'm sure holds true for many therapists. My personal and professional experiences of homophobia and internalized homophobia for instance, allow me to identify with and validate many of my clients' personal challenges. I also have an implicit understanding of the creative opportunities we have as queer people, as there are fewer societal expectations for us. I can help each client to be in touch with their own natural resources, and to construct their own narrative with this in mind.

Narrative mirroring is generally a pivotal tool to use with all clients whose voices are marginalized. We all need external validation to help us through the doubt and shame and fear that surfaces at those times when we must challenge the dominant narrative in order to be recognized. For example, an actor client of Korean descent who feels constantly stereotyped and diminished recently asked me if his self advocacy—with directors, producers, fellow actors, and friends—was "too strident" or "inappropriate." I first mirrored back that his specific experience as a full human being is largely unappreciated by his peers, the entertainment industry, and our society in general. I then said, "Who gets to determine whose voice and concerns are appropriate? In order to turn the tide of a normative narrative, one has to face and induce discomfort. It sounds to me that your self advocacy, however 'strident,' is a means to connect, not to push people away." This suggested narrative helped him to stop internalizing the social power hierarchies that conspire to keep him down. It also validated his self-promotion efforts, which were not at all intended to cause havoc, but designed to simply have a seat at the table.

Couples, both gay and straight, also find it helpful to hear that their conflicts are not unique. There is so much fear of failure and shame when it comes to the inevitable challenges of relationships and marriage—related to sex, communication, and unhealed childhood wounds—and these topics are therefore rarely openly discussed. For many couples, therapy is the first place they will have their struggles not only mirrored back to them, but validated as being common. I am always deeply moved when my couples shift their narrative about attending therapy from a story of weakness and failure to one of resilience and the willingness to ask for help.

Rewrite

The process of narration provides clients the opportunity to *rewrite* their stories—which may be what many CBT therapists mean by "modifying cognitions."[16] By *rewrite* I mean to free oneself from a narrative that has shackled them, preventing them from maximizing their full potential. Like an actor who is empowered by the chance to doctor their script and shape the destiny of their character—as I described Maggie Gyllenhaal doing for her character in *The Deuce* in Chapter 12. To *rewrite* in therapy is to doctor the script handed to you by family, peers, and society, and to make your character a protagonist with a story arc that you find freeing and fulfilling, without having to disavow the aspects of the story that cause you pain.

For some clients, this may mean giving voice to emotional ruptures that have thus far only manifested in their bodies. For example, an actor client who developed severe neck pain after playing a character that required her to contort her body was able to find words in our sessions for the first time in her life to describe childhood relational traumas, which she had stored in her body. This emotional pain was always available to her, and helped her embody characters brilliantly throughout her career, such as the one that caused her injury. But her body could no longer take it. By finding words for her childhood trauma in our sessions, and narrating how she had coped for so many years, she was able to free the pain from her body—albeit through a great deal of grief which took a good amount of time to process carefully. These narrative performances in our sessions have helped her discover a whole palette of options to channel and process her pain—beyond contorting her body to play characters.

Another client constantly blamed himself for his sexual desires, which he feared were "perverse." I was particularly struck by how the behaviors for which he reprimanded himself all seemed common, if not tame—e.g., protected intercourse, oral sex, mutual masturbation via smartphone. When he would describe his sexual encounters with remorse, my initial instinct was to validate his desires and behaviors like a reassuring parent. But this made him more anxious because I failed to recognize his severe, subjective feelings of shame. Over the course of two years, I began to grasp his pattern of referencing an event that took place when he was a tween, which symbolized much of how he felt about himself. He only ever brought it up briefly and vaguely in session, but I attempted to catch it (like a butterfly), to hold it, and to help him to express it fully—which he eventually did.

In his memory, he was playing with an eight-year-old child, and at one point he wanted to hold him close, so he did. Suddenly, the client's older sister entered the room, and stared at him. "Her face and voice were chilling. Judgmental. Like I had violated the boy. She called out, 'What are you doing?'…I don't think I was harming him, but the shame she induced is still in me."

Over several weeks of playing with this narrative in my head, I came up with an opportunity for him to rewrite it. I had to keep in mind several sensitive factors: 1) If I was too validating he would remain anxious, fearing I was simply condoning the aspects of his behavior that he believed bordered on violating a child; 2) If I was too critical, I would simply join his sister and pile on judgment that made him feel "perverse" for having desires. But after trying out different versions of how the event could have gone differently, I finally landed on a narrative that would allow him to take responsibility for his actions without a life sentence of self-punishment for wanting to touch another body. The next time he brought up the event, I said in a grounded, nurturing, and calm manner (having rehearsed the delivery several times), "Your whole life would have been so different had your sister simply said, 'Careful. You're bigger than he is.' Right?" He warmed to this, and gradually developed the confidence to rewrite his narrative in future sessions, not only rethinking what happened in that fateful moment years ago, but also of reimagining his entire adult experience of sex, touch, and desire.

Edit

Most actors hate to be directed to say a line in a particular way—which is known as a "line reading." Likewise, most people hate to be told what we feel and think by a therapist—or anyone else. And yet, sometimes the words we choose to tell our stories are illuminated when another person says them. As Brecht said of both art and life, "The smallest social unit is not the single person but two people. In life too we develop one another."[17] I sometimes try to help my clients develop and clarify their narratives in a way I call *editing*.

Editing is a tricky word in therapy, especially since, for the most part, the client's experience takes priority over ours (What right do we have to edit their words?). But there are times when our collaboration yields a narrative that is closer to their intended expression of self than they could have achieved alone. I liken this to the times as a writer when great editors (like the friends, peers, and husband who gave me feedback on this book!)

cut, distill, or re-word a passage I've written in a way that not only better reveals my intended meaning, but allows it to sing. As writer/editor Susan Mary Malone says, "a great editor helps you hone [your] voice until it is truly uniquely yours."[18]

My husband and I once had a couples therapist who was a remarkably talented *editor*. Like a human "autocorrect," she could easily translate what each of us meant to say to the other in ways we could both hear. I have since been inspired to try that sort of editing with my clients. But since I will never be as good at this as our therapist was, I always acknowledge that my "line reading" will be flawed, and ask them to say it better in their own words.

My *edits* usually include words the client has chosen, even if they are not grammatically correct, as I presume they have chosen each word for some inspired reason. For example, a client might say she enjoyed the "pompousness" of an event; even if I think she meant to use the word "pomp," rather than to simply correct her, I might suggest that as someone who struggles with self esteem and who often desires to bolster her own self image, she may have indeed been interested in the "pompousness" she witnessed at the event. This comment not only draws her attention to the word choice, but also gives her the option to play with various ideas rather than to be stuck in one narrative.

In other cases, I may introduce a word the client did not use if I feel it will expand the truth of their narrative. For example, an actor client of mine, whose brother had recently died, described how his brother was one of the few people who offered him unadulterated listening and support. As a way to process his grief, my client channelled those qualities of his brother into the role he was playing in a professional production of a classic play. The character is typically thought to be a devious Lothario, but much to my client's delight, the audience seemed to like his otherwise unlikable role. When I performed my version of his narrative for him, I introduced a word to him. I said, "In making the audience **recognize** the empathic side of your character, you also helped them to **recognize** your brother, and to **recognize** you—the part of you that misses him. It sounds like he was one of the few people who truly **recognized** you, and you have honored him with your **recognition** of him in this performance." The following week he began the session asking, "What was that word you used last time?..." "Recognition?," I asked. "Yeah!," he said, as his eyes lit up. "That's it."

In still other cases, I might use words to describe the client's mimetic performance. For instance, if I witness a string of affect-laden facial expressions, I might say, "Now that's the silent movie version. What would the subtitles say?" If they just shrug their shoulders, I will share some suggestions.

One of the most extreme edits I made was for a couple who had been together for over a decade, and were struggling to communicate any of their true feelings to one another. This lack of communication kept them in a holding pattern of avoidance, with one escaping into his work and the other into late night partying. In session, they would both look at me, and rarely at each other. Sometimes I would say, "I guess you're wondering why I called you here…," to not only mirror their apparent "stage fright," but also to invite their participation through play. And though they often "Yes, and-ed…" me with humor in response, these exchanges only exacerbated their avoidance. One of them would summarize their challenges in wordy monologues from his head chakra, while the other would laugh uncomfortably, blink his eyes like a cartoon, and say in a high-pitched, comic voice, "I agree." Then they would look to me and ask, "What do you think?"

My eyebrows reactively furrowed as I strained to discern what was actually going on between them. I began to look away from them so I could actually hear what they were saying—and, more importantly, how they were saying it (their subtext)—without distraction. "I need to hear you like a radio play," I would say.

After six months of listening to their dialogue without visual distraction, I intervened with a provocative bit of narration. The more talkative client had spent the first half of the session saying his usual, "We are both stuck, but we both want the other one to be happy…" Suddenly, I interrupted: "But what do you *really* want to say to him?" Silence.

"Instead of all of those words you said over the past thirty minutes, you could have said one line." Silence.

The talkative partner finally responded, "I…I'm not happy. I…might want to…explore other options…"

"Yes," I said. "I think that's what you really want to tell him. But you're terrified of hurting him. And I understand. You've been together a long time. You love each other a lot. There is security in the life you've built together, and a primal fear of losing that. But I promise you both it will be a lot less scary if you can talk openly about how unhappy you are. You need to tell the other one how you feel without the fear of breaking them. This therapy space can help you practice that. But I don't think you can move anywhere if we don't start using the word *separation*."

Well, that woke them up! The following week, they both began by thanking me for my provocative *edit*, and proceeded to talk to each other directly. Their voices resonated in their solar plexus as they discussed what was next, and though separation was not necessarily their goal, the word got them talking. It was hard, painful, and sad, but also liberating. And there was a newfound security in their will to tell each other their truth. At that point, I could not take my eyes off of their performance.

Let Them Hear Themselves

The choice we make to let the client hear their own performance—and to be astonished and curious about it—is an artful form of editing (akin to the editing of a film, in which distinct meanings can be emphasized in an actor's performance by virtue of when the scene is cut). An example of this is our timing when it comes to when to end a session. When a client says something self-reflective and poetic, especially a revelation that has taken them years to discover—such as the man who is always moving apartments who says, "I'm learning that the deeper I grow my roots, the easier it is to transplant myself," or the woman who always needs to be told what to do, who says, "I need to be the choreographer of my own dance"—I might let that be the last line of our scene, so they can be their own audience.

Or, as is more frequently the case, I may choose to leave them with an open-ended line to reflect on, such as, "I know I should let people know that I'm here too…but I don't like to cause a fuss…"

14 Direct

Sometimes we *direct* our clients to take some form of action. But whenever we assume the role of director, we are also their scene partner. We can't tell a client what to do without playing a transferential character for them. To *direct* is to perform multiple roles by default, both in the private mind of your scene partner and in the interpersonal dramatic action that unfurls between you. Whenever I intrude upon my client's process with a specific direction, I therefore think of myself as a director who is also an actor.

A particular actor/director who inspires me is award-winning director Liesl Tommy. Her strong choices on stage and screen reveal riveting stories about a wide spectrum of people—especially those whose truth has been marginalized. I know first-hand what it is to collaborate with Liesl on multiple levels. We did our graduate conservatory acting training together, and she directed me in a play that I also produced when I first moved to New York City years later. More significantly, I also know Liesl as a living, breathing human, and her capacity to follow another person with compassionate curiosity while she simultaneously leads them with her own strong creative vision translates directly to her work as an artist.

I'll never forget one challenging day during my first year of drama school when I was only twenty. A teacher was trying to direct me in a scene in which my character was in conflict with his mother. Like a family therapist, my teacher wanted me to share my genuine underlying emotions with my scene partner, free of angry defensive tension. But the abrupt and gratuitous way in which they directed me to open up actually shut me down. The teacher had taken a prop letter that my character read in the scene and written highly specific, horrible names on it; ones that I had been called as a child—names which I had shared with this particular teacher in a private conversation, unrelated to school. When I opened the letter during the scene and saw what the teacher had written, I instantly felt unsafe, which only made me more defensive than before. I stormed out of the studio, and as I ran through the halls, I saw Liesl standing in a doorway, strong and grounded, with welcoming energy radiating from her heart chakra. Without thinking, I dove into her arms and cried.

"What are they doing to you?," she said in a compassionate, playful tone, as she held me. I told her everything. Only now, safe in her arms, was I able to release my inhibitions. I explained how I understood the teacher's intention, but also how their approach had sabotaged my trust, dignity, and creative agency. Liesl listened. I can't recall if she continued to hold me physically or not, but I remember somehow feeling entirely held by her as I spoke. "You got all of that out," she said. "You're gonna have a healthy life."

Liesl directs in much the same manner: Not necessarily by hugging each of her collaborators literally, but by using herself to make them feel safe enough to participate, openly, creatively, and expansively. She always holds her ground as a director, but she never forgets what it is to be an actor—like a therapist who never forgets what it is to be a client.

Here are a few different ways the actor/director approach helps me to direct my clients when that approach seems productive or necessary.

Dictate

Some performers/clients enter a rehearsal room/office wanting to be told where to stand, what to say, and how to say it. And depending on the circumstances and our clinical approach, we may attempt to give such a person the direction they demand. For example, if we follow the guidelines of a cognitive-behavioral modality, we may instruct someone with social anxiety to take deep breaths (see Chapter 5, and **Exercises V & VI**), prescribe a cardio exercise regimen for them, or assign readings to them on mindfulness and being present in their minds and bodies (see Chapter 4). And these directives may or may not reduce their symptoms of anxiety. But even if they do, this is only the first step. We will then want to play back the dailies of our interaction in our minds as our work progresses, and reflect on how that intervention has affected them. Did it shut down their will to participate, foster dependence on us, or empower them to explore and discover their own creative agency? Did it make them storm out of the studio, or encourage them to bloom in our arms?

Crisis Management: Obviously, if clients are in imminent danger, we must direct them to safety before we can work with them further. If they inflict self harm, make suicidal gestures, or pose a threat to us or another person, we have to tell (not ask) them to seek medical attention—or call 911 for them. As psychoanalyst/family therapist Virginia Goldner has said, there are times as therapists when we have to use our "enormous if implicit moral authority."[1]

For example, I once had to insist—with a grounded, confident use of my voice—that a couple move to separate apartments before we could work together because the risk of them being physically violent with each other was too great. They both agreed to these terms, like lost children in need of a guide. This arrangement allowed them to think in future meetings, and to hear each other without the impediment of fear, hostility, or angst. In this particular case, I did not need to know these people for very long before I gave that *direction*, as safety is always the priority, no matter what. Of course it's great if we get the opportunity to rehearse with our scene partners for a while before dictating such an unwavering prescription. Nevertheless, we can always reflect on the character(s) we become for clients whenever we dictate a safety plan, and be actively curious about the significance of that enactment between us. Did the unambiguous command represent secure, comforting arms to them—or a straight jacket from which they must wriggle free? We will never know for sure until we give future scenes between us time to breathe. Only then will the roles we play during those pivotal moments in the client's story take form through our scene work.

Symptom Management: As I have described above, there are myriad directions we can give to clients to reduce symptoms of anxiety, depression, anger, panic, or other forms of discomfort or distress. These include helping them to directly resolve relational impasses in their interpersonal lives.

Like the actor who needs to be told where to stand, how to stand, to sit, or to gesture before they can play freely with the other actors, some clients need such technical blocking in order to relate to their family, partners, and friends with mental and emotional freedom. Family therapy techniques like those developed by Murray Bowen are a great example of this kind of directing. For instance, there are times when we might advise clients explicitly to detriangulate[2] from family members, and specifically to refuse to talk to one family member about another in order to strengthen dyadic relationships in the family system. Or we might literally block a scene between partners or family members—i.e., tell the players where to sit or stand—in the playing area of our office in order to facilitate their interaction.

For example, while working with a teenager who was severely depressed and whose parents worried he might inflict self harm due to gestures he had made in the past, I chose to meet with all of them in various combinations. This way, we could maximize the potential of their scene work as individuals, as pairs, and as a group. When it became clear that the mother was a "scene stealer," and did most of the talking for all of them, I became laser focused on the symptom of tense, palpable silence between father and son. When I arranged a two-person scene with father and son, they stared at me like deer in headlights, frozen, waiting to be thawed by my direction. At one point the father said, "I just don't know why he would be afraid to tell us how he feels." In response, I not only directed him to say his line to his son directly, but more specifically, I asked him to shift his seat to face him as he spoke. In this new configuration, the boy could feel the warmth of his father's focus, and felt compelled to respond. "I guess I was afraid to hear myself say the words... 'Sometimes I want to die,'" he replied. The father could not help but receive not only the words, but also his son's emotional energy, given the open physical positions in which I had directed them to sit. He teared up. For a flash, he looked back to me, but I commanded him to *stay in there* with his son. As he looked back to the boy, the words came to him naturally: "It's better to verbalize thoughts like that than to keep them to yourself. Even if it's scary. It has less power over you if you verbalize it." The boy retreated, overwhelmed by the heightened emotions induced by the closeness of his father. But I directed him to *stay in there*. As they made eye contact, the father found his own flicker of inspiration to take the scene further. He moved closer to his son, put his arm on his shoulder and said, "Hey, you don't have to be afraid to tell me anything. You're everything to me." The boy teared up as he received this invitation. This was a message his father had intended to send to him for some time, but he needed choreography to follow it through.

Invite Creative Participation

As an actor, I find it helpful when directors show me a bit of their creative process as a way to deepen and expand my own. I do not necessarily want a line reading or to be told how to get from point A to point B, but it can be motivating, encouraging, and liberating when I am invited to play in ways I may not have thought to do on my own. For instance, a director might say "Your character makes me think of a sweet little dog who just wants to please her owner but keeps getting kicked. Does that resonate with you?", or, "I know this scene is sad, but let's try doing it like it's ridiculous, or full of rage, or ecstasy, or try it with an Australian accent, just to see what happens," or, "Try expressing non-verbally what you wish you could say to your scene partner, even though your character doesn't have lines here."

My version of this as a therapist often intends to direct my clients to choose words to describe feelings they have so far expressed only in sounds and gestures, or to encourage them to think of themselves as characters they must play. Actors have so much more fun playing people like Virginia Woolf, Margaret Thatcher, or Abraham Lincoln than those real people likely had living their lives. This is because actors have the advantage of looking at those lives with creative distance. Many actors love to talk about their process of identifying with another life, even with characteristics that are unlikable, agonizing, or inscrutable. As therapists, we can give our clients the wonderful creative opportunity to be both the living person/the character, as well as the actor. In this vein, I sometimes encourage clients to watch interviews with great actors like Meryl Streep, James Earl Jones, Viola Davis, Cate Blanchett or Daniel Day Lewis, and listen to the passionate curiosity they have about their characters—especially their interest in the characters' imperfections, flaws, and idiosyncrasies that make them challenging but utterly human. I then ask my clients to look at themselves with that same curiosity, to be creative detectives investigating their own lives, to enjoy the fun of asking themselves, "What's it like to be me?"

I may also model curiosity for them by asking follow-up questions about topics they would otherwise gloss over. For example, a gay client of mine who was extremely reserved with other people, including his close family, briefly mentioned his gay uncle who had died, and then quickly moved on to another topic, as if having a relative who shared his gay identity was insignificant. I interjected, "Was Uncle Seymour the only out gay relative you had?" "Yes," he replied, somewhat taken off guard. "But he wasn't really out. People just…knew. They never used the word 'gay.' But they always emphasized his eccentricities: he was 'rich' Uncle Seymour, or 'fashionable' Uncle Seymour, or 'garish' Uncle Seymour." As I shared my enthusiastic interest in all that had gone unsaid about Uncle Seymour, my client began to find the creative exercise contagious. His curiosity grew, not only about the aspects of his uncle's life that had been obfuscated, but also about aspects of himself. As we continued to explore this topic, he eventually said, "I guess by 'rich' they really meant, 'his life is better off closeted.' Which is *so* like my family. We are Jewish. And we have a history of hiding, conforming, and avoiding, to survive. That sort of thing percolates through generations of a family…"

Another way I encourage creative participation is to walk clients through a version of the energy meditation we discussed in Chapter 5 (**Exercise VIII**), and explore their childhood attachments and how those influence their use of body, voice, and self. This is something I direct my couple clients to do in particular because it helps them to appreciate each other's emotional histories in a safe, creative, and fun way.

For instance, after completing a meditation during which I ask each partner to imagine a childhood bedroom and who they see in the doorway, Partner A might say, "I didn't see anyone there. I only heard arguing in the next room." Partner B, on the other hand, may chime in with, "Both of my parents were there, watching my every move." Now we have evocative images to access each of their experiences of primal attachments. And we can play with these the next time they are in conflict. When Partner A insists, through tears, that Partner B is "rejecting" her pleas for help around the house, I can ask her to consider that Partner B may experience her like his parents, staring at him through his bedroom door. Or when Partner B is furious that Partner A won't "stop nagging" him, I ask him to consider that she may experience him like her parents, abandoning her as they argue in the next room.

I may then ask each of them to play the part of the other's defense attorney—to have fun with the role, maybe even impersonate their favorite *Law & Order* character—and to make a case for why their partner (or client, as it were) behaves the way they do. I encourage them to be empathic as they do this. If I sense one of them is too detached as they defend the other, I might play the part of "the judge" and say, "Council, I'm aware of the facts of the case… What I need is for you to walk in your client's emotional shoes. Make me feel what it's like to be them." This spirit of play allows us to go to emotionally challenging places while holding multiple perspectives and possibilities at once.

Encourage Emotional Commitment

It's easy for an actor to deliver their lines without emotional cost, personal investment, or with a vocal affectation that protects them from meaning what they say. But such performances deny collaborators and audiences access to the character's truth. Similarly, every one of us may be tentative to lay bare our emotions with conviction, even in therapy, for fear of getting rejected. Like actors, it's our *selves* we put on the line, and it's our *selves* the person sitting across from us invalidates when our feelings are not received (e.g., a client can so easily feel like an actor who is brutally rejected at an audition when we seem unattuned or unempathic). But when clients rise above their vulnerable emotions with defensive anger, humor, or intellect—or an odd contortion of their speech or body—like a compassionate director, we can encourage them to drop into their thoughts and feelings (without calling them the dehumanizing names they were taunted with as children, like the aforementioned acting teacher did to me).

For example, when I ask Partner A in a couple to reflect back what they heard Partner B say, I will listen not only to what they say, but how they say it. Is there a distance or judgment in their voice? Sometimes you can hear the trace of whininess in Partner A's version of Partner B (like a self-conscious actor who plays Ophelia with an affected voice that betrays judgment of Ophelia's emotional dilemma—caught between Hamlet and her father—rather than one that personally connects to her struggle). In this case, I would encourage Partner A to observe their sound, where their voice is placed in their body, and to reflect on why that is the case. I would then help them to say the words with their voice resonating deeper in their body, and to connect to the feelings as personally as possible; to drop in, to *stay in there*. I encourage them to use their imaginations if they must, but most importantly, to make sure they capture the essence of their partner/ character's feelings, no matter how foreign those feelings may seem to them. I may point out at these times that Meryl Streep did not agree with Margaret Thatcher's politics when she played her, but still managed to find deep levels of emotional identification with Thatcher's point of view.

Couples and families present more palpable opportunities for us to direct in this manner than do individual clients, though I also encourage individuals to speak their thoughts with conviction, from deep within their bodies, when I sense they are trying to rise above vulnerable emotions.

Direct Them to Direct Themselves

As long as everyone in the studio/the theater/the office is safe, we can direct by not directing, do by not doing. We can trust the players to not have immediate answers, to be silent, to breathe, to regress, make a mess, throw paint on the canvas, and figure out what they're painting as they go. We can trust ourselves to see them in all of their truth, and to hold their needs, desires, obstacles, strengths, gifts, and frustrations—the good, the bad, and the ugly—in our compassionate, curious minds. As Oscar winner Viola Davis describes her journey as an artist and a person, "It was good to see how other people see me, because then I began to have an inner gauge as to how to direct myself."[3] But it is not as easy as it sounds to make our clients truly feel seen.

To direct in this manner, we have to approximate my description of Liesl Tommy at the start of this chapter. We have to find enough of a sense of center, of our breath, of our mental, physical, and emotional presence, of our insight, intuition, and imagination to be confident in our own skin. Only then can we invite our creative collaborators to feel safely held in our rehearsal room.

For instance, one day my client Peter (who I described as having trouble breathing and living in Chapter 5) discussed his difficulty sleeping…which he linked to his overuse of his smartphone…which he linked to his over-abundance of ambition to move his career forward…which he linked to his childhood anxieties about not being good enough for his parents. He then looked to me, breathless and defeated, and said, "I have no idea what to make of all this."

"Don't you?," I said calmly and groundedly.

Behind my deceptively simple performance in this moment were the several years spent in rehearsal with Peter—trying, failing, failing again, and failing better.[4] During that time, I grew into the role of his much-needed scene partner,[5] a character that is part unconditional listener, recognizer, and validator, part tough love parent, part self-possessed gay man (with whom he can identify), and part creative collaborator. All of that history supported my simple delivery of that line.

"No," Peter replied, playfully defiant. I simply smiled back, patiently, still in character. He took a moment. Breathed. And thought about everything he had shared. Then he said, "I'm asking you for the answers, like I'm the student who isn't good enough. And maybe that's what I need to let go of. The role of student. After seventy years I do have some answers within me. I have to pull myself out of the rat race more often. To stop chasing the cheese. And appreciate that the reward is actually in my reach." He took another breath, "The real reward is to enjoy my daughter, my granddaughter. To enjoy every run I take along the beach. To feel the sun and the breeze on my skin. To enjoy my life while I'm alive."

I listened intently to every word. And as the session ended, I suggested that the exchange that took place between us—the dramatic dialogue,[6] including our words and our silences—was instructive for us both. It showed us that he can trust himself as much as I trust him to navigate his life creatively and meaningfully, and to live a livable life.

I effectively improvised an even more subtle bit of direction in a session with my adolescent client, Coco—whom I discussed in Chapter 8. Coco was experiencing severe challenges in her relationships with her peers, as well as her parents. Though in many respects her parents are great providers, they often fail to recognize or validate Coco's emotions, which has been devastating for her throughout her life. "I can't tell my mother when I feel hurt by her without her feeling criticized and reminding me of EVERYTHING she's ever done for me," Coco explained, continuing, "But on the flip side, she has no problem criticizing *me*…"

During a family session, I tried to help Coco's parents to recognize and mirror back her feelings to her, without letting their own feelings interfere. My efforts were mostly unsuccessful, but at one point, Coco's mother blurted out: "Look, I know you're having a hard time with your friends, but they're probably just jealous of you…I mean, you're not exactly the most unattractive thing…" I made eye contact with Coco just as her mother delivered this line, and we exchanged a nuance of a smile.

Ordinarily, Coco would have reacted to her mother with frustration at a moment like this, focusing on what she had missed (e.g., "Mom that's not the point. Can you at least acknowledge that my feelings have been hurt?…"). But something about our silent, dramatic exchange inspired her to stop, breathe, and reflect on the complexity of the scene.

In future sessions, Coco and I would eventually discuss the significance of her mother's comment—both her genuine attempt to compliment Coco and her limited ability to do so directly or with emotional openness. And although articulating these insights in words would prove to help Coco better understand her relationship with her parents, a far more pivotal event had already played out through our eyes (see Chapter 2) in that one brief moment. During that live piece of theater, Coco got to experience me witness her mother's love as well as her limitations allowed. Coco also received my implicit bid to play with these multiple realities creatively rather than to be stuck in a single one of them; she has since navigated emotional ruptures in her life with a similar approach. However, I can't take as much credit for her performance on the stage of life as I would like.

At our last session before she left for college, I wanted to empower Coco with my observation of her resiliency. I chose words I thought could be useful for her to hear, and attempted to deliver them without too much emotion of my own—so as not to replicate her familiar experience of her parents. I breathed, centered my body and voice, and validated her internal resources—specifically her capacity to stay connected to her parents while being able to survive them at the same time. But as I spoke, I realized that my grounded, calm, and simple performance belonged to her even more than it did to me. Throughout our years of rehearsal, Coco had listened this version of me into existence. Together we had materialized a caregiver for her who could say a lot with very little. A director who trusted her to direct herself.

15 Publicize

How does the internet impact the psychotherapeutic exchange? How do the growing demands for therapists to promote our businesses impact our thinking on self disclosure? What must we share publicly about ourselves in order to attract the clients we hope to reach? And how do we protect our privacy in the midst of all of this confusion?

Actors and other performing artists can help us to navigate these dilemmas.

I find that the more I participate in the creation of my online presence—like an actor who engages the public eye rather than one who runs for cover—the better. In one respect, it is necessary to *publicize* who I am, what I do, and how I do it, if I want clients to find me. But also, in my experience, clients tend to project and get things wrong about me no matter what I post or do not post about myself. At the very least, I can choose *what* they find about me in this age of too much information.

Pop performer Lady Gaga takes a similar approach to managing her public presence in a way that simultaneously attracts her desired audiences and protects her privacy. She calls it "art directing" her life.[1] I call it *The Lady Gaga Approach*. I recommend you try it too, and call it whatever you like.

As therapists today, we have much in common with Lady Gaga, and we can learn a great deal from her. Her awareness that "the public is almost always watching"[2] falls in line with psychoanalyst Stephen Hartman's observation that therapist self disclosure "happens all the time, whether you know it or not,"[3] and psychoanalyst Steven Kuchuck's insight that therapists "are never really invisible—even if they try."[4] If there ever was a blank screen in psychotherapy, the internet has surely torn it down, revealing more of our personal information to clients than we can control. Where we once thought disclosure was an action we could perform at will whenever we judiciously chose to emerge from backstage, we now find ourselves center stage without a curtain. And to disavow what our clients clearly see about us—on and off line—becomes a performance in itself, one of closetedness and shame, if not buffoonery—like the emperor in his new clothes (think movie star Frances McDormand shooing away cameras at the 2018 Golden Globe Awards, at which she won Best Actress, or Jodie Foster winning a lifetime achievement award at the 2013 Golden Globes, and *coming out* by insisting defiantly that she does not need to *come out*).

One way therapists can use The Lady Gaga Approach is by creating a website and making use of social media—on both a professional and personal level. This interface allows us to not only be aware of our online selves, but to craft them (not unlike what we discussed in Chapter 2: Know What You Look Like). On our website, we can decide *what* we share in terms of professional experience and expertise, and *how* we share it. Rather than simply reposting our LinkedIn profile or stating that we help clients reduce "anxiety" or "depression," or that we are trained in CBT, EMDR, or Existential Humanistic Psychotherapy, we can describe how and why we do what we do in our own unique voice. We can share articles and blog posts we've written, interviews we've done, and videos and podcasts of us speaking on topics that interest us. On our personal Twitter and Facebook accounts, we can share articles on mental health issues we care deeply about, pictures of us participating in social activism, performing music, or acting in plays. Such an online presence can give potential clients who vet us a sense not only of our expertise, but also our values and the kind of scene partner we might be for them.

For example, when potential clients flip through therapist profiles online, my gay identity is as knowable as the color of my hair. This identity is not presumed based on shards of my personal data scattered throughout the web, but because I have taken steps to assemble the puzzle for them every time I use words like "gay" or "husband" in essays, interviews, and social media posts. This clarity obviates an anxiety-riddled build-up toward a moment of "self-disclosure" in session. There is no need for me to "come out" to them because I'm already out, on my own terms. The same is true for my colleagues whose personal lives blend with their clinical specializations in terms of their religious journeys, racial and ethnic identities, gender expressions, HIV statuses, experiences navigating acculturation, adoption, or fertility issues, eating disorders, disabilities, or specific forms of trauma—just to name a few. By sharing personal reflections on their particular life experiences in varied ways online, they are able to *be out* to their clients before they even meet them.

In my own experience, *being out* online allows clients to show up to our first session with a sense of what to expect from the person who will listen to them each week. No matter their orientations or identities, my clients have the opportunity to know from the start that their therapist is an openly gay man who writes advocacy essays about women, queer lives, race, family conflicts, gender and sexual expression. Inevitably, not all of their expectations will be met when we meet—which we can explore clinically, as we will do with everything they bring to the playing area. But at least they know enough about me from the start to feel safe as we begin.

People want to cast someone with whom they feel a connection in the role of their therapist. They may even wish to select someone with whom they share a significant identity. But most importantly, clients want to work with someone they believe will recognize them and help them to feel alive. The internet gives each of us the opportunity to both show and tell prospective clients how we might be that person for them.

In this sense, clients are like casting directors who need more than an actor's resume in order to cast a role effectively. They need to see a headshot and have a sense of what the actor is like, both as an artist and a person, before calling them in for an audition.

And like Lady Gaga, most actors don't just sit back and wait to be called based on what other people have said about them. Instead, they make use of the public gaze to share various versions of themselves—e.g., in interviews, at events, and on social media. They understand psychoanalyst Stephen Mitchell's insight that, "There is no 'me,' waiting to be captured, either by an artist or an analyst or even by myself."[5] Rather than wasting energy trying to be anonymous when they are out of character (though some actors do try this, just as some therapists shortsightedly believe they can successfully create a "blank screen"), they take the bull by the horns and communicate with audiences directly via the internet. Ironically, this active use of the spotlight not only protects the actor's privacy (who needs to know where they eat breakfast when you can engage with their blog, vlog, or Twitter account?), but it also gives them some agency in how they are perceived.

Rather than sit back and let our personal information become narratives written by other people, therapists can create our own online selves, just as actors do. We can foreclose the moments of "getting caught" backstage by choosing what to share via social media, whether in the form of personal essays we have written about our own identity struggles, or pictures of us marching for someone else's rights.

And perhaps even more importantly, we can get ahead of our anxieties about *being out* by approaching our lives and our work as though our naked selfies have already been seen.

Anxiety About Being Out

Though many therapists have an active online presence, many others actively do not. There is a collective anxiety about "self disclosure" in our field due to decades of discussions about its pitfalls. No doubt, the more that is known about us, the more challenging it can be for our scene partners to dream us into the characters they want us to play. As Meryl Streep says, it is a burden to start a new job with the reputation of being "the world's greatest actress" preceding her, "like a big gorilla before I arrive on set, and I have to escort him out and introduce myself."[6] Similarly, therapists share a collective anxiety about our work becoming too much about ourselves and not enough about our clients. A memorable *Saturday Night Live* sketch comes to mind in which a psychoanalyst repeatedly pops up in her patient's free associations, invading his stream-of-consciousness with, "And I'm here too."[7] We laugh because this invasion is precisely what we all hope to avoid: the client should not be more concerned with the therapist than herself. But no matter how much our own presence, desire to be known, or narcissistic qualities make us cringe, we are there whether we acknowledge it or not[8]—regardless of our relationships to social media. I suggest that we minimize the potential obstacles that our subjective presence contributes to the therapeutic situation when we acknowledge it, check it, and harness and make creative use of it,[9] both on and offline.

Participating in the construction of my own public presence has become second nature for me. My years as an actor have certainly helped with this process, but so too has being born a gender nonconforming gay male in a homophobic world; hiding was never an option for me. I once had a chuckle when a senior psychotherapist gave me some critical feedback on a clinical paper I wrote, encouraging me to take a page from "experts" in the field who believe self disclosure should be deployed carefully and minimally—all of whom happen to be straight white men. Perhaps these "experts" understood disclosure to mean one's choice to reveal personal information—e.g., whether or not to wear a wedding ring to the office—and that by not making that choice they would appear to be perfectly blank slates. I, on the other hand, never had the privilege of such a choice—as a therapist, an actor, or as a proto gay boy. If I didn't want other people to narrate my life for me based on societal stereotypes, or to spend all my energy trying to hide/pass/cover/closet myself for fear of being "outed," I had to show people who I was. And like many queer people, I learned that working *with* my authentic self was much easier than working against it. Ever since I left the closet behind at age sixteen, I have found that being open about who I am takes the spotlight off of me and directs it onto the subjects about which I am most interested. The more practice I have with this process, the easier it becomes for me to exist—and therefore, the easier it is for other people to exist in my presence.

Ultimately, what does it matter what clients think they know or do not know about us as long as they feel they can exist freely in our presence?

I believe our own anxiety about self-disclosure gets in the client's way more than the disclosure itself. As psychoanalyst Steven Kuchuck writes, the still relative paucity of literature on therapists making use of the internet, may in part be explained by how uncomfortable it makes us feel.[10] Furthermore, he opines that the surrender we feel when our clients try to know us—when they catch a glimpse of us backstage and want to process that with us—can get too easily confused with masochistic submission and loss of power. In other words, our anxiety about not being able to control the uncontrollable—or to effectively hide inside the emperor's new clothes—may disrupt our scene work more than any other aspect of *being out* online. This dynamic is true for all of us, regardless of our identity or orientation. Straight, white, "normative" therapists are also only a Google search away from public scrutiny. All therapists must choose how to portray ourselves to our potential scene partners.

Clinical Benefits of Being Out

I believe we can be inspired to turn our anxiety into creativity—to art direct our lives—by looking to our predecessors. Therapists who had marginalized orientations and/or identities are particularly inspiring and instructive, and had no choice but to grapple with questions of being out vs. closeted.

For example, Charles Silverstein helped make a place for queer people in mental health in 1973 by advocating for the deletion of homosexuality from the DSM, and, founding an LGBT-affirmative psychotherapy clinic and a scientific journal about queer lives. Being out himself was a huge factor in these achievements. Not only did he inspire many therapists and clients to extricate themselves from the "pernicious effects of hiding in the closet,"[11] but he also spurred profound changes in clinical practice. Gone were the days of whispers surrounding the psychotherapy closet—such as those about Harry Stack Sullivan, who founded interpersonal psychoanalysis and was never out in his lifetime. In the years since, influential psychoanalysts like Richard Isay, Ken Corbett, Jack Drescher, Mark Blechner, and many others have increasingly made room for a variety of LGBTQ+ people in psycho-analysis through their clinical work, their writing, and by virtue of simply *being out*. As Mark Blechner has said, "The understanding of homosexuality could not have advanced were it not for the contributions of openly-gay and lesbian psychoanalysts."[12]

Blechner has also noted that it wasn't until psychoanalysts wrote clinical papers from a feminist bent—including Jessica Benjamin, Nancy Chodorow, Jody Davies, Muriel Dimen, Virginia Goldner, and Adrienne Harris—that attitudes toward women changed significantly, observing that "[t]he greatest strides in our understanding of the psychology of women [has] come from women psychoanalysts."[13] Significantly, Jessica Benjamin paralleled the movement in psychotherapy from a *one* to a *two person* model, with the awakening of women in our culture (mothers in particular) as active subjects from their former designation as quiet, containing objects—not unlike the classic psychoanalyst. Benjamin emphasized that as the therapeutic relation-ship reconfigures to recognize the therapist's subjectivity, it actually provides more opportunity (not less) for the client to collaborate in the therapeutic process, and to *out* herself as a subject, separate from the therapist.[14]

Legendary singer Joni Mitchell describes a similar parallel process between her role as a performer and her audience. She says, "The trick is if you listen to [my] music and you see me, you're not getting anything out of it. If you listen to that music and you see yourself...you'll learn something about yourself, and now you're getting something out of it."[15]

When my prospective clients find me online, they typically see themselves—whether they are queer, or straight men who want to work with a "sensitive" man, or straight women who want to work with a man who is "safe." And for the most part, they need very little of my help to get something out of our scene work. But when they do, I encourage us both to carve out reflective space with our own, individual curiosity (much as I described in Chapter 12). I invite them to participate in our co-created performance, to art direct their own lives, to be seen while seeing—to say to themselves, to me, and to the world, "I'm here too."

16 Present

Academic presentations are often boring. This includes the ones we give as psychotherapists (Google "academic presentations are boring," and behold the endless commentary on the subject).

Much like a boring therapy session or a boring scene in a play, a boring presentation indicates a block between scene partners—in this case between presenter and audience. The performer has somehow denied their listeners an invitation to engage in the event with their own creative imaginations. As presenters, we too often take our audience for granted. We lack interest in who is listening or how our performance affects them. And while in the rehearsal studio/therapy office we get to explore how and why we impact each other and learn to be more present and collaborative over the course of weeks and months, when we're at the podium with a mic, a crowd, and twenty minutes to speak, we don't have time to discover why we fail to connect. Our scene partners either feel invited to the party or they do not.

I find that to present my work effectively, I must keep my audience awake and invite them to participate in a live, transformative event. When we are open and attentive with our collaborators, our presentations can expand our own minds, not just theirs, and deepen our understanding of our work, our clients, and ourselves.

Actors and other performing artists can show us how to make the most of our presentations; they can help us to receive our audience's observations even as we share our own, and to not only perform, but to listen, reflect, and mutually exchange ideas.

Here are a few actorly guidelines I use to help *present* my work in different mediums.

Ask "Why?"

There is nothing to fear about performing for an audience if you know why you are doing it.

"Why?" is the first question great theater directors ask when they begin work on a play: "Why this play, why now?". Similarly, before I do any kind of presentation, I ask who is listening, what story I want to tell them, and

why that story is interesting, relevant, and necessary? The answers to these questions become my core intention and guide me through the storm of inevitable obstacles such as stage fright, fear of failure, criticism, judgment, embarrassment, or shame—or even technical problems like a bad mic, low attendance, or a large, cranky, crowd with an especially low attention span.

We get lost in the smog of fear when we don't create a lighthouse of intention. We fear "looking stupid," "bombing," or getting "eaten alive by the crowd." We then shield ourselves with the lifeless words of our "scripts." We read our scholarly papers (in their entirety) defended with a veneer of intellectualism, with a dull voice that lacks resonance and breath support—because, as we discussed in Chapter 5, to breathe is to risk experiencing a range of feelings, including vulnerability. We indulge in monotonous, guarded speech that lacks enough varying emphasis, color, or imagery to effectively translate our abstract thoughts into a live event. Or, on the flip side, we might focus all of our efforts on being entertaining, with the singular goal of *not* boring the crowd. We pander with bells and whistles and animated PowerPoint slides, which can be great if those pyrotechnics actually invite our listeners into the stories we wish to share. If not, they are merely shiny distractions from our fear and their boredom—they address a surface symptom, but fail to solve the underlying problem.

Similar dilemmas occur in therapy, plays, and movies when participants reflexively mask their fear of rejection with surface solutions. This includes clients who fear they will bore their therapist if they don't entertain them or present them with a "worthy problem" to "fix." The same is true for therapists who offer "quick fixes" to prove their worth, as well as actors who play a scene for superficial laughs or tears.

The key to avoiding these traps is to prioritize the live connection between everyone present as opposed to assuming the role of wise sage to your audience's empty vessels, or the role of shiny star to their groundlings. It doesn't matter if the performance takes place in an office, an arena, a parking lot, a conference room—or whether there are elaborate props, proper lighting, or a fancy set. What does matter is the connection between you and your scene partner in real time. And that connection is born from your confidence of knowing *what* you want to say, *who* you want to say it to, and **why** you want to say it.

Prepare

Once we specify our intention, we can prepare our instruments to perform it. Before I do any presentation, I always prep my body and voice to help me connect with my scene partners. To that end, I choose from the various exercises (see **Exercises**) discussed in Act I of this book. Knowing what we look and sound like (as per Chapter 2 and 3) and our tendencies as idiomatic individuals—as well as the content of our intended presentation and the medium in which we will perform it—helps determine what we should work on.

For example, as I prepare, I keep in mind my tendency to shrink before live crowds. Without preparation, I will likely apologize for my presence and speak with deference—a tightness of my vocal cords, a shortness of breath, a lack of energy in my center, and a pinched, nasal resonance. My core will collapse, posture get slouchy, shoulders tense up, and jaw tighten from smiling too widely—a reflexive attempt to beg my listeners not to judge me for wanting their attention. At that point, the words I speak don't matter because everything else about me will scream, "Don't look at me!"

Fortunately, years of my own therapy and acting training help me to get ahead of all this, and to choose exercises that prepare me to be confident, clear, and generous in my live presentation. This includes a grounding meditation (**Exercise VIII**), breathing deeply and freely (**Exercises I–VI**), and transforming the tension in my upper body to energy that can flow from my chest and core down to my feet. As I do this I allow my mind to imagine listeners with whom I want to connect. This exercise helps me to present a confident body and voice that invites attention and participation as opposed to one that pushes people away.

If I'm preparing for an on-camera presentation, I do these same exercises, but I also address how tense and overly expressive my face can get, especially when I am caught between many thoughts (as is my tendency), which can be distracting for a screen audience. I'll want to loosen my jaw muscles, practice speaking one thought at a time with clear diction, practice breathing between each thought, and remind myself how much is conveyed to an audience onscreen simply through the presenter's eyes and facial muscles—and therefore how important it is to have clear, focused thoughts in mind, and to truly listen to how I am received.

It's easy to underestimate the importance of this kind of technical preparation—but don't. As public speaking coach Terri Trespicio has said, "Be really, really prepared. Don't mistake being unprepared for being 'authentic.'…The most prepared speakers are the most comfortable and 'seem' casual, but they're not—they're confident."[1]

Rehearse

I like to type out a list of bullet points before my presentations, as well as questions for my audience—which reminds me that my endgame is not to share conclusions, but to invite discovery. I then rehearse various ways to share those thoughts. As I rehearse, I keep in mind aspects of other presentations I have seen that inspired me, bored me, repelled me, or left me wanting more. I imagine a live audience, or I practice speaking to a camera if the presentation will be on screen, and remind myself that when I actually do it, live subjective beings will be on the other end, receiving everything I say and do—not unlike in a therapy session or acting performance. I might also try out bits of my presentation on another person (I often share some of my key points with my husband over dinner, without him realizing what I'm doing, or I may work it into conversations with peers). I take notes on what seems effective, what lands for various people, what opens up creative thinking, and what does not, not only in terms of the words I choose to say, but how I say them—the variations of tone and emphasis I use in my speech, the timing, and the pauses I take for effect. I practice supporting my voice and speech with breath, and try to maintain vocal energy through to the end of each thought. I also try to use pitch to clarify my points, and to create images and events out of my words—keeping in mind the listener's experience of my delivery. If some thoughts seem vague or unclear, I ask myself if this is a problem I can fix technically through my voice and speech exercises, or if there is something that can be sharpened in the underlying thought I'm trying to share—in which case I will revise the words I plan to speak.

If the presentation will be filmed, I pay extra special attention to the distinct points I want to make, the exact words I want to say, and the way I want to say them—since there will only be one take, one cut-and-print, and I will have to live with what I say and do forever. I also rehearse potentially provocative questions I might be asked ahead of time to prepare myself to not be thrown off my game by saying something which I don't necessarily mean or haven't fully processed and which could undermine my intention.

Through this process of repetition, I give myself the opportunity to discover the most accessible ways to share my message. I also allow the presentation to become muscle memory. This way, when it's showtime, my mind and body have a map of where to go, no matter how rocky the ride. Most importantly, this preparation gives me the confidence to look each of my live scene partners in the eye and invite them to engage with my ideas and questions, no matter what actually happens.

Collaborate

"The audience is my collaborator,"[2] says actress Glenn Close, and this is true for me as well. This means that when I am face to face with my listeners, I loosen my expectations for the presentation and adapt what I rehearsed to create a connection with particular participants in a particular moment. I practice being present (as per Chapter 4), the same way I try to find my way into an improvisational dance with each client in session, each actor on stage, or each neighbor I bump into when I run in the park.

This does not mean I simply throw out my preparation. We need our technical prep work to be confident when we're in the hot seat. After all, "Craft," as Glenn Close says, "will keep you at a certain level of performance. But from there," she adds, "you are always searching for nuance."[3] That nuance can only be discovered between yourself and others when you are present.

"To be a compelling speaker," says professor/writer Randy Laist, "you must adjust your delivery to suit the audience. A face-to-face encounter requires at least a minimal degree of rhetorical improvisation, which is unavailable to a speaker reading verbatim from a prepared text."[4]

Likewise, when I face my live audience and take in their unique, subjective gazes, I adapt my technical preparation in order to connect with them. I emphasize chosen words with my use of pitch, not to "blow them all away" with my impressive speech skills, but to invite each of them into my ideas. And though I enter the presentation with an intention or superobjective, I don't take for granted exactly how I will generate each thought, each sound, in each moment, or how each thought will hit each person. Instead, I remain alert and receptive to the energy that comes back to me, and allow that dynamic to motivate my next thought, my next sound, my next move. Again, in the words of Glenn Close, "You set up literally an energy field and you shoot [a thought] out into the audience. And they shoot things back, and then it becomes this great exchange."[5]

It is in this unique, live exchange of energy that we can discover potential truths about our clients, our work, and ourselves that would otherwise remain unavailable to us. This is only possible if we allow ourselves to be present with our listeners and accept that our unique idiosyncrasies will affect them no matter what we do or don't do. The ways they respond to us, both explicitly and implicitly, gives us valuable information to take back to our clinical work and to our lives.

The best illustration of this concept is actors playing real people. For example, as I discussed in Chapter 10: Play, Meryl Streep doesn't magically bring the actual Margaret Thatcher or Julia Child to life when she plays them any more than we share completely accurate depictions of our clients in our case presentations. Nor does Streep merely perform her roles precisely as she rehearsed them at home when she shows up on set. She ultimately finds the idiomatic truth of her characters in response to her live scene partners. "I take my entire performance from them,"[6] she has explained of her process. From this performance and our personal reactions to it, we are given a window into Margaret Thatcher and Julia Child that neither Thatcher, Child, Streep, her scene partners, or any one of us in the audience could have found alone.

In this same sense, we can think of our presentations not as conclusive dead ends, but as transformative opportunities. After all, the whole point of our job as therapists is to engage participants in a reciprocal dialogue, not to bore them to death with complicated lessons. When we (are) *present*, we can show and not just tell our scene partners and audiences about our work.

17 Take a Bow

The scene work of therapy transcends our offices much like a performance lives beyond the walls of the theater. The relationships we cultivate in our intimate time together—between performers, audiences, and characters—do not terminate, but evolve inside each of us.[1] And though the visits to the therapist end and not the therapy itself,[2] we still must face one final live moment with our scene partners and decide what to *do* with it.

As the curtain closes on each treatment and each session, I always wonder how I can best help each client transition from the safety of our mutual presence to the world beyond. What can I do to remind, encourage, and inspire them to take all of our scene work and its reverberating effects with them?—all the hope and dread, the playfulness, frustration and despair, the verbal exchanges and shared silences and that which has been performed and processed as well as that which (for now) remains inchoate.

As clinical performers, how do we effectively **take a bow**?

Intend

Separations of any kind remind us that we can't be together forever, and there is no perfect way to gloss over that fact. What we can do is *intend* to remain in each other's minds and hearts after we part. And we can let that intention shine through our words, gestures, and eyes.

It took me years to trust the simple power of my intentions, both as an actor and as a therapist; even today, I still have to remind myself to trust them.

The instant a play ended, I would feel naked and anxious without the protective shield of a character and a story. I would have to walk across the stage as myself (which actress Helen Mirren calls the most difficult thing to do as an actor), and acknowledge the audience with a gracious bow that would hopefully send them on their way with an enduring reminder of the event we shared. If my bow had too much technique or flourish, it could be jarring, more about me than about *us*. If it was too casual, it could read as an apology for my efforts, and discredit the whole play.

I was equally anxious as a rookie therapist during the final moments of sessions and treatments. If I was too technically precise as I wrapped things up, I risked disrupting our natural flow or impeding the client from choosing their own ending. But if I was too loose and open ended, I might disorient them.

Yet having learned to think of my work as an art over the years, I now let go of the need to "get it right," and instead engage in a daily practice of craft (after all, as therapists we call our business a "practice"). I have come to accept that as performers, *what we do* in each millisecond is less important than *how we think about*[3] *and practice* what we do on a continuum (Much like the endless challenge of being in the present, as per Chapter 4).

Just as my years of practice as an actor have taught me to be present when I take a bow, regardless of my exact moves, the same has proven true as a therapist. Sure, my timing may be off when I say, "Our time is up," or my voice may betray ambivalence about cutting clients off as I fumble through broken sentences like, "Oh no, look at the clock…," or "And, on that note…," or I might even impersonate one of my former therapists with a verbatim line reading such as "We ARE out of time," spoken with breathy stodginess. And all of these idiosyncrasies may elicit nervous laughter. But I realize now that the discomfort is not necessarily born from me and my inadequacy as a clinician, but more from our mutually unsettling awareness that the intimate scenes we co-create must fade to black. Even if I could smooth over that harsh reality with a perfect-ten performance, it would be in vain. On the other hand, rather than try to "get it right," if I **intend** to acknowledge our collaboration and its potential to endure inside me and my scene partner, they may receive that message on some level—whether through my explicit performance, or through my subtext, of which I may not even be entirely conscious.

Even if my parting word choice or delivery does not effectively summarize our work over the years, my intent might still appear in my eyes or the tone of my voice. It might also appear in a whole range of ineffable efforts to show my deep appreciation, respect, and love for my scene partner, as well as my confidence in their capacity to carry on without me. And if, upon reflection, I feel my intention is unexpressed even after we say goodbye, I can convey it with a follow up email—perhaps when I send a final bill or receipt. Further, I can trust that if and when the client next reaches out to me—either to ask for a referral, share news, or to resume meetings—my intention can appear in the way I receive their contact. Again, no matter what I do or do not do, I can intend for my underlying message to acknowledge the following: **"The time we had together is valuable. The work is yours, take it with you. We can always work together again, if you choose. But either way, what we have done will always have a life of its own inside both of us."**

To illustrate this sentiment, let's compare and contrast two screen performances of a *goodbye*. First, Winona Ryder as Spock's mother in the 2009 feature film, *Star Trek*. Spock is a science fiction character who is half human and half Vulcan—a creature that is ruled by logic over emotions—and his human mother symbolizes the imperfect, emotional side of him. Though Ryder is literally only on screen for a few minutes, her presence is felt throughout the film just from one flicker of her eyes during a short scene in which she sends her son off into the world with love and confidence. And though there is nothing particularly sophisticated or polished about her use of voice and body, her internal connection to her character's intent is palpable and moving. There is almost something meta about Ryder in this role since she is an utterly human, inconsistent actor who has been guided more by instinct than technique throughout her career. Her career stands in contrast to the work of an actor like Cate Blanchett, whose palpable technical discipline—vocally, physically, and analytically—allows her to perform with more versatility, gravitas, and consistency than Ryder, but who also can lean too far in a technical direction and "perform" with a capital P. But to be fair, Blanchett typically performs with both masterful technique and emotional depth, as she does in her Oscar-winning portrayal of Katherine Hepburn in *The Aviator*. For instance, in a scene in which she breaks up with her lover, Howard Hughes (played by Leonardo DiCaprio), Blanchett impersonates Hepburn with a polished, over the top, musical precision of diction (like a top-notch drag queen). The effect is almost alienating as she delivers her brusk lines to end their affair. And yet, her love, compassion, and intention to maintain a connection with Hughes radiates genuinely through her eyes. In contrast, many of Ryder's performances can seem like messy rehearsals that never quite take shape. But when Ryer does find moments of connection with her characters, however erratic her process, she, like Blanchett, forms an extraordinary human connection with her audience. Both of these actresses show that when an artist's underlying intention is put into practice, it finds its way to her scene partners regardless of her tendency to pay too much or too little attention to technical perfection.

Fortunately for us as therapists and clients, neither our messy rehearsals nor our grandiose performances are filmed, packaged, or sold as entertainment. As artists, we have the advantage of being able to reflect on our technical and empathic imperfections in the safety of the rehearsal room, and to use that awareness to strengthen our connections with one another even as we separate. And we get better and more natural at such parting moments the more we put our intentions into practice.

Award-winning actor Willem Dafoe has observed that "[t]he older I get, the less I want to be an actor who seems like an 'actor'"; similarly, the older I get, the less I want to be a therapist who seems like a "therapist"—especially when the curtain falls on a long-term, therapeutic relationship.

Have Faith

Faith in our intention is often the only bow we get to take as performers. Audiences may exit the theater mid-show, or clients may discontinue therapy abruptly, leaving only a curt email or no explanation at all. Wonderful as it is to share a cathartic end to a dramatic journey, we cannot take such neat closure for granted as performers. Part of our job is to never know how effective or appreciated our work will be. But much like we practice being present, we must also have faith that our intention to help our clients will reach and inspire them, even if we do not receive the instant reward of their applause.

We practice such acts of faith in each session, not only when we say "Our time is up," but whenever we feel the palpable sting of differentiation from our scene partner. Each mini-separation of sorts prepares us for the inevitable super-separation, however and whenever it may arrive. Every misunderstanding about payment or cancellation policies, every empathic failure, and every defensive wall between us conjures feelings akin to those that arise at termination—e.g., fear, embarrassment, longing, frustration, resentment, rage, sadness. But we also learn to have faith at those times that no matter how distant we may feel from one another, our relationship will ultimately have value and meaning for us both—even if it takes years before we understand how. Similarly, actors must have faith that even their toughest crowds will be influenced by their performances in various ways throughout their lives, whether or not they clap during the curtain call.

Robin Weigert performs this act of faith in her sublime portrayal of a therapist on the series *Big Little Lies*. For most of the first season, her character creates a safe holding environment for her client, a survivor of domestic abuse played by Nicole Kidman. As the two of them plan Kidman's escape from her husband, they seem joined in a therapeutic dance, what Jessica Benjamin calls a rhythmic third. But in the season finale, as Kidman storms wildly into Weigert's office to declare an abrupt change of plan, they are torn apart. Weigert reaches for Kidman reflexively in an effort to reconnect, as well as to calm and comfort her. But this gesture only triggers Kidman to scream, "Don't touch me!," as she storms out, leaving them in what Benjamin calls a doer/done to dilemma.

How will this event affect their relationship? Will Kidman permanently break with Weigert and discredit all of their work? Will she return next week to repair the rupture? Or will she discontinue sessions but take the fruits of their relationship with her—the good and the bad, the comfort and the conflict, the "Yes, ands..." and the "Nos!"? Like Weigert's character, we can only wonder, theorize, and wait to see what happens next.

In a personal conversation, Weigert told me she received feedback from viewers that her character seemed like a great therapist until she touches Kidman—an arguable boundary violation for a survivor of abuse. She then explained that the touch was not in the script, nor was it her own instinct as a performer, but the director told her to do it on the day they shot; Kidman reacted to it instinctively, leaving Weigert feeling ambivalent, both as an actor and a "therapist." But I told her that I, for one, found that pivotal scene to be credible. The dramatic circumstances are far more heightened than a typical session, and who knows what any of us would do in the moment if our client was in such imminent danger. I also said I felt connected to her character, despite the questionable touch, due to the palpable clarity of her intention to care for her scene partner, even if it could not be received or appreciated in the moment.

Like Weigert, we all at times try dramatic actions, sometimes against our natural instincts, which divide us from our scene partners. And if we don't get the chance for a do-over, we can at least have faith that they will receive our intention on some level, eventually, and make use of it. Again, refusing our help is sometimes part of that process.

As Benjamin has observed, recognition requires differentiation, not just oneness.[4] And as Robin Weigert's grandmother, psychoanalyst Edith Weigert wrote, years before, therapist and client should aim to swing between identification and "a differentiating and detached object relationship"[5] in order to prepare for the end.

And though we may never know the extent of the transformational impact our scene work has on former clients, we can use our own experience as a proxy.

Like all artforms, therapy is an apprenticeship profession. We learn our craft by absorbing the work of mentors, peers, and a variety of artists. And through years of integrating all of that inspiration into our own practice, it eventually becomes *us*. For example, ten years after I graduated from drama school, I could finally use the techniques, relationships, trials, and failures I soaked up at that time to reveal *me*, not just my ability to *act*. I came to realize that this was what my teachers had intended all along. I had a similar awakening through my journey as a client in therapy.

I was at a pivotal point in my life and had been without a therapist for some time when my father passed away. I then found myself caught in a toxic web of dysfunction with several family members. I have since discovered that many, many people experience this kind of crossroads. To play your role the way your family of origin expects of you is to feel dead. But to assert yourself in a way that feels awake and alive is to feel guilt for saying "No," for playing "against type," and for separating from the ensemble of stock characters with whom you were raised.

As I sat alone on a beach at sundown, I felt like the Little Mermaid, caught between two worlds—land and sea, past and present, my family and myself. I thought of my last therapist—not only what she would say, but how she would say it, how she would look at me, her comforting energy. Most significantly, I recalled the emboldening trust in me and my instincts that she conveyed through her ineffable subtext.

But could I trust myself?

I imagined how I might maintain connections with my family without being harmed by them. I breathed in the loss of the past, but also the strength of being centered in the present. I breathed in the many people in my life with whom I have cultivated secure relationships, and consider to be my family, my future. My therapist had no idea how our rehearsals and performances would save me that night, years after our last scene. As the waves crashed, I breathed in the bitter sweetness of being alone in a liminal space, yet deeply connected—in two places at once.

18 Audition

Audition: to give, watch, or listen to a short performance that tests whether a performer's skills are suitable for a particular event.

(Cambridge Dictionary)[1]

No sooner do the lights fade on one transformational journey, than they rise on another. Such is the life of every performing artist. We feel the pang of separation from one scene partner as we *audition* for the privilege to collaborate with someone new.

Audition skills are often taught toward the end of drama school because, crucial as they are to get a job, they do not necessarily help us navigate the untrodden rehearsal process we enter once we book the role. In fact, the inherently myopic mindset that helps us nail the audition can, ironically, undermine the creative openness we need to embody our roles over time.

In some cases—such as productions with tight schedules or short-term, symptom-focused psychotherapy treatments—the director or client will expect you to perform in each scene exactly as you did at the audition (or *initial consultation*). But this situation is the exception. In most cases, the audition is merely a means to an end: a formal performance that helps directors and clients make informed guesses as to **who will be the best fit for the role they need to cast, who will rise to the specific challenges their project presents, and who seems trustworthy enough to embark on an intimate, collaborative, uncharted voyage with them**.

Here are some of the ways my experience auditioning as an actor helps me perform *initial consultations* as a therapist.

Be Prepared

The greatest obstacle to a good audition is fear. A casting director once told me, "If they smell fear on you, it's over." But how can you avoid fear when you are being scrutinized, evaluated, and judged by another person? In short, you can't. But you can manage it by being prepared.

The first bit of audition prep I recommend to any performer—in order to minimize fear and help focus both you and your scene partner—**is to remember that whoever you are meeting** *wants* **you to succeed.** Producers, directors, and clients won't necessarily show you this desire explicitly. But part of our job is to know that deep down, they want, if not need, us to solve their casting problem no matter how intimidating, disinterested, or devaluing they appear on the surface. This thought helps me focus my energy on each prospective client's presenting problem, rather than to needlessly stress about how inadequate a provider they might find me to be.

For the actor, this kind of prep includes memorizing your *sides* (the lines you've been asked to perform for the audition), and then asking yourself what the character wants in the scene, what various tactics they will use to get what they want, and what various ways they will listen and respond to their scene partner as they get or do not get what they want. Without asking these questions about your character, you will enter the audition armed only with what *you* want and your fear of not getting it. Your performance will then, by default, tell the story of an insecure actor who desperately wants a job, though the role may be an empowered leader who commands respect by doing very little.

As a therapist, the closest thing I have to "sides" are the questions I have for prospective clients after listening to their initial emails or voice messages. The questions I prepare for each "audition"—which, for me, is a free twenty-minute phone consultation—are derived from my years of experience doing psychotherapy intakes (e.g., What does this individual client want? What is their mental health history? What are their relationships like with family, friends, and romantic partners? What are their stressors and strengths?). I also have specific questions in mind tailored to the content of their first message. I consider not only the particulars of their reported struggles, but also their gender and gender expression, race, sexuality, love life, ethnic origin, family, and career status. I wonder what they hope to gain from our scene work (and what conversations they want to have,[2] as Adam Phillips puts it), what they fear could go wrong between us, and why they may have chosen me specifically. Then, I prime myself to listen for implicit clues about all of these things as we talk. The specificity of my compassionate curiosity here not only helps me focus on the purpose of the exchange without anxiety about my "performance" being judged, but, more importantly, it similarly invites the client to participate free of self-consciousness.

Another crucial bit of audition prep I recommend is to remember that auditions are imperfect procedures intended to predict the unpredictable, and therefore we must not overly internalize their outcomes, one way or the other.

For example, the director who casts you may have reduced their idea of a great performance to the actor's capacity to use a deep, resonant voice, which you happened to achieve brilliantly at the audition, only to prove during the rehearsal several weeks later that your voice is not enough, and that the emotional depth that the character must express is beyond your immediate skills. Likewise, the client who says "you're the one" with excitement sets you both up for a let down several sessions in when they realize they feel just as hopeless talking to you as they do talking to their emotionally distant parents.

Ideally, we hope that our scene partners will accept and appreciate that a creative process entails disappointments, detours, and missteps along the way. But if they don't, we need to remind ourselves that **process is more important than product**, and that we alone are not to blame for their unmet expectations.

No doubt, many directors and clients blame the performer for not delivering what they promised. Rarely, if ever, does it do us any good to defend ourselves with logical observations like, "You were expecting the impossible. How can I produce exactly what you envision on the first try? I'm not psychic. That's not how this works. I need space to play so that we can figure this out together over time." This will only fan the flames of mutual victimhood, and keep us stuck in a "doer/done to" dilemma.[3] But at the same time, it equally does not behoove us to submit to their proposed narrative that we are complete "failures" unless we give them exactly what they demand, on cue. This is particularly difficult given that they often don't know exactly what they want.

What they actually want, of course, is for the scene to work. And if it doesn't, they will find a symptom to blame, whether or not it addresses the underlying problem (e.g., the director who says, "Something's not right… can you butch it up a bit?…", or the client who says, "I'm frustrated. I thought you were an expert on this topic…you're supposed to tell me what to do").

I try to get ahead of all of this by accepting in advance that I will inevitably be disappointing in some way at the audition—and if not, the disappointment will come eventually. I try to accept that the director or client won't necessarily agree with me about the reasons for said disappointment, and then I try to have a sense of humor about all of this as I do my best to give them what they want in the most authentic way I can—using my unique instrument. I try to be in two places at once: with their desired outcomes and respecting my own process.

As an actor, this means that when the director says, "This character is like a drill sergeant, he's gotta be in charge," rather than think, *ooh, I'm awful. I'm not right for this. I better impersonate the actor from Full Metal Jacket,* I breathe and give myself a moment to adjust. I then interpret what the director is actually asking me to do—which, in this case, is very possibly just to find more grounding, authority, and conviction within myself than I currently appear to possess. Then, I give the scene another go using whatever specific flicker of inspiration I think will get me to that place in a genuine and interesting way—as opposed to tensing up defensively and becoming a wooden stereo-type of a "drill sergeant." For example, as I read the lines, I might find the innate assertiveness I have when I command my male cat to stop bullying my female cat—which I often have to do, and which conjures a familiar side of me that is not only in-charge, but also infused with my unique sense of passion, concern, and love. The director need not know how I made the scene work, how I increased my status[4] and brought their "drill sergeant" to life, or how I may have even transcended their idea of the character by portraying someone more layered and complex than they could have imagined on their own.

As a therapist, this could mean that during a consultation call, when a client says, "I know what my problem is: I self sabotage. But I don't need to talk about my childhood. I just need to get out of my own way. Can you help me?," rather than think, *uh oh, I don't have the skills they need, I better impersonate an uber-confident CBT therapist, life coach, or self-help guru,* I breathe and give myself a moment to adjust. Then, I interpret what the client is actu-ally asking of me—which, in this case, is very possibly just to assure them that I am actively listening to their unique concerns. Next, I give the scene a go, using whatever specific flicker of inspiration will help me to attune to the client genuinely in the moment—as opposed to tensing up defensively and becoming what I presume to be their idea of a "behavioral therapist." For example, as I ask the client questions like "Have you had therapists in the past who focused on your childhood? What was that like?," and say things like, "I do think I can help. A lot of our work will be to give you the oppor-tunity to share your struggles with me in a safe environment. We'll also come up with strategies to get you out of your own way," I might imagine myself talking to a friend who just found out that a reckless bully was elected presi-dent of our country. In such a moment, that person would not find it the least bit helpful to be analyzed or to hear clinical explanations for *why* this bully was elected. More than anything, they would need their feelings to be validated, have assurance that steps will be taken to help solve their problem, and in the meantime, they must feel safe enough with you to explore the uphill battle ahead of them (This particular scenario is, of course, familiar to me, as I had to support friends, family, clients, and myself through the American presidential election of 2016). The client need not know what made the audition work, how I brought their desired "life coachy" character to life, or perhaps even how I transcended their idea of that character by personalizing it for myself.

Remember this as you prepare to audition: Nothing matters more than the foundation of trust we establish with our potential creative collaborator. From there, we can begin our rehearsal process. We may stick to the original objectives we discuss in that twenty-minute call throughout the therapy process, or we may discover new objectives altogether, but our creative alliance is what will yield the healing transform-ation we both seek.

See While Being Seen

Like actors, therapists sometimes forget that we are auditioning the other person as well. While actors must remember to inquire about the demands of each prospective job, and what measures will be taken to promote safety, respect, and fair compensation, therapists too must determine with whom we are working, what they are asking of us, and how we feel about this particular arrangement.

As we ask detailed questions about the client's symptoms and mental health history, for example, we may discover that we do not have the training or resources to accommodate them in our practice, and may need to refer them to a more specialized setting. We also may want to do some minimal vetting in the way of an internet search, just to make sure they are who they say they are (one can never be too sure these days, in the age of "Fake News," "Fake Profiles," and "Fake Identities"). I also tend to do a brief scan of social media to see if I have any mutual connections to the client. This helps me determine if working with them might compromise them or me in some way. And if you feel uncomfortable about undertaking such a digital search, just remember, your client has already done one on you; this is the world in which we live.

Show *And* Tell

It's not only what we say or do in auditions that matters, it's how we do it: how we enter the room, or the call, how we take or do not take direction, and more generally, how we get along with other people.

When I was much greener, I would stress about every word I said in a consultation. I wanted to be sure to convince clients that I was a consummate professional who knew exactly what he was doing. Now, with the confidence of experience, I focus more on setting up a basic frame for our potential collaboration, on finding a genuine rapport between us, and on trying not to get too hung up on what I say or don't say beyond necessary due-diligence (e.g., asking about medication, hospitalizations, and thoughts or attempts of self-harm). For example, during a recent consultation on a very busy day, I found myself distracted and fumbling over my words. *This guy must think I'm an idiot*, I thought. But after breathing, apologizing through my humiliation, and finding my way to the present, I was able to tell him what I had heard him say so far, and how I had heard it. "Huh," he said, "I guess that's right. I never thought about it that way before." This was not at all how I had hoped the audition would go, and yet, it showed the client what our rehearsal process might be like together better than I could have described in words. I showed him that even in a moment of distraction, I could recover with humility, apologize, and let him know that above everything else I am listening.

It's also important to remember that we are showing people what kind of therapist we are all the time in the way we interact with every person in our lives. The explicit and implicit ways we engage another therapist— or a doctor, bartender, friend, friend of a friend at a party, or LinkedIn connection whom we've never met—informs them what it might be like to be in a therapy scene with us. And they will recall that information when they consider referring us to someone in their life. In short, we are always auditioning, whether we intend to or not. With this in mind, it behooves us to listen, to know what we look and sound like, to stay present, breathe, and move and speak with a genuine connection to ourselves and to other people as we inhabit the world.

Please use any of the suggestions I share with you throughout this book to help you feel like *you* in your life, work, and art. And if my suggestions don't help you feel more authentically yourself, find something else that will. As Stanislavski wisely and passionately encouraged all performers, "create your own method, don't depend slavishly on mine. Make up something that will work for you. But keep breaking traditions. I beg you."[5]

Now, get back to work—and this time, don't forget to play.

Epilogue

MY CLIENT: *[At the start of a video session] Wait…I can see you, but I can't see myself.*
ME: *[Playfully] I know. That's why you're in therapy. We're working on that very thing. [We laugh]*

"Because art is important," I say with an exaggerated Australian accent. I have surprised my client, Emily—a painter—with an impromptu impersonation of Nicole Kidman winning the Academy Award, back in 2002.

I remember that night vividly: Kidman was wearing black in sorrowful solidarity with the troops who were deployed to Iraq, and their families. As I re-enact this moment for Emily, I emphasize Kidman's message: that our creativity is worth sharing with one another, even in the face of disaster and loss.

Only later, upon reflection, will I realize what I am up to with this improvisation. I will think back to the moment just before I said, "Because art is important," and recall Emily asking, "Why should I bother to paint? If the world blows up, who's gonna care about my painting?" And I will better understand my response to her (including my Aussie accent).

I want Emily to recognize that both she and her creativity are important. I also want her to laugh, and to know that she is not alone—that I am with her, even if the world blows up. If she doubts this, at least she will have my portrayal of Nicole Kidman to play in her mind. And maybe, just maybe, my idiosyncratic performance, and my intention behind it, will inspire her to make other people feel less alone—as she does for me each week with her humor, her unique observations, and her art.

My client Wade sits across from me, more despairing than usual: "Are you watching *Big Little Lies*?," he asks. "It's a show about women who appear to have perfect lives but… Nicole Kidman's character is in an abusive marriage, and when her husband hurts her she justifies it. There are some amazing scenes with a therapist…"

I too am in despair. After years of working together, I fear I am not helping Wade. But I make note of this TV show he mentions—a playful invitation for me to access him.

It's Sunday night and I am working feverishly on this book—trying, failing, failing again, pulling out my hair. My husband Justin suggests I stop working and start playing. As my primary scene partner in life—the person who knows me best—he had encouraged me to write this book, and now with equal confidence he recognizes it's time for a break. I feel the loss of accomplishment as I close my laptop and surrender to the couch. "What do you want to watch?," Justin asks. "How about *Big Little Lies*?," I suggest, thinking of Wade.

As we watch I'm enthralled; the therapy scenes jump off the screen. The actors listen to each other with their entire bodies. The silences between them are burgeoning with conflict, fear, hope, and possibilities. "Who plays the therapist?"

I write to Robin Weigert, the actress who plays Nicole Kidman's therapist on *Big Little Lies*, and whose performance captivates me inexplicably. This is a bold move as she doesn't know me, but I feel roused to engage her in a dialogue about acting and therapy.

Meanwhile my sessions with Wade open up. With the therapy scenes in *Big Little Lies* as a playful reference, we are able to talk more openly about his pain, as well as possibilities for him to live a livable life.

Robin writes me back. She invites me to send her pages from my book. I do and she reads them—attentively, generously—the way she listened to Nicole Kidman in their scene work. As we exchange dialogue by email and phone, she lets me know not only that she understands the ideas I have put forth, but that she connects to them personally. She tells me that her grandmother, Dr. Edith Weigert, was a formidable foremother of psychoanalysis—who held her own in debates with Freud about gender equality!—and that Edith believed psychotherapy is an art in and of itself. Robin tells me that her father, Edith's son, was also a psychoanalyst, and that creative artists greatly influenced his life and work. She agrees with me that the role of listening serves a similar function in both the art of acting and of therapy. She asks me guiding questions to help me connect with my intended audience. I receive her responses—I am both validated and transformed by them. I send her new pages that could never have existed without her listening—her empathy, her self-awareness, and her sense of play.

She sends me feedback just as Nicole Kidman wins the Emmy Award for *Big Little Lies*. In her acceptance speech, Kidman shares how indebted she is to her "scene partners," including Robin.

I am in a weekly reading group led by psychoanalyst Lewis Aron—a master of the art of teaching. We discuss his book about clinical "scene work," *Dramatic Dialogue*, and a particular chapter on psychoanalyst Howard Searles—who was known to be provocative if not offensive, despite his great influence on the art of therapy. As Lew discusses the history of Searles, I retreat into the role of empty-vessel student, not expecting to be impressed by this repellent man's biography. Lew tells us that when Searles began to train as a therapist no one wanted to work with him because of his odious comments and behaviors. But, he was encouraged by his supervisor—a woman who recognized something creative and generative in him, beyond his alienating remarks; a quality he could use to help other people see themselves. "Her name," Lew says, "was Elizabeth Weigert." I wake up. "*Edith* Weigert?..." "Oh, yes, that's right...Edith." I have been invited into this scene. I tell Lew what I know about Edith—based on what Robin has told me, and the literature I have since read by and about her—and I receive what Lew knows of her as well. The fact that "Dr. Eda," as she was affectionately known—pioneer of empathy, equality, and creativity that she was—saw potential in Searles, helps me to consider him from a different perspective.

Robin writes to let me know that our dialogues have made a significant difference in her "ever evolving understanding of why being an actor has value." She tells me I am with her, "in a sense," as she films challenging new therapy scenes on *Big Little Lies: Season 2*.

She is also with me as I write and rewrite.

Each day I discover new roles to play with my clients, as I invite each of them to perform their own lives.

And when I return home, I carve out intentional time to be with my husband. I take pleasure in *his* creative projects, even as I bombard him with my own. And we watch TV together, on purpose.

I continue to find and expand myself through other people, in art and in life. I observe how we all inspire each other's capacity to create and to live, through our attention, imagination, and generosity. We learn and relearn that our very existence matters, through the presence of listeners, audiences, and scene partners—some of whom we may never meet.

And speaking of scene partners, I haven't forgotten *you*, dear reader. I am writing this in what is your past while you are in my future, but we have been present together throughout this journey. These stories, ideas, and images are yours now; ours. No matter how they have affected you, I trust you will do something creative, generative, and loving with them, in your own unique way.

After all, you're here too.

Exercises

No artists are above keeping their physical apparatus in order by means of necessary technical exercises.

(Constantin Stanislavski, *An Actor Prepares*, 1946a, p. 172)

I. Book Rest (Drawing 1)

This is known as the "semi supine position" in Alexander Technique.[1]

- Place a book, 2–3 inches thick on a comfortable surface on the floor. Rest the back of your skull comfortably on the book. Make sure that your head is not pushed too far back or too far forward.
- Bend your knees and place your feet flat on the floor in front of you. Think of your knees pointing towards the ceiling. Let your back rest flat on the floor, and allow your neck to release. Notice if you tense your muscles to keep your back or neck in place; let that effort go, and allow gravity to do the work.
- Without *doing* anything, notice if your shoulders and neck tense and from the control center of your head, give your body directions to release that tension. Give your body the directions to lengthen and widen. *Do* by *not doing*.
- The release of your neck allows your head to release subtly forward and up so that your head is not tightening back and down, which then gives the message to your spine to lengthen, your back to widen and your breathing to open.
- Notice breath flowing naturally in and out of your body, and allow it to fill your ribs and diaphragm—just observe this, don't do anything physically to force your breath. As you allow breath to enter and exit, notice what is happening in your body in the here and now. Give yourself the direction to get out of your own way. Let the body breathe you.
- Allow the breath to seem as if it is visiting the seat bones as well, so that your whole back breathes.

- Give your back and ribs the direction to lengthen and widen as breath enters and exits. Allow your body to expand and contract naturally, as if you are a happy baby.

II. Baby Pants

- Stand with your feet hip width apart, shoulders relaxed—you might want to shake your body out and flail your arms and legs around a bit, to let go of tension.
- Open your mouth wide, as if you're looking at a baby. And if you think about it, when we make wide open faces at babies, we're actually sort of *being* the baby—joining them where they are, and showing them how to take their natural excitement, or *flicker*, a little further (an engagement between adult and baby that some psychotherapists call reverie, which transcends verbal communication—and can also occur between therapist and client, actor and scene partner, and actor and audience.)
- Exhale short and fast on the whispered sound of "ha." Try to surprise yourself. Make the sound in reaction to something random and exciting, the way a baby might react to a happy thought, a familiar face, or a shiny toy. Focus on the exhale, the "ha," and then notice how your body involuntarily takes air back in. Allow the incoming air to fill up your rib cage, but don't force it; don't *do* anything on the inhale. Exhale your staccato, whispered "ha" again, and again. Keep your intention in mind each time.
- Speed this up a bit, so that you're fully panting like a baby. Let the rhythm have a life of its own. As you continue, intensify your intention—like the happy baby crawling closer and closer to her destination—and as your excitement increases, let the breath fill your lower ribs and back. You can even put your hand on your diaphragm—the muscle just between the lower ribs—to feel it expanding and contracting as you pant. This will give you a very intuitive sense of how your body wants to breathe, from the diaphragm, without any extraneous effort, pushing, or tension.

III. Fly in Place (Drawing 2)[2]

- Stand with your feet hip width apart. Let your hips be stacked directly on top of your feet, and your shoulders directly over your hips. Let the entire bottoms of your feet flatten onto the ground, and surrender them to gravity. Let your knees be relaxed and springy, and your core/lower abdomen to slightly engage, so that if you were surfing or standing on a bumpy train, you would find balance.
- Imagine helium-filled balloons tied to each of your wrists. Allow the balloons to float your arms forward and up, without any muscular effort. Notice your shoulders wanting to help lift your arms, and let that tension go. Allow the balloons to take your arms with them.

- As you float, bend slightly at the waist, and let your torso follow your arms forward and up. The bottoms of your feet remain entirely secured to the floor and your core continues to engage. You would fly away if not for gravity.
- Notice how your body automatically wants to breathe. Allow air to fill your diaphragm, and find the natural rhythm, "the pulse." Observe the tension in your ribs as your body breathes, and release it. Breath will naturally enter and exit on "the pulse," as you continue to float forward and up, and as your feet, and legs continue to ground down into the floor. Let the air rush in on its own, all the way to your lower back, with no muscular effort. Let the body breathe you.
- After a good minute, imagine the balloon strings cut, and let your wrists drop. Followed by your elbows. And, with your feet still planted and held by gravity, let your head roll forward and down your spine, vertebrae by vertebrae, until you are fully bent over at the waste.
- Imagine you are hooked up to a harness at your coccyx that swings you from side to side. (**Drawing 3**). Then roll back up, slowly, vertebrae by vertebrae.
- Repeat these steps two more times. Each time see if you can let even more tension go, and allow more breath to expand your lower ribs more and more. Think of being strong with breath as opposed to tension.

IV. Vacuum

As an acting coach once said to me, "If you do nothing else before you go onstage, *Vacuum!*" True to its name, this exercise literally turns your diaphragm into a vacuum, allowing your body to automatically fill up with air without effort.

- Stand with your feet hip width apart. Stack your hips over your feet, and shoulders over your hips.
- Exhale completely. Notice your diaphragm cave in as it empties the last of its air.
- Now, hold your nostrils closed with your left hand, reach toward your left with your right hand (forming an arch with your arm) and lean your torso to the left as far as you can go, as you bend at the waist.
- Be present. Allow yourself to be pulled by gravity in two directions at once. Live in this dynamic contrast, but not long enough to pass out.
- When you're ready, let go of your nostrils. Air will involuntarily rush into your diaphragm. Let your upper body roll down your left side and around to the front of your body, until you're hanging over your waist, facing your shins. Imagine a harness around your waist that swings you from side to side. (**Drawing 3**). Roll up, slowly vertebrae by vertebrae. Repeat on the right side.

V. Breath Capacity

- Find a sense of center. (See **Drawing 4**). Inhale on a count of ten. Think of the breath expanding your rib cage.
- Hold the breath on a count of ten, keeping your ribs expanded. As you do this, try to think of holding it deep in your body, and not in your throat. (Sometimes it helps me to imagine that my torso is actually one long throat. This releases tension in the upper body, and engages the core. You can also watch yourself inhale in the mirror—to see what you look like, as per Chapter 2—to get a clearer sense of your lower ribs expanding).
- Keep your ribs expanded as you exhale on a count of ten, and use your hands to push against them. This will strengthen your intercostal muscles and ensure that you are using your diaphragm.
- Repeat a couple more times. As you challenge yourself to take in more and more air, and to expand your ribs wider and wider, remember to find a personally motivating ★flicker★ each time.[3]

VI. Breath Control

- Find a sense of center. Inhale on a count of four.
- Exhale on four counts, using a "sh" sound. As you exhale, imagine a lit candle in front of you. You want the flame to flicker as you exhale, but not to blow out entirely. (You can also use a real candle).
- As you repeat this, gradually increase the exhale counts and decrease the inhale counts, so that you work toward taking quick expansive breaths.[4]

VII. Structural Center (Drawing 4)

- Stand with your feet hip width apart. Stack your bones on top of each other: hips directly over ankles, shoulders over hips, ears over shoulders. (Note: Try to do this without effort, and find an intentional, internal flicker of motivation to stand this way, using images that inspire you.)
- Let the back of your head be pulled by an imaginary string, and at the same time and in the same way, let your chest be pulled forward. In this dynamic state of moving in two directions at once, allow your core to engage.
- If there is a mirror or reflective surface nearby, check out what you look like (as per Chapter 2), so you can get both an internal and external sense of your center.

VIII. Energy Meditation[5]

A) Energetic Center

- Stand with your bones stacked, as in **Exercise VII,** and with your eyes closed. Let yourself breathe naturally.

- Observe the tippy top of your head. Notice the tension there. Now imagine that tension transforming into free flowing energy. Give that energy a color of your choice.
- Let the colorful energy drip down the back of your head and the front of your face, transforming all muscular tension into energy as it moves. The energy releases your jaw; your facial muscles; your neck and throat.
- Observe the colorful energy dripping down around your shoulders and upper back, as well as your torso; your mid back; your lower back; and your abdominal region. This area, between shoulders and lower back is particularly tense for most people, so pay extra special attention to the tension there, and take your time transforming it into energy.
- The color also drips down your biceps, elbows, wrists, and fingers. It drips into your buttocks and pelvic region, and moves down your thighs, into your knees, your shins, and calves, into your ankles. The energy then spreads throughout your feet, your toes, and the balls of your feet.
- At this point the color becomes a grounding, energy cord, that sinks into the floor beneath your feet. There is no need for any tension in your body at this point, whatsoever, as the grounding cord is keeping you sturdy, poised, and connected to the earth through your heels.
- The grounding cord sinks into the foundation of where you're standing, into the earth below that, and the sediment below that. All the way down through the layer and layers and lava, until it reaches the center of the earth.
- The center is filled with white light. Take a moment to be there, stay there, and let yourself breathe.

B) Emotional Center

- From the bright white light of the center of the earth, imagine yourself on a bed from childhood. Is there a door? Is it open or closed? If open, imagine someone looking in the door at you. Look at their face(s). Notice all the subtleties of their expression, and take that in. How do you feel?
- Let that feeling carry you to an open outdoor space from your childhood. Imagine yourself moving freely through this space, however you would naturally want to move.

C) Poise and Possibility Without Tension

- Let all of the feelings you experience transform into the colorful grounding cord once again. Imagine it moving up from the center of the earth through the lava and layers and layers of plates and sediment, through the earth, into the foundation of the building you are in, into the floor, and let it absorb into your feet.
- Let the energy have a life of its own as it moves from your feet up your ankles, into your calves and shins, up through your thighs, and pelvis and

buttocks, up your fingers, wrists, elbows, and biceps, your lower back abdominal region and torso, through your upper back and shoulders. Your neck, the back of your head, your jaw and face, up through the tippy top of your head. You should now have a sense of your entire body filled with energy, with poise and possibility, and absolutely no tension. Let the body breathe you.

D) *Energetic Self States: Chakras (Drawing 5)*

- From where we left off—with your colorful energy radiating from the bottoms of your feet up through the tippy top of your head—put the palms of your hands together and rub them for about twenty seconds. Slowly pull your hands apart and notice the hot energy flowing between them.
- Move your hands down to face the front of your thighs, and move them around behind you to face your tailbone, and then back again. Observe the energy in this lower part of your body, rooting you to the ground. This is your **Root Chakra (#1)**, and is associated with survival, stability, grounding, and the foundations of your life. What is it like to be grounded? Is this familiar to you or is it a new bodily experience? What does grounding do to the rest of your body, and to your sense of self? Do you feel more in charge than usual, more secure? Or is it painful to connect to the ground; does it bring up doubt and insecurities? Let your body breathe as you experience this and consider the times in your life when you are more or less grounded than others. Consider the reasons for this. And then consider the same for other people in your life.
- You might want to refresh the energy field between your hands at this point, so rub them together once again. Then face them toward your groin/pelvis/lower abdominal region. This is your **Sacral Chakra (#2)**, and is associated with your sense of openness to new experiences, sexuality, emotion, and the capacity to derive pleasure from your life. What is it like to experience an open energy flow in this area of your body? Is this a part of yourself that you keep open in the company of other people, or do you shut it down, and if so in what ways do you shut it down? What happens to your body when you block the energy in this region? What happens to you physically and emotionally when you open it up? Consider people in your life who seem very open here, or closed off, and consider the reasons for that.
- Move your hands up to face your upper abdomen/stomach area. This is your **Solar Plexus Chakra (#3)** and is associated with confidence, power, will, self-worth, and self-esteem. Let yourself breathe, with energy radiating here. Very often we over compensate for our lack of energy in this region by emphasizing other areas of our body, e.g., such as puffing out our chests or tightening our shoulders, or straining our throats and raising our voices unnecessarily. But when we genuinely

experience confidence in our bodies, it is in this chakra. What is it like to experience this part of your body? Where in your body do you tend to compensate for confidence? Keep this in mind for the future, so that you can radiate true confidence in various situations, at will.

- Turn your hands toward your chest and feel the energy flowing between your hands and your body. As you breathe, observe what it's like to live in this part of your body, with energy radiating but without muscular effort. This is known as the **Heart Chakra** (**#4**), and is associated with love, healing, affinity, and generosity. Consider the times you operate from this part of your body, and the times you shut it down, and consider the same for other people in your life: e.g., family, friends, clients.

- Move your hands up to your throat, and as you breathe and feel the energy there, let any remaining tension go. This is the **Throat Chakra** (**#5**), and is related to our creativity, perceptiveness, and authentic self expression. We tend to tense throat muscles in an effort to control how we are heard and perceived. In fact, this is one of the major areas in which we overcompensate when we lack confident energy in our solar plexus. Notice what it's like to let your throat tension go, and to let energy flow freely here. Consider the people in your life who tense their throats when they communicate, people whose voices are nasal, shrill, or otherwise strained (as my own can often be), and contemplate reasons for that.

- Rub your hands together again, and face them toward your forehead, right between your eyes. This is your **Third Eye Chakra** (**#6**), and is associated with thought, intuition, and imagination. We tend to clench the muscles here—like my client Peter furrowed his brow, as I described in Chapter 5—when we don't trust our intuitive mind, and instead cling tightly only to our logic and intellect. But by allowing energy to flow freely here, we can access and make use of a greater range of mind.

- Move your hands to the tippy top of your head. This is your **Crown Chakra** (**#7**). This is our connection to higher power, spirituality, sense of wonder, and all things greater than ourselves. Think about the times in your life when this is open. What does it feel like to have this part of you open? Think of the people in your life who tend to be more open here than others, and consider the implications of that.

IX. Idiomatic Gesture

- After completing the **Energy Meditation** in a quiet space, begin to walk around freely. Don't think, just walk.

- Notice how you walk: e.g., your pace; where you are tense and where you are relaxed; where you are heavy and where you are light. As you move, observe what happens to the energy in your body. Where is it most present or absent?

- Think of a spontaneous/psychological/idiomatic gesture for one of your clients. (Perhaps the way they furrow their brow when they speak; or the particular ways they blink or widen their eyes or curl their lip, when they listen; or the way they use their hands in an effort to make you understand something). Choose a movement that affects you. Either because it is puzzling, annoying, irritating, tickling, titillating, sweet, pathetic, elating, or evocative in any other way. Do the gesture as you walk. How does that feel? How does it affect the rest of your body, from your head to your toes? As Viola Davis says, "When you're acting, you're feeling everything—every last receptor in your body is alive, one-hundred percent alive, and you're not hiding anything because everything is used as a tool to make the character a fully realized human being."[6] Along these lines allow yourself to have what improvisation expert, Viola Spolin, calls an *organic response* to the gesture: a "head to foot response where mind (intellect), body and intuition function as one unit."

- As you continue walking, let the rest of your body become the client's body. Where are they heavy, tense, and/or guarded? Where are they light, relaxed, and open? What energy centers do they tend to live in? How is that different from or similar to your physical life?

- What do those similarities and/or differences imply about you and about them? What is your/their body trying to say? What are their bodies trying to protect? What do they desire? How do they go about getting what they desire? (These are what Michael Chekhov referred to as *Leading Questions*,[7] which help actors to cultivate their imaginations, and increase personal connections to bodily experiences outside of their own range of everyday self.)

- Observe where your/their body is blocking or contorting what they want to say (along the lines of a "False Self"). Exaggerate those areas of the body as you move. What does that feel like? Consider any blocks or splits between body and mind due to some specific form of trauma[8] the client may have experienced. Imagine walking through the world like this?

- Note: When I guide actors/clinicians through this exercise together in group workshops, they get the benefit of experiencing how the presence of other people influences the ways we live in our bodies. You might try to embody your client while taking a yoga, pilates, dance, or some other movement class, so that you can play with the creative reflections, inquiries, and explorations I suggest above, in relation to other people, without anyone necessarily knowing what you're up to.

X. Take a Seat (Drawing 6)

This exercise is based on Utkatasana (or "chair pose") from yoga,[9] which is Sanskrit for "intense and powerful." This word in itself reminds me to be poised, active, and engaged in the stillness of my seated body, as opposed to collapsed, lifeless, and unfocused.

- Stand with your feet about hip width apart, exactly as you do to find your center.
- Let your hands float forward and up, similarly to Exercise III, so that your arms are stretched out in front of you.
- Let your knees bend and ever so slightly and take a seat into an imaginary chair.
- As you sit back, find center anew in this position. Smile, throughout your body as you do this. Allow yourself to breathe into your center. With each inhale, take in something interesting, inspiring, and/or nourishing, real, or imagined—(e.g., a happy puppy on a beach, the smell of fresh lavender, the sound of a loved one's voice). With each exhale, let go of unnecessary tension in our body and static in your mind.
- As you sink deeper back into the chair—without letting your knees get in front of your toes—continue to find center and feel the energy redistribute throughout your body. This will ensure you are not hurting your knees or back, and will keep you focused on the action of taking a seat—the action of listening.

XI. Sound Mind and Body

A) Find your Voice

- Begin with your *sound check* from Chapter 3. Keeping that self assessment in mind, do whichever of the breathing exercises (**Exercise I–IV**) best help you to find your natural breathing rhythm. Blend this with the exercise to find your *physical center* (**Exercise VII**), and of course, approach all of these exercises with the guidelines for *being present* from Chapter 4.
- Move into the *Energetic Center* meditation (**Exercise VIII**), maintaining awareness of your inhale and exhale as you go. Consider what the sound of your voice tells you about the tension in your body, and do your best to locate and convert that tension into energy.
- You will likely have tension in your jaw, so press the joints of your pointer fingers into your jaw muscles (the masseter muscles, just behind your cheeks). Massage those muscles around in circles. Then take hold of your chin between your thumb and pointer finger, and gently open and close your mouth with it, releasing sound as you do.
- Let the energy from this jaw workout turn into a color and flow into your body. Where is energy most vibrantly present in your body at this moment, and where is it absent?
- Allow colorful energy to flow throughout your whole body, notice how that affects you, and try to *stay in there*.

- With a sense of center, and a sense of your energy flow, do the breath *Capacity* and *Control* exercises (**Exercises V** and **VI**). Keep in mind where tension continues to block your air flow—based on your self assessment of sound and your energy meditation—and see if you can continue to turn that static tension into dynamic energy as you breathe.

- You might also see *what you look like* in the mirror as you breathe, as per Chapter 2, to get an external sense of where your body expands, and where you are blocked. Use this information to help yourself breathe more deeply into your lower ribs and back. This will increase your breath support, which will help you to vocalize—fully, naturally, and without effort.

- At this point I like to envision myself inhaling from various parts of my body to help me get a sense of ease and flow throughout my whole instrument. This is based on Kristin Linklater's suggestion to keep the body "light and diaphanous" so breath can move in and out freely, and to simultaneously "imagine mouths opening out from each part of the body"[10] as you breathe—especially the low parts, as that will help you to support your voice.

B) Use Your Voice (Drawing 5)

- Move into the *Energetic Self States* exercise (**Exercise VII: D**). Rub your hands together and feel the energy radiating between them, and then hold your hands in front of your thighs and pelvis/around Chakras #1 and #2.

- On your next inhale, allow the breath to enter as if from that region of your body, and as you exhale, release sound in the form of a long open vowel. Allow the energy in that chakra to vibrate as you do this; you can even put your hands on your body to feel the vibrations there.

- As you vocalize, be reminded by Patsy Rodenburg's, "God doesn't mind a bum note."[11] Don't try to make a perfect sound. We're trying to connect to our bodies in a truthful way, and to express intentional sounds from there. If your voice is tense or blocked in some way the first time, allow yourself to breathe more deeply the next time, and use your imagination to open up your instrument and to specify your flicker of inspiration even more. Remember, *the present*, and *your center*, are not static states; they are dynamic, and always moving toward something.

- Imagine the energy in your body as a color, as you did in the last chapter, and as you exhale on the vowel, imagine the air and sound as that color, as if you are painting the world in front of you with your voice.

- Ask yourself what it is like to make sound from this part of your body. What feelings come up? Do you feel like your everyday self here, or more like someone else? Is there an actor or someone in your life who tends to express her or himself from this part of their body? Play with the experience of being like that person. Stay in there with this experience, and get a sense of what it would be like to speak from this center for long stretches of time.

- Try to communicate different thoughts, ideas, or expressions through this colorful vowel sound, and as you do, get a sense of your own power to communicate simply through bodily vibration and sound.

- Rub your hands together again and move them up to your stomach/ solar plexus, Chakra #3, to generate energy there. Repeat the steps above: inhale, exhale on a long vowel sound, feel the vibration in your body as you do so, and give the energy and sound a color that you paint the world with as you vocalize. Observe how it feels to express yourself from this part of your body.

- Remember, as with *being present, breathing,* and *finding center* in your body, we are not aiming for perfection here. (Consider the talented, well-trained singers who make perfectly, beautiful, clear-as-a-bell sounds, but who are not great actors because they do not necessarily connect to their specific mind/body experience in the present moment.)

- Move up to Chakra #4 and similarly work with your chest and heart, on the sound of "Ha-hum-mah." Try making fists and lightly tapping on your chest, like King Kong, as you release the sound to increase the vibration.

- Move up to your throat chakra, #5, and as you repeat the energy/voice ritual here, release a short vowel sound. You can even play with moving between your throat chakra here and your chest: notice the vibration moving between the two energy centers of your body as you do this, as well as the corresponding feelings you have to the different sounds you make. As you slide between vocal vibrations in different parts of your body, imagine moments in session when such a move could effectively enhance your communication—e.g., A time when you want to assure a client that you understand his intellectual point, as you offer him heart-felt empathy.

- As you warm up the energy in your third eye chakra, #6, vocalize the sounds of "EE," and "AY." Notice the vibration in your cheekbones. This is your mask resonance, and it helps you to focus and project your sound, particularly when you want to emphasize specific thoughts and ideas. To enable the greatest vibration here, you'll want to raise what's known as your *soft palate*, located in the back roof of your mouth. It's easy to locate the soft palate by opening your mouth and inhaling on the sound of "Hah." The soft tissue in the upper back of your mouth is the soft palate. And when it's open, you have more access to air, and more room for vocal vibrations in your mask. What is it like to operate from this part of your body? Think of the people who tend to live here in the extreme, and why that may be (e.g., kindergarten teachers; television journalists; people who want to be easily understood).

- Repeat the energy/voice ritual on your crown, Chakra, #7, on a short vowel sound, like "Na, na, na." You'll need to raise the soft palate high to get a full resonance through the top of your head. This is a sound we typically hear when we are singing, or preaching, or connecting in some way to higher power.

- Remember to breathe as you do all of these exercises, in a way that keeps you supported, in the present, inspired, creative, playful, and connected to the emotions in your body.

XII. Words Words Words

A) *Tongue Warm ups*

- After completing some version of the vocal warm up above, find a sense of center in your body, find your breath, and then with your mouth closed move your tongue in circles around the front of your mouth. Do this with intention.
- Open your mouth and stick the tongue out as far as it can go. Let it retract and then repeat.
- Hold the tip of the tongue behind the lower teeth and at the same time, pulse the top of your tongue forward and out of your mouth several times.
- Put the tip of the tongue on the bottom of your top teeth and make an "L" sound. Then pull the tip of the tongue back behind the top teeth and directly on the edge between the roof of the mouth and the teeth, and make an "N" sound. Move the tongue back for the "L" sound, and then the "N" sound again. Repeat several times.
- Make the sound of "Tuh" three times, followed by the sound of "Duh," one time. ("Tuh, Tuh, Tuh, Duh.") Repeat this several times.
- In a similar fashion, make the sound of "Kuh" three times, followed one beat on the sound of "Guh." ("Kuh, Kuh, Kuh, Guh.") Repeat several times.
- Now do the same thing with the sound of "Puh" three times, followed by one beat on the sound of "Buh." ("Puh, Puh, Puh, Buh.") Repeat.
- As you practice articulating these consonants, remember to have a flicker of inspiration. Imagine yourself creating color with your sound, or that you are saying communicating a powerful, tickling, or insinuating message through this sound.

B) *Text Warm up*

- Take your tongue workouts further by speaking words that emphasize specific consonants. Try this favorite Speech 101 exercise: "Red leather, yellow leather. Red leather, yellow leather…" Repeat several times. Don't stress about being perfect. Just allow yourself to seek a clearer articulation of sound each time (the same way you endlessly seek center, or a full breath, or a sense of being present) and find a personal and specific motivation to create each sound, each time. As you do this, keep in mind this advice from Kristin Linklater to observe "the autonomy of each word" and to find variety in your pitch and pronunciations, but not necessarily volume or emphasis. The goal isn't to push out sound at random, but to find a range of specific expressions of emotion, imagery, and thought that convey meaning through your instrument.

- Continue playing with any of your favorite tongue twisters to sharpen the sound of, and intention behind, your consonants. E.g., "Betty Botter," "Peter Piper," "She Sells Sea Shells," "Lilly Lolly Lou."
- As you practice your speech making muscles, continue to seek more specific thoughts, emotions, and images with each word.
- Practice reciting entire poems that are chock full of consonants. E.g., "The Bells," by Edgar Allen Poe; "Sir Beelzebub," by Edith Sitwell; "About Socks," by Dr. Seuss. As you speak the words, consider the thoughts you are trying to share in addition to the imagery. What is the story you are trying to tell with this text? The thrust? The action? **The connection you intend to make with your listener?** Remember Hamlet's advice to "suit the action to the word, the word to the action," as you play.

Drawings

Drawing 1

Drawing 2

Drawing 3

Drawing 4

Drawing 5

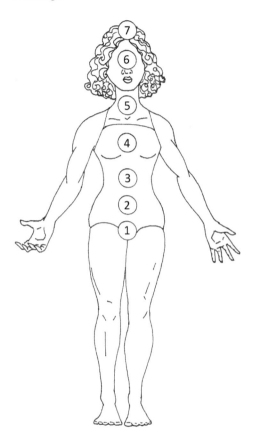

Drawing 6

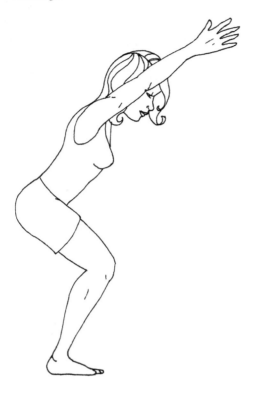

Notes

Prologue

1 Bollas (1992), p. 17
2 Phillips (2016)
3 Moore (2016)
4 Weigert (1962), p. 4
5 Benjamin (1990), p. 33
6 Benjamin (2018), p. 23
7 Ibid.
8 Ghent (1990) and Benjamin (2018), p. 23
9 Personal communication, August 31, 2017
10 Kermode (1985), p. 9; and Mitchell (1993), p. 59
11 Winnicott (1968), pp. 592–593, and p. 596
12 Mitchell (1993), p. 59
13 Mitchell (1993), p. 58
14 Stern (1994), p. 338
15 Atlas & Aron (2018)
16 Kindler (2010), p. 225; and Chaplin Kindler (2005)
17 Humphrys (2017)
18 Personal communication, August 31, 2017

Act I Prepare

1 Listen

1 Faires (2010)
2 Freud (1912), p. 112
3 O'Connell (2012)
4 Headlee (2015), 03:15

2 Know What You Look Like (And Use Your Subtext)

1 Bach (2016), p. 56
2 In *The Enigma of Desire* (p. 168), Atlas invokes Laplanche's concept of *enigmatic messages* (Laplanche, 1992:1995)—implicit, unconscious information delivered from parent to child, as well as therapist to client—to explore how therapists can unwittingly be seductive to clients. Atlas suggests that the therapist's awareness of her own implicit "seductions" is critical to the therapeutic process.

3 Lahr (2015)
4 Ibid.
5 Miller (1997), p. 33
6 O'Connell (2014), pp. 156–164
7 Bach (2016), p. 57

3 Know What You Sound Like (And Face Your Inner Critic)

1 Harris (1998), p. 41
2 Rodenburg (2002), p. 385
3 Bollas (1997), p. 366
4 On each episode of his/her popular, award winning reality show, *RuPaul's Drag Race*, celebrated entertainer RuPaul shares the following affirmation with each of the drag queen contestants competing for the crown: "If you can't love yourself, how in the hey-ell you gonna love somebody else."
5 Harris (1998), p. 40
6 Rodenburg (2015), p. 11
7 English National Opera (2015), p. 18
8 Rodenburg (2015), p. 10
9 Mamet (1986), "Introduction," p. xi
10 Rogers (1961), p. 341
11 Hornby (1992), p. 22

4 Be Present

1 This expression refers to a short comic play by Christopher Durang, in which an accountant is mistaken for an actor, and forced to perform in a play for which he doesn't know any of the lines
2 Rose (2004), 1:43
3 Stanislavski (1946a), Chapter 15
4 Actor/director/teacher Mark Alan Gordon, a former mentor of mine, uses this mantra as he warms up his mind, body, and voice before any performance.
5 Riviere (1952), p. 172
6 Phillips (2013), "Introduction," p. xiii
7 Klein (1935), p. 155
8 Erikson developed a theory of development that suggests we each need to move through eight linear stages in order to live a full life.
9 A version of this case example was originally published on *Psychotherapy.net*, see O'Connell (2017).

5 Breathe

1 Winnicott (1965), p. 148
2 You will further learn breathing techniques from training in yoga, Alexander Technique, singing, and/or books by great voice teachers such as Kristin Linklater and Patsy Rodenburg.
3 Gill Malik (2016)
4 Gill Malik (2016); Brook (1968), p. 109

5   Beckett (1983), p. 7
6   Humphrys (2017)
7   Benjamin (2018), p. 27
8   Rank (1924)
9   Corbett (2014), p. 301
10   Winnicott (1953), p. 91

6 Embody

1   Marcus (2010), p. 761; Johnson (1995), p. 88; and Goffman (1959)
2   Marshall (2001), p. 89
3   Schwartz (2011)
4   Milner (2010), p. 29
5   Hlavsa (2006), p. 153
6   These descriptions are based on my graduate classes with actor/director/voice teacher, Julia Carey.
7   Spolin (1986), p. 42
8   Winnicott (1965), p. 145
9   Richards (1995), p. 94
10   Chekhov (1953), pp. 71–75
11   Christie (2017)
12   Asi (2011)
13   Winnicott (1965), p. 34
14   Weigert (1962), p. 14
15   Lahr (2016)
16   Marcus (2011), p. 74, and Meisner (1987)
17   Stanislavski (1946a), p. 71
18   Brown/ Trinity Rep. Retrieved from https://vimeopro.com/user15409844/f-anne-scurria-intro
19   Streep (2010)
20   Ibid.
21   Ibid.
22   'This scene from *Outside Providence* is available on YouTube at https://youtube/G3k_Z4o4nEc
23   Furness (2016)
24   "The MELT Method," Retrieved from https://www.meltmethod.com/
25   Parker (2017)
26   Furness (2016)
27   Stern (2017), p. 159

7 Speak

1   Winnicott (1965), p. 167
2   Linklater (2010)
3   Warner (2017)
4   Grotowski (1968)
5   Bady (1985), p. 482
6   Goldner (2005), p. 110 and Harris (1998), p. 54

7 Bady (1985), p. 483

8 Green (1995), p. 210

9 Green (1974), p. 421

10 Van Bark (1953), p. 90

11 Kramer (1994), p. 42 and Stanislavski (1946), pp. 129, 130

12 Berry (2001), Chapter 4

13 Harris & Aron (1997), p. 526

14 To supplement your vocal preparation, you will benefit from the books *Freeing the Natural Voice* by Kristin Linklater, *The Actor Speaks* by Patsy Rodenburg, and *Text in Action* by Cicely Berry, as well as by taking voice classes from trained professionals near you.

15 See *The Hours*, DVD, Bonus Features: Actors Commentary

16 Bollas (1987), p. 209

17 Skinner (1990), p. 4

18 Harris (1998), p. 45

19 Freud (1913), p. 176

20 Bollas (1987), p. 234

21 Ibid.

22 Schechner (1998), p. 55

23 Bollas (1987), p. 234

24 Green (1986), Chapter 11

25 Benjamin (2018), p. 23

26 'Personal communication, August 31, 2017'

8 Warm Up

1 Freud (1913), p. 183

2 Bion (1970), especially pp. 34 and 69

3 *Newsweek's 2011 Oscar Roundtable: 2011*, Retrieved from Youtube: https://youtu.be/VTT1RvznHas?t=8m11s, 8:11

4 Hagen (1991), p. 134

5 Adler (2000), p. 80

6 White (2017)

7 Schechner (1998), p. 55

8 Lyttelton (2014)

9 Gorman (2002)

10 Benjamin (2018), p. 76

11 Benjamin (2018), p. 91

Act II Rehearse

9 Frame

1 Benjamin (2018), p. 26

2 Rizzo (2014)

3 Johnstone (1979), p. 42

4 This concept is not unlike Jessica Benjamin's idea of the *differentiating third,* (Benjamin, 2018), p. 84

5 Johnstone (1979), p. 35

6 Bion (1957), especially pp. 268–269

10 Play

1 Milner (2010), p. 192
2 Dale (2012)
3 Freud (1920)
4 Erikson (1961), p. 156 and Fromm (2009), p. 192
5 In my psychoanalytic review (O'Connell, 2014a) of the play, *A Kid Like Jake* (now a movie starring Claire Danes, Jim Parsons, and Octavia Spencer), about a gender nonconforming child, I invoked Philip Bromberg's concept of "standing in the spaces" (Bromberg, 1998)—which refers to one's capacity to make room for various parts of self—and explored the idea of "playing in the spaces," which is to maintain playful access to our self experience while acknowledging the inevitable pain that comes with negotiating self-states.
6 Ringstrom (2014), p. 9
7 Shurtleff (2003), p. 23
8 Winnicott (1968), p. 591
9 Toohill (2015)
10 Selman (2015), p. 32
11 Marcus (2011), p. 82
12 Winnicott (1971), p. 54
13 Ringstrom (2014), p. 31
14 Ringstrom (2014), p. 32
15 Hornby (1992), p. 57
16 Hornby (1992), p. 58
17 Ringstrom (2014), p. 138
18 Beckett (1983), p. 7
19 Ghent (1990): and Benjamin (2018), p. 23
20 Ghent (1990), p. 108
21 Milner (2010), p. 83
22 Dukakis (2012), p. 30
23 Dukakis (2012), 1:30
24 Hagen (1973), p. 20
25 Hagen (1973), p. 19
26 Ringstrom (2014), p. 36 and Benjamin (2018), p. 52
27 Ringstrom (2014), p. 182
28 Spolin (2001), p. 8
29 Ringstrom (2014), p. 140
30 Bogart (2015)
31 Stanislavski (1946a), p. 250
32 Bogart (2015)
33 Tronick (1989)
34 Benjamin (2018), p. 7
35 Spolin (1985), p. 3
36 O'Connell (2016)
37 Ringstrom (2014), p. 142
38 Mitchell (1993), p. 149
39 Stanislavski (1946a), p. 166
40 Stanislavski (1946a), p. 46

41 I found Jessica Benjamin's writing on the therapist's acknowledgment of failures to be a great source of support and inspiration here, particularly the idea that "embracing the inevitability of failures prevents bigger failures, and lets the analysis embody the principle of rupture and repair" (Benjamin, 2018, p. 62

11 Find the Characters

1 Personal communication, August 31, 2017
2 Lachmann (2003), p. 343
3 Ibid.
4 Brando, p. 199
5 Freud (1920), p. 29
6 Benjamin (2018), p. 51
7 Mirren (2017), p. 10
8 Hart (1999), p. 196
9 Riviere (1952), p. 172
10 Safer (2012)
11 Chefetz & Bromberg (2004), pp. 419–420
12 Linklater (1997), p. 6; Chefetz & Bromberg (2004), p. 420
13 Chefetz & Bromberg (2004), p. 420
14 Winnicott (1980), p. 353
15 Kafka (2008)
16 Searles (1973), 30:00
17 www.lynxtheater.org

12 Love

1 Belloni & Galloway (2011)
2 Schechner (1998), p. 234
3 Adler (2000), p. 26
4 Rotte (2000), p. 30
5 Rotte (2000), p. 36
6 Meissner (1972), p. 247
7 Grotjahn (1967), p. 445
8 Winnicott (1949), p. 72
9 Ibid.
10 Belloni & Galloway (2011)
11 Artaud (1938), p. 162
12 Artaud (1938), p. 84
13 Artaud (1938), p. 7
14 Freud (1912a), p. 249
15 Winnicott (1971), p. 56
16 Goethals (1976), p. 538
17 Schechner (1998), p. 55
18 Davies (1999), pp. 187–188
19 "Workshop: Directing Physical Danger with Moritz Von Seulpnagel," Primary Stages, Retrieved from http://primarystages.org/espa/directing/workshop-directing-physical-danger

20 Barrett (2015)
21 Travers (2014)
22 Mulkerrins (2017)
23 Ibid.
24 Winnicott (1965), p. 29
25 Hetrick (2014)
26 Blechner (2009), p. 92
27 Hagen (1973), p. 20
28 Atlas (2015), p. 129
29 Benjamin (2018), p. 191; Ringstrom (2016)
30 Kirkland (1996)
31 Benjamin (2018), p. 12
32 Hugo (1982)
33 Benjamin (2018), p. 3
34 Yalom (1980), p. 371

Act III Perform

13 Narrate

1 narrate. 2018. In *Merriam-Webster.com*. Retrieved from https://www.merriam-webster.com/dictionary/narrate
2 Benjamin (2018), p. 186
3 "The Albert Ellis Institute." Retrieved from http://albertellis.org/rebt-pamphlets/Techniques-for-Disputing-Irrational-Beliefs.pdf
4 "Beck Institute for Cognitive Behavioral Therapy." Retrieved from https://beckinstitute.org/get-informed/what-is-cognitive-therapy/
5 "Narrative Therapy Centre." Retrieved from www.narrativetherapycentre.com/narrative.html
6 "Lee Strasberg Theatre and Film Institute." Retrieved from https://newyork.methodactingstrasberg.com/what-is-method-acting/
7 "The Drama Teacher: Meyerhold's Biomechanics" Retrieved from www.thedramateacher.com/meyerholds-biomechanics-for-theatre/
8 "The Viewpoints Project." Retrieved from https://theviewpointsproject.wordpress.com/a-brief-history-of-viewpoints/
9 "Atlantic Acting School." Retrieved from https://atlanticactingschool.org/about/
10 Brooker (1988), p. 63
11 Brooker (1988), p. 44
12 Kohut (1968), pp. 100 and 109
13 McLaren (1993), p. 80; a similar statement was first made by Leon Trotsky in *Literature and Revolution* (1924; edited by William Keach (2005), Ch. 4: Futurism, p. 120)
14 Benjamin (2018), p. 169
15 "TJ and Dave: Official Website." www.tjanddave.com/
16 "Beck Institute for Cognitive Behavioral Therapy." Retrieved from https://beckinstitute.org/get-informed/what-is-cognitive-therapy/
17 Brecht (1950), p. 197
18 "Malone Editorial: How to Edit Your Work Without Losing Your Voice" Retrieved from https://www.maloneeditorial.com/edit-your-work-without-losing-your-voice/

14 Direct

1 Goldner (2004), p. 350
2 Bowen (1978), p. 524
3 Beckett (1983), p. 7
4 Stern (2017)
5 Atlas & Aron (2018)
6 Lahr (2016)

15 Publicize

1 Cooper, A. (2011). Mastering the art of Fame [Television broadcast]. *60 Minutes*. New York: CBS.
2 Davisson (2013), p. 6
3 Hartman (2006), p. 275
4 Kuchuck (2014), Introduction, p. xix
5 Mitchell (1993), p. 12
6 "Meryl Streep's Young Co-Stars 'Get Nervous,'" *Female First*. Retrieved from www. femalefirst.co.uk/movies/movie-news/Meryl+Streep-64359.html
7 "SNL Digital Short: Relaxation Therapy," *NBC*. Retrieved from https://www.nbc. com/saturday-night-live/video/snl-digital-short-relaxation-therapy/n12882
8 Kohut (1956); Chused (2012)
9 Kohut (1966), pp. 258–261; Lachmann (2003), p. 342
10 Kuchuck (2014), p. 65
11 Silverstein (2011), p. 160
12 Clarke & Blechner (2011), p. 376
13 Clarke & Blechner (2011), p. 377
14 Benjamin (1997), Introduction, xv
15 Ghomeshi (2013)

16 Present

1 Trespicio (2017)
2 Colbert (2017), 3:32
3 Colbert (2017), 3:36
4 Laist (2017)
5 Colbert (2017), 4:54
6 Gross (2012)

17 Take a Bow

1 Bonovitz (2017), p. 230
2 Witenberg (1976), p. 336; Bonovitz (2017), p. 230
3 Atlas & Aron (2018)
4 Benjamin (2018), p. 28
5 Weigert (1952), p. 473

18 Audition

1 Epigraph: audition. 2018. Cambridge Dictionary. Retrieved from https://dictionary.cambridge.org/us/dictionary/english/audition.
2 Phillips (2016)
3 Benjamin (2018)
4 Johnstone (1979), p. 43
5 Moore (1984)

Exercises

1 These instructions are based on my memory of working with Carol Gill Malik at Trinity Rep Conservatory, and on a personal communication with Carol and actor/movement expert, Lian-Marie Holmes, August 5, 2017. For more information visit https://alexandertechnique.com/
2 These instructions are based on my memory of working with director/actor/voice teacher, Julia Carey, at Trinity Rep Conservatory.
3 Personal communication with singer/songwriter Allison Langerack, September 15, 2017
4 Ibid.
5 These instructions are based on my memory working with Julia Carey at Trinity Rep Conservatory.
6 Lahr (2016)
7 Chekhov (1953), p. 23
8 Bach (2016), p. 247
9 These instructions are my version of "chair pose," based on how it has been taught to me by my yoga instructor, Nancy Elkes.
10 Linklater (2010)
11 Rodenburg (2015), p. 10

Bibliography

Adler, S. (2000). *The Art of Acting*. (H. Kissell, Ed.). New York, NY: Applause Books.

Arlow, J.A. (1961). Silence and the Theory of Technique. *J. Amer. Psychoanal. Assn.*, 9:44–55.

Aron, L. (1992). Interpretation as Expression of the Analyst's Subjectivity. *Psychoanal. Dial.*, 2(4):475–507.

Artaud, A. (1938/1958). *The Theatre and Its Double*. New York, NY: Grove Press.

Asi, H.S. (2011). "Meryl Streep: I'm the Ironing Lady." *UK Screen*. Retrieved from www. ukscreen.com/articles/interviews/meryl-streep-im-the-ironing-lady/

Atlas, G. (2015). *The Enigma of Desire: Sex, Longing, and Belonging in Psychoanalysis* (Relational Perspectives Book Series). London & New York: Routledge.

Atlas, G. and Aron, L. (2018). *Dramatic Dialogue: Generative Enactment in Contemporary Clinical Practice*. London & New York: Routledge.

Bach, S. (2016). *Chimeras and Other Writings: Selected Papers of Sheldon Bach*. New York, NY: IP Books.

Bady, S.L. (1985). The Voice as a Curative Factor in Psychotherapy. *Psychoanal. Rev.*, 72(3):479–490.

Balsam, R.H. (1997). Active Neutrality and Loewald's Metaphor of Theater. *Psychoanal. St. Child*, 52:003–016.

Barrett, K. (2015, Oct. 30). "Actors Anonymous Step 10: Establishing Boundaries." *Backstage*. Retrieved from www.backstage.com/advice-for-actors/the-working-actor/actors-anonymous-step-10-weeding-out-negative/

Basch, M.F. (1986). Can This Be Psychoanalysis?. *Progr. Self Psychol.*, 2:18–30.

Beckett, S. (1983). *Nohow On*. London: John Calder Publishers.

Belloni, M. and Galloway, S. (2011, Nov. 9). "THR's Actress Roundtable: Six A-Listers Sound Off on Bad Reviews, Nudity and Playing Hitler." [Transcript from broadcast on Oct. 24, 2011.] *THR*. Retrieved from www.hollywoodreporter.com/news/charlize-theron-michelle-williams-the-help-oscars-roundtable-258936

Benjamin, J. (1990). An Outline of Intersubjectivity. *Psychoanal. Psychol.*, 7S(Supplement): 33–46.

Benjamin, J. (1997). *Shadow of the Other: Intersubjectivity and Gender in Psychoanalysis*. New York, NY: Routledge.

Benjamin, J. (2018). *Beyond Doer and Done to: Recognition Theory, Intersubjectivity and the Third*. London & New York: Routledge.

Bernstein, J.W. (1999). The Politics of Self-Disclosure. *Psychoanal. Rev.*, 86(4):595–605.

Berry, C. (2001). *Text in Action: A Definitive Guide to Exploring Text in Rehearsal for Actors and Directors*, London: Virgin Publishing Ltd.

Bion, W.R. (1957). Differentiation of the Psychotic from the Non-Psychotic Personalities 1. *Int. J. Psycho-Anal.*, 38:266–275.

Bion, W.R. (1970). *Attention and Interpretation*. London: Tavistock, 1–130..

Blechner, M.J. (2009). Erotic and Antierotic Transference. *Contemp. Psychoanal.*, 45(1):82–92.

Bogart, A. (2015, March 24). "The Art of Adjustment." SITI. Retrieved from www.siti.org/content/art-adjustment

Bollas, C. (1987). *The Shadow of the Object: Psychoanalysis of the Unthought Known*. New York, NY: Columbia University Press.

Bollas, C. (1992). *Being a Character: Psychoanalysis and Self Experience*. London: Routledge.

Bollas, C. (1997). Wording and Telling Sexuality. *Int. J. Psycho-Anal.*, 78:363–367.

Bonovitz, C. (2007). Termination Never Ends. *Contemp. Psychoanal.*, 43(2):229–246.

Bowen, M. (1978). *Family Therapy in Clinical Practice*. New York: Aronson.

Brando, M. (1994). *Brando: Songs My Mother Taught Me*. New York: Random House, Brecht.

Brecht, B. (1950). "The Modern Theatre is the Epic Theatre: Notes to the Opera *Aufstieg und Fall der Stadt Mahagonny*." *Brecht on Theatre: The Development of an Aesthetic*. Ed. and trans. J. Willett. London: Methuen, 1964.

Bromberg, P. (1998). *Standing in the Spaces*. Hillsdale, NJ: Analytic Press.

Brook, P. (1968). *The Empty Space*. London: Penguin.

Brook, P. (1994, June 13). "Ernest Jones Lecture given by Peter Brook at The Edward Lewis Theatre, UCL, London." *The British Psycho-Analytical Society Bulletin*, Vol. 34, No. 1, London, 1998. Retrieved from www.ciret-transdisciplinarity.org/bulletin/b15c1.php

Brooker, P. (1988). *Bertolt Brecht: Dialectics, Poetry, Politics*. London: Croom Helm.

Chaplin Kindler, R.C. (2005). Creative Co-constructions: A Psychoanalytic Approach to Spontaneity and Improvisation in the Therapy of a Twice-Forsaken Child. *Clinical Applications of Drama Therapy in Child and Adolescent Treatment* ed. Weber, A.M. and Haen, C. New York: Brunner-Routledge, pp. 87–103.

Charles, M. (2001). Nonphysical Touch. *Psychoanal. Q.*, 70(2):387–416.

Chefetz, R.A. and Bromberg, P.M. (2004). Talking with "Me" and "Not-Me." *Contemp. Psychoanal.*, 40(3):409–464.

Chekhov, M. (1953). *To the Actor: On the Technique of Acting*. New York: Harper and Row.

Christie, J. (2017, Jan. 14). "Interview: Natalie Portman on making her new film, Jackie." *The Scotsman*. Retrieved from www.scotsman.com/news/interview-natalie-portman-on-making-her-new-film-jackie-1-4338938

Chused, J.F. (2012). The Analyst's Narcissism. *J. Amer. Psychoanal. Assn.*, 60:899–915.

Clarke, J. and Blechner, M. (2011). Interview with Dr. Mark Blechner. *Psychoanal. Psychother.*, 25:361–379.

Colbert, S. (2017, March 23). "The Late Show with Stephen Colbert: Glenn Close," CBS. Retrieved from www.youtube.com/watch?v=lqmYSSQiL8Y

Cooper, A. (2011). "Mastering the art of Fame [Television broadcast]." *60 Minutes*. New York: CBS.

Corbett, K. (2009). *Boyhoods: Rethinking Masculinities*. New Haven: Yale University Press.

Corbett, K., Dimen, M., Goldner, V. and Harris, A. (2014). Talking Sex, Talking Gender— A Roundtable. *Stud. Gend. Sex.*, 15(4):295–317.

Dale, A. (2012, March 14). Audre Tatou Seeks the 'Virgin Pleasure of Acting' in Her New Film 'Delicacy'. *IndieWire*. Retrieved from www.indiewire.com/2012/03/audrey-tautou-seeks-the-virgin-pleasure-of-acting-in-her-new-film-delicacy-48762/

Davies, J. (1999). Getting Cold Feet, Defining "Safe-Enough" Borders. *Psychoanal. Q.*, 68(2):184–208.

Davis, V. (2017). "Academy Awards Acceptance Speech Database." February 26. Retrieved from: www.aaspeechesdb.oscars.org/

Davisson, A. (2013). *Lady Gaga and the Remaking of Celebrity Culture.* McFarland Books.

Dukakis, O. (2012). "I Am Theatre: Olympia Dukakis." *TCG.* Retrieved from Youtube: www.youtube.com/watch?v=XBjsJZMk_-s

Eagle, M.N. (2011). Psychoanalysis and the Enlightenment Vision: An Overview. *J. Amer. Psychoanal. Assn.*, 59(6):1099–1118.

Ekstein, R. (1965). Working Through and Termination of Analysis. *J. Amer. Psychoanal. Assn.*, 13:57–78.

English National Opera (2015). Glenn Close—Preparing for the Role | Sunset Boulevard at ENO. *YouTube*, Nov. 20, 2015. Retrieved from www.youtube.com/HLWe_GYICj8?t=18s.

Erikson, E. (1961). The Roots of Virtue. In: ed. J. Huxley, *The Humanist Frame.* New York, NY: Harper, pp. 145–165.

Faires, R. (2010, Nov. 12). "Good Listening: Meryl Streep speaks on the keys to acting and its importance to life." *The Austin Chronicle.* Nov. 12. Retrieved from www.austinchronicle.com/arts/2010-11-12/good-listening/

Ferenczi, S., and Rank, O. (1923). *The Development of Psychoanalysis.* Madison, CT: International Universities Press.

Frank, K.A. (1997). Reply to Commentaries. *Psychoanal. Dial.*, 7:347–361.

Freud, S. (1912a). Contributions to a Discussion on Masturbation. *The Standard Edition of the Complete Psychological Works of Sigmund Freud, Volume XII (1911–1913): The Case of Schreber, Papers on Technique and Other Works*, 239–254.

Freud, S. (1912b). Recommendations to Physicians Practising Psycho-Analysis. *The Standard Edition of the Complete Psychological Works of Sigmund Freud, Volume XII (1911–1913): The Case of Schreber, Papers on Technique and Other Works*, 109–120.

Freud, S. (1913). The Claims of Psycho-Analysis to Scientific Interest. *The Standard Edition of the Complete Psychological Works of Sigmund Freud, Volume XIII (1913–1914): Totem and Taboo and Other Works*, 163–190.

Freud, S. (1920). Beyond the Pleasure Principle. *The Standard Edition of the Complete Psychological Works of Sigmund Freud, Volume XVIII (1920–1922): Beyond the Pleasure Principle, Group Psychology and Other Works*, 1–64.

Fromm, M.G. (2009). Potential Space and Maternal Authority in Organizations. *Organ. Soc. Dyn.*, 9(2):189–220.

Furness, H. (2016, June 23). Curse of Richard III: actors bear 'scars' for rest of career. *The Telegraph.* Retrieved from www.telegraph.co.uk/news/2016/06/23/curse-of-richard-iii-actors-bear-scars-for-rest-of-career/

Ghent, E. (1990). Masochism, Submission, Surrender: Masochism as a Perversion of Surrender. *Contemp. Psychoanal.*, 26: 108–136.

Ghomeshi, J. (2013). "Portrait of an Artist: Joni Mitchell [Television Broadcast]." *The National.* Vancouver: CBC. Retrieved from www.youtube.com/watch?v=cWEz_hpOQME

Gill Malik, C. (2016). "Voice for the Actor." *Direction: A Journal on the Alexander Technique.* Retrieved from www.directionjournal.com/bright-16/

Goethals, G.W. (1976). The Evolution of Sexual and Genital Intimacy. *J. Am. Acad. Psychoanal. Dyn. Psychiatr.*, 4(4):529–544.

Goffman, E. (1959). *The Presentation of Self in Everyday Life.* New York, NY: Doubleday.

Goldner, V. (2004). When Love Hurts. *Psychoanal. Inq.*, 24 (3):346–437.

Goldner, V. (2005). The Poem as a Transformational Third. *Psychoanal. Dial.*, 15(1):105–117.

Gorman, H.E. (2002). Growing Psychoanalysis. *Can. J. Psychoanal.*, 10(1):45–69.

Green, A. (1974). Surface Analysis, Deep Analysis (The Role of the Preconscious in Psychoanalytical Technique). *Int. Rev. Psycho-Anal.*, 1:415–423.

Green, A. (1986). *On Private Madness*. London: Hogarth.

Green, A. (1995). Summary: Affects versus Representations or Affects as Representations?. *Brit. J. Psychother*, 12(2):208–211.

Gross, T. (2012, Feb. 6). "Meryl Streep: The Fresh Air Interview." *NPR*. Retrieved from www.npr.org/2012/02/06/146362798/meryl-streep-the-fresh-air-interview

Grotjahn, M. (1967). *Sigmund Freud and the Art of Letter Writing in Freud as We Knew Him* ed. H.M. Ruitenbeek. Detroit, MI: Wayne State Univ., 1973, pp. 433–447.

Grotowski, J. (1968). *Towards a Poor Theatre*. London: Methuen.

Guskin, H. (2003). *How to Stop Acting*. New York, NY: Faber & Faber.

Hagen, U. (1973). *Respect for Acting*. New York, NY: Wiley Publishing, Inc.

Hagen, U. (1991). *A Challenge for the Actor*. New York, NY: Scribner.

Harris, A. (1998). Psychic Envelopes and Sonorous Baths: Sitting the Body in Relational Theory and Clinical Practice. In: *Relational Perspectives on the Body*, ed. L. Aron and F.S. Anderson, pp. 39–64.

Harris, A. and Aron, L. (1997). Ferenczi's Semiotic Theory: Previews of Postmodernism. *Psychoanal. Inq.*, 17(4):522–534.

Hart, A. (1999). Reclaiming the Analyst's Disruptive Role. *Contemp. Psychoanal.*, 35(2):185–211.

Hartman, S. (2006). Disclosure, Dis-closure, Diss/clothes/sure. *Psychoanal. Dial.*, 16(3):273–292.

Headlee, C. (2015, May 1). "10 Ways to Have a Better Conversation." Presented at TEDx Creative. Retrieved from: www.ted.com/talks/celeste_headlee_10_ways_to_have_a_better_conversation   /transcript?awesm=on.ted.com_c0Era&utm_medium=on.ted.com-facebook-share&utm_content=awesm-bookmarklet&utm_source=direct-on.ted.com&utm_campaign=

Hetrick, A. (2014, Dec. 12). "Stage Manager Paralyzed in London Theatre Accident Awarded Millions in Historic Settlement." *Playbill*. Retrieved from www.play-bill.com/   article/stage-manager-paralyzed-in-london-theatre-accident-awarded-millions-in-historic-settlement-com-337390

Hlavsa, D. (2006). *An Actor Rehearses: What to Do When—and Why*. New York, NY: Allworth.

Hornby, R. (1992). *The End of Acting: A Radical View*. New York, NY: Applause. Theatre Books.

Hugo, V. (1982 [1862]). *Les Misérables*, Harmondsworth: Penguin.

Humphrys, J. (2017). "Today at 60: Judi Dench [Radio Broadcast]." BBC Radio 4. September 11.

Hurt, M. (2014). *Arthur Lessac's Embodied Actor Training*. Oxon and New York: Routledge.

Johnson, A.G. (1995). *The Blackwell Dictionary of Sociology: A User's Guide to Sociological Language*. Malden, MA: Blackwell.

Johnstone, K. (1979). *Impro: Improvisation and the Theatre*. New York, NY: Routledge.

Kafka, H. (2008). The Man Who Could Not Cry and the Psychoanalyst Who Could: Mutual Healing in the Maternal Transference/Countertransference. *Am. J. Psychoanal.*, 68(2):156–168.

Kermode, F. (1985). Freud and Interpretation. *Int. Rev. Psycho-Anal.*, 12:3–12.

Keveny, B. (2015). "Morgan Freeman Has Double Duty in CBS' 'Madam Secretary.'" *USA Today*. Retrieved from www.usatoday.com/story/life/tv/2015/09/30/ morgan-freeman-has-double-duty-cbs-madam-secretary/73050472/

Kindler, A. (2010). Spontaneity and Improvisation in Psychoanalysis. *Psychoanal. Inq.*, 30(3):222–234.

Kirkland, B. (1996, Dec.). "Nice 'n' Nasty." *Toronto Sun*. Retrieved from www.winona-ryder.org/library/1996-2/nice-n-nasty/

Klein, M. (1935). A Contribution to the Psychogenesis of Manic-Depressive States. *Int. J. Psycho-Anal.*, 16:145–174.

Kohut, H. (1966). Forms and Transformations of Narcissism. *J. Amer. Psychoanal. Assn.*, 14:243–272.

Kohut, H. (1968). The Psychoanalytic Treatment of Narcissistic Personality Disorders—Outline of a Systematic Approach. *Psychoanal. St. Child*, 23:86–113.

Kondazian, K. (2001). "Lee Strasberg: Method Acting." *New York Architecture*. Retrieved from www.nyc-architecture.com/MID/MID120.htm

Kramer, S. (1994). "The Promise of Family Therapy." *British J. Psychother.*, 11(1).

Kumiega, J. (1985). *The Theatre of Grotowski*. London: Methuen.

Kuchuck, S. (2008). In the Shadow of the Towers. *Psychoanal. Rev.*, 95(3):417–436.

Kuchuck, S. (2014). *Clinical Implications of the Psychoanalyst's Experience*. New York: Routledge.

Lachmann, F.M. (2003). Supervision. *Psychoanal. Dial.*, 13(3):341–353.

Lahr, J. (2015, Sept. 21). "The Sphinx Next Door: Julianne Moore and her Imagination," *The New Yorker*. Retrieved from www.newyorker.com/magazine/2015/09/21/the-sphinx-next-door-profiles-john-lahr

Lahr, J. (2016, Dec. 19 & 26). "Viola Davis's Call to Adventure." *The New Yorker*. Retrieved from www.newyorker.com/magazine/2016/12/19/viola-davis-call-to-adventure

Laist, R. (2017, Dec. 5). "Academic Conference Panels are Boring." *The Chronicle of Higher Education*. Retrieved from www.chronicle.com/article/Academic-Conference-Panels-Are/241970

Laplanche, J. (1992). Psychoanalysis, Time and Translation. In: *Jean Laplanche: Seduction, Translation, Drives*, ed. J. Fletcher and M. Stanton. London: Institute of Contemporary Arts, pp. 161–177.

Laplanche, J. (1995). Seduction, Persecution, Revelation. *Int. J. Psycho-Anal.*, 76, 663–682.

Linklater, K. (1997), Thoughts on Theatre, Therapy, and the Art of Voice. In: *The Vocal Vision: Views on Voice*, ed. M. Hampton and B. Acker. New York: Applause Books, pp. 4–12.

Linklater, K. (2010). "The Art and Craft of Voice and Speech Training." *Linklater Voice*. Retrieved from www.linklatervoice.com/resources/articles-essays/42-the-art-and-craft-of-voice-and-speech-training

Lyttelton, O. (2014, Oct. 29). "The Gyllenaissance: 5 Recent Roles That Have Re-Established Jake Gyllenhaal's Career." *IndieWire*. Retrieved from www.indiewire.com/2014/10/The-gyllenaissance-5-recent-roles-that-have-re-established-jake-gyllenhaals-career-270848/

McLaren, P. and Leonard, P. (1993). *Paulo Freire: A Critical Encounter*. New York and London: Routledge.

Mamet, D. (1986). *A Practical Handbook for the Actor*. New York, NY: Vintage.

Marcus, P. and Marcus, G. (2011). *Theater as Life: Practical Wisdom Drawn From Great Acting Teachers, Actors and Actresses*. Milwaukee, WI: Marquette University Press.

Marcus, P. and Marcus, G. (2010). Psychoanalysis as Theater: The Practical Application of Acting Theory to Psychotherapy and Real Life. *Psychoanal. Rev.*, 97(5):757–787.

Marshall, L. (2001). *The Body Speaks: Performance and Expression*. London: Methuen.

Meisner, S. and Longwell, D. (1987). *On Acting*. New York, NY: Vintage Books.

Meissner, W.W., S.J. (1972). Notes on Identification—III. The Concept of Identification. *Psychoanal. Q.*, 41:224–260.

Melzer, D. (1967). *The Psycho-Analytic Process*. London: Heinemann.

Messer, R. (2011, March 24) "Amy Ryan Exclusive Interview." *Collider*. Retrieved from www.collider.com/amy-ryan-interview-win-win-the-office/

Miller, A. (1997). *The Drama of the Gifted Child: The Search for the True Self*, revised edition. New York, NY: Basic Books.

Milner, M. (1952). Aspects of Symbolism in Comprehension of the Not-Self. *Int. J. Psycho-Anal.*, 33:181–194.

Milner, M. (2010). *On Not Being Able to Paint*. London and New York: Routledge. (Original work published 1950).

Mirren, H. (2017). "Helen Mirren Teaches Acting." *Master Class*. Retrieved from www. youtube.com/watch?v=-hYDmRq_PHY

Mitchell, S.A. (1993). *Hope and Dread in Psychoanalysis*. New York: Basic Books.

Modell, A.H. (1992). The Private Self and Private Space. *Annu. Psychoanal.*, 20:1–14.

Moore, S. (1984). *The Stanislavski System—The Professional. Training of an Actor*. Harmondsworth: Penguin Books.

Moore, T. (2016). Why Theater Majors Are Vital in the Digital Age. *Chron. High. Ed.*, 62(30), A48.

Mulkerrins, J. (2017, Sept. 30). "Maggie Gyllenhaal: 'Pornography is an Art Form.' *The Guardian*. Retrieved from www.theguardian.com/tv-and-radio/2017 /sep/30/maggie-gyllenhaal-pornography-is-art-form

O'Connell, M. (2012). Don't Act, Don't Tell: Discrimination Based on Gender Nonconformity in the Entertainment Industry and the Clinical Setting. *J. Gay & Lesb. Ment. Heal.*, 16:241–255.

O'Connell, M. (2014a). Review of '*A Kid Like Jake*' by Daniel Pearle. Lincoln Center Theater, New York, 2013. *J. Amer. Psychoanal. Assn.*, 62(2):363–371.

O'Connell, M. (2014b). *Modern Brides & Modern Grooms: A Guide to Planning Straight, Gay, and Other Nontraditional Twenty-First Century Weddings*. New York, NY: Skyhorse Publishing.

O'Connell, M. (2016). "Queer Couch for the Straight Girl." *Psychotherapy.net*. Retrieved from www.psychotherapy.net/article/queer-therapy-for-straight-people

O'Connell, M. (2017). "Straight Life Cycle/ Queer Life." *Psychotherapy.net*. Retrieved from www.psychotherapy.net/article/gay-marriage-adoption-psychotherapy

Parker, I. (2017, June 26). "Bobby Cannavale's Workplace Injuries." *The New Yorker*. Retrieved from www.newyorker.com/magazine/2017/06/26/bobby-cannavales-workplace-injuries

Phillips, A. (2013). *Missing Out: In Praise of the Unlived Life*. London: Penguin.

Phillips, A. (2016, March 12). Conversion Hysteria. *A Conversation with Adam Phillips*. Conference presented by CMPS, New York.

Rank, O. (1924). The Trauma of Birth in its Importance for Psychoanalytic Therapy. *Psychoanal. Rev.*, 11(3):241–245.

Richards, T. (1995). *At Work with Grotowski on Physical Actions*. London: Routledge.

Ringstrom, P. (2014) *A Relational Psychoanalytic Approach to Couples Psychotherapy*. London & New York: Routledge.

Riviere, J. (1952). The Unconscious Phantasy of an Inner World Reflected in Examples from English Literature. *Int. J. Psycho-Anal.*, 33:160–172.

Rizzo, F. (2014, April 20). "Meryl Streep's Summer at the O'Neill." *The Hartford Courant*. Retrieved from www.articles.courant.com/2014-04-20/entertainment/hc-Meryl-streep-oneill0420-20140420_1_monte-cristo-award-eugene-o-neill-theater-center- meryl-streep

Rodenburg, P. (2002). *The Actor Speaks: Voice and the Performer.* New York, NY: Palgrave Macmillan.

Rodenburg, P. (2015). *The Right to Speak*, 2nd ed. London: Methuen Drama.

Rogers, C. (1961). *On Becoming a Person: A Therapist's View of Psychotherapy.* Boston, MA: Houghton Mifflin Company.

Rose, C. (2004, Dec. 1). "Mary-Louise Parker Examines Her New Role in the Broadway Play, *Reckless." Charlie Rose.* PBS. Retrieved from www.charlierose.com/videos/8520

Rotte, J. (2000). *Acting with Adler.* New York, NY: Limelight Editions.

Safer, M. (2012, Jan. 23). "The Many Meryls." [Transcript of broadcast on Dec. 18, 2011]. *CBS.* Retrieved from www.cbsnews.com/news/the-many-faces-of-meryl-streep-23-01-2012/

Seneca, L.A. (1969 [n.d.]). *Letters from a Stoic*, trans. R. Campbell. London: Penguin.

Schechner, R. and Wolford Wylam, L. (Eds.). (1998). *The Grotowski Sourcebook.* London: Routledge.

Schwartz, R. (2011). "Is Mindfulness Enough." *Psychotherapy Networker* Retrieved from www.psychotherapynetworker.org/magazine/recentissues/2011-septoct/item/1518-is-mindfulness-enough

Searles, H. (1973). "Case Study: Commentary." YouTube video published Dec. 12, 2017. Retrieved from www.youtube.com/watch?v=77Zvp31HYzA

Selman, M. (2015). Getting 'Withness'-Thinking Through Theatrical Improvisation. *Context.* 138, 32–34.

Shurtleff, M. (2003). *Audition: Everything an Actor Needs to Know to Get the Part.* New York, NY: Walker & Company.

Silverstein, C. (2011). *For the Ferryman: A Personal History.* New York, NY: Chelsea Station Editions.

Skinner, E. (1990). *Speak with Distinction.* New York, NY: Applause Theatre.

Sontag, S. (1966). *Against Interpretation, and Other Essays.* New York, NY: Farrar, Straus & Giroux.

Spolin, V. (1985). *Theater Games for Rehearsal: A Director's Handbook.* Evanston, IL: Northwestern University Press.

Spolin, V. (1986). *Theater Games for the Classroom: A Teacher's Handbook.* Evanston, IL: Northwestern University Press.

Spolin, V. (2001). *Theater Games for the Lone Actor: A Handbook.* Evanston, IL: Northeastern University Press.

Stanislavski, C. (1946a). *An Actor Prepares.* Trans. E.R. Hapgood. New York, NY: Theatre Arts.

Stanislavski, C. (1946b). *Creating a Role.* Trans. E.R. Hapgood. New York, NY: Theatre Arts.

Stanislavski, C. (1958). *Stanislavski's Legacy. A Collection of Comments on a Variety of Aspects of an Actor's Art and Life.* Trans. and ed. E.R. Hapgood. New York, NY: Theatre Arts Books.

Stanislavski, C. (2008). *An Actor's Work: A Student's Diary.* Trans. and ed. J. Benedetti, New York, NY: Routledge.

Stern, S. (1994). Needed Relationships and Repeated Relationships: An Integrated Relational Perspective. *Psychoanal. Dial.*, 4(3):317–346.

Stern, S. (2017). *Needed Relationships and Psychoanalytic Healing: A Holistic Relational Perspective on the Therapeutic Process.* New York, NY: Routledge.

Streep, M. (2010, May 18). "Commencement Speech." *The Huffington Post.* Retrieved from www.huffingtonpost.com/2010/05/18/meryl-streep-barnard-grad_n_580335.html

Stewart, S. (2007, July 1). "What Makes Dame Judi Run?" *The New York Times*. Retrieved from www.nytimes.com/2007/07/01/arts/television/01stew.html

Suzuki, T. (1995). Culture is the Body, in *Acting (Re). Considered*, P. Zarrilli (Ed.). New York, NY: Routledge.

Toohill, K. (2015, Sept. 11). "So Funny, It Doesn't Hurt: Can Improv be a Form of Therapy? Some Psychologists Think So." *The Atlantic*. Retrieved from www. theatlantic.com/ health/archive/2015/09/comedy-improv-anxiety/403933/

Travers, B. (2014, July 29). "Maggie Gyllenhaal on 'The Honorable Woman' and Why 'The Indie Film Community is Working in TV.'" *IndieWire*. Retrieved from www. indiewire.com/2014/07/maggie-gyllenhaal-on-the-honorable-woman-and-why-the-indie-film-community-is-working-in-tv-23712/

Trespicio, T. (2017). "I've Taught Public Speaking to Hundreds of People—and They All Make the Same Mistakes." *Business Insider*. Retrieved from www.businessinsider.com/common-public-speaking-mistakes-2017-2

Tronick, E.Z. (1989). Emotions and Emotional Communication in Infants, *Am.Psychol.*, 44:112–119.

Van Bark, B.S. (1953). The Meaning of Silence in the Analytic Situation, *Am. J.Psychoanal.*, 1953, 13:89–90.

Warner, B. (2017, Aug. 10). "Why Do Stars Like Adele Keep Losing Their Voice?" *The Guardian*. Retrieved from www.theguardian.com/news/2017/aug/10/adele-vocal-cord-surgery-why-stars-keep-losing-their-voices

Weigert, E. (1952). Contribution to the Problem of Terminating Psychoanalyses. *Psychoanal. Q.*, 21:465–480.

Weigert, E. (1962). The Role of Sympathy in the Psychotherapeutic Process. *Am. J. Psychoanal.*, 22(1):3–14.

Weigert, E. (1964). The Goal of Creativity in Psychotherapy. *Am. J. Psychoanal.*, 24(1):4–14.

White, A. (2017, Feb. 27). "From Abject Poverty to Oscar Winner: How Fences Star Viola Davis Took on Hollywood, and Won–in Pictures." *The Telegraph*. Retrieved from www.telegraph.co.uk/films/0/viola-davis-life-career-movies-pictures/

Winnicott, C. (1980). Fear of Breakdown: A Clinical Example. *Int. J. Psycho-Anal.*, 61:351–357.

Winnicott, D.W. (1949). Hate in the Counter-Transference. *Int.J. Psycho-Anal.*, 30:69–74.

Winnicott, D.W. (1953). Transitional Objects and Transitional Phenomena—A Study of the First Not-Me Possession. *Int.J. Psycho-Anal.*, 34:89–97.

Winnicott, D.W. (1965). *The Maturational Processes and the Facilitating Environment*. London: The Hogarth Press and the Institute of Psycho-Analysis.

Winnicott, D.W. (1968). Playing: Its Theoretical Status in the Clinical Situation. *Int. J. Psycho-Anal.*, 49:591–599.

Winnicott, D.W. (1971). *Playing and Reality*, 1–156. London: Tavistock Publications.

Witenberg, E.G. (1976). Problems in Terminating Psychoanalysis (A Symposium)— Termination is no End. *Contemp. Psychoanal.*, 12:335–337.

Yalom, I. (1980). *Existential Psychotherapy*. New York, NY: Basic Books.

Index